A Horseman for the Emperor

A Horseman for the Emperor

A Cavalryman of Napoleon's Army on Campaign Throughout the Napoleonic Wars

Jean Baptiste Gazzola

A Horseman for the Emperor: a Cavalryman of Napoleon's Army on Campaign Throughout the Napoleonic Wars
by Jean Baptiste Gazzola

Published by Leonaur Ltd

Text in this form copyright © 2007 Leonaur Ltd

ISBN: 978-1-84677-386-0 (hardcover)
ISBN: 978-1-84677-385-3 (softcover)

http://www.leonaur.com

Publisher's Note

The opinions expressed in this book are those of the author and are not necessarily those of the publisher.

Contents

Lost in Translation?	7
Preface	11
The Rencontre	13
La Ballerina	19
The Confirmation	23
The Flight	28
The Discovery	33
The Siege of Mantua	38
The Place of Mantua	44
The Advance	49
The Voyage	57
Boulak	62
Cairo	67
The Passage of Mont St. Bernard	72
The Fort of Bard	81
The Repulse	85
The Passage of the Tessin	90
Milan	95
The Ball	101
Passage of the Po	106
Marengo	112
Marengo II	118
San Juliano	126
Turin	131
Liege	137
Liege	142
Mayence	148

The Eve of Austerlitz	153
The Sun of Austerlitz	159
The Night After the Battle	164
La Belle France	169
Paris	175
Paris II	180
Weimar	185
Jena	190
Berlin	195
Prussia	201
Eylau	206
Osterode	212
Friedland	218
The Hospital	222
The Estaminet	227
Eckmuhl	233
Essling	239
The Passage of the Danube	246
Wagram	252
Russia—the Advance	256
Smolensk	261
Borodino	267
Moscow	274
The Retreat	279
The Passage of the Beresina	283

PUBLISHER'S NOTE
Lost in Translation?

Jean Baptiste Gazzola's book is something of a curiosity. The author of the English edition remains unusually anonymous—even at the end of his preface—where he explains to his readers that he took the book down in dictation from Gazzola, who was at that time his Italian language teacher.

There may be an element of truth in this, but the reader will have the impression as the text is read that it contains references to matters probably better to known to an Englishman than they would be to a Piedmontese—Gazzola's actual nationality. At the very least, one must suspect a heavy elaboration on the kernel of a genuine story. The question is—how much of this book is attributable to Gazzola and how much is the English author's embellishment?

It has be admitted that Gazzola's is a rollicking adventure that includes several changes of cavalry regiment, encounters with the Emperor, love affairs, duels and battlefield experiences. Campaigns are faithfully recounted, though not necessarily in a manner that would deny the possibility of reference to historical accounts by another author.

Readers of Marbot's autobiography may find similarities with this book and indeed Gazzola apparently served in the same regiment of Chasseurs a Cheval for a period according to his own account. It would be a brave advocate who claimed complete authenticity for the Marbot account, however!

Nevertheless, this story has a ring of authenticity to it and so could easily have been inspired by the experiences of a real

Napoleonic Wars soldier. If there are 'tall tales' within it, then that would hardly differentiate it from the tales of many other soldiers, from all periods of history, who have recounted their experiences 'with advantages' as the bard pointed out in Henry V.

Still, Gazzola is not so easy to track down—which is understandable in the case of an ordinary soldier. As his career progresses and he achieves promotions and awards he puts himself within the ranks of those whom history has seen fit to record in more detail. So whilst it is possible that the record does not list every recipient of 'the medal of honour', the fact is there is no record of it having been conferred on one 'Gazzola'.

This can be easily explained by the substitution of one name for another for the sake of anonymity However, towards the end of the account—according to Gazzola himself—he has achieved the rank of colonel in a cavalry regiment of the Imperial Guard. Whilst the absence of his name could be explained in the same way—upon the most casual examination of the lists of those who achieved that distinction—it is difficult to identify who the Italian principal character of the book you are now holding might be.

It is slightly more unsettling to learn that his regiment was 'The Cuirassiers of the Guard!' The non-existence of such a unit will not be lost on most students of the era. But, again, this could be nothing more than an incorrect attribution by the anonymous translator of Gazzola's story.

So, to be sure, this book is not the 'Gospel truth'. Very few biographies come accompanied by that guarantee. Perhaps some are not so easy to criticise or discover where 'recollection' has parted company with accepted 'fact'. It goes without saying, therefore, that this book no more comes with a certificate of authenticity than any other memoir that published by Leonaur or any other publisher.

Who was Gazzola? What is the element of truth within his book? Quite simple, we do not know. If this volume is entirely a work of fiction, its actual author should be congratulated for his efforts, because it is not so far away in style and content from those works of the era and subject that many have come to accept as authentic.

It is, no matter what else it may be, a highly entertaining account of life in Napoleon's cavalry and we hope you will enjoy reading it.

The Leonaur Editors

Preface

It has been well said that a preface should resemble a fair porch through which all must pass before entering a good-looking mansion; but as the building to which I would introduce my friends may not possess attractions the most alluring, I will not detain them at the entrance. My acquaintance with the writer of these sketches commenced in November, 1828, exactly in the manner described in the first chapter. I wrote them from dictation, as exercises in the language he professed to teach me, and on my return to England, translated some of the earlier chapters, which were sent to the *New Monthly Magazine,* then under the management of Sir Lytton Bulwer; they were returned to me as inadmissible, and thrown aside; and there perhaps they might have remained, but in tumbling over some papers they came to light, and were sent to the editor of the same journal some four or five years since. Mr. Hood at once accepted them, but after Mr. Colburn had them in his possession some year and a half, they were returned to me, and were then sent to my friend, the Editor of the *Worcestershire Chronicle,* in the pages of which journal they have since appeared.

As the only merit I can claim is that of a translator, it must of necessity be small; the faults, I am willing to think, are all my own, for I cannot but remember (even at this distance of time) the interest with which I listened to the narrative of events, in which my instructor had played so prominent a part—an interest which I fear may not be conveyed to the reader.

Should it be otherwise, I shall at some future period resume the subject, and continue the narrative of the scenes through which he passed, to that sad eventful one when we parted on the Ponte St. Trinita at Florence, he to pursue the drudgery of teaching the Italian language for a living, while I returned to the bosom of my family.

Chapter 1

The Rencontre

"Long years have passed away since the first dawn of youth, and silver hairs are o'er my forehead stealing, yet am I still in heart and soul a boy, though Hope, the most esteemed inmate of Pandora's box, was in vain restrained for me, and, losing her, I have little else to sigh for besides rest, that everlasting rest found only in the grave.

"When I reflect upon what I have been, and contrast it with what I am—I who, in the ever-varying walks of life, have wandered on regardless alike of the future and the past—I who, from a soldier of fortune, with no heritage save my courage, no possessions save my sword, cut my way to the highest honours—I who have been held by the button by the ruler of nations, the creator of kingdoms, the setter up of kings, the greatest man of any age or country—when I look at these decorations and recall to my recollection Mantua, the Pyramids, Marengo, Austerlitz, Moscow, and the thousand other battles where our valour triumphed or his genius rendered a retreat almost equal to a victory—when I contrast his brilliant successes with his last reverse—the imperial splendour with his ocean prison and early grave, I dare not murmur; I cannot repine. What has been my fate compared to his, since I am here in some comfort, enjoying health and strength, if not competency; and having exchanged the sabre for the ferule, and thrown over the gay uniform of the light dragoon the more sober mantle of a teacher of languages, am still able to pour into the ear of my first pupil this record of my youthful follies, instead of unceasing and unavailing regrets.

"What boots it now, that life has lost its freshness—that youth and joy are gone; none can rob me of the glory I have obtained, as none can relieve me of the miseries I have endured. Away then care, the, present moment is our own, and who would distress himself about aught beside?"

Such, in the impassioned language of his country, which I have but feebly rendered into English, were the words of my Italian master, as seated by a cheerful wood fire in the sitting room of my apartments on the Arno at Florence, we conversed on his present situation; but as they were the prelude to the history of the scenes I am about to describe, it may perhaps be as well if I here pause and say a little concerning the narrator.

I was walking round the harbour of Genoa, admiring the beautiful quays which form that port, some ten days after my arrival there, when I was accosted by a man in the garb of a sailor, who, in a sort of *Lingua Franca*, compounded of Genoese, French, and Italian, with, for aught I can tell, a smattering of Spanish, neither very melodious to to the ear nor comprehensive to the understanding, asked if I wanted a passage to Leghorn? I had been roaming over the north of Italy for the last three months, without any definite object or fixed destination, one moment resolving to start for Greece, the next determining to proceed to Spain. The choice was a matter of caprice, not necessity, for I cared little whether I went to the icy regions of the North, or the burning climes of Africa—"the world, was all before me where to choose"—so I soon made up my mind, asked the terms of the passage, and the time of sailing, and depositing a gratuity in the hands of the sailor, was entered as a passenger on board the good felucca *La Sucra Famiglia,* under the command of *Il Capitano* Tarabotto. I run quite aware that many of my readers would condemn this off-hand method of acting, for although the weekly steamer to Leghorn and Naples had only left the harbour on the previous evening, I had declined the pressing invitation of a friend on board to accompany him to the metropolis of the south, since I had no immediate intention to die, and therefore preferred obeying the Neapolitan proverb[1]

---

1. *Vedi Napoli et poi mori.*—(See Naples, and then die.)

at some future period. I felt, however, a desire to float "o'er the glad waters of the dark blue sea," and therefore resolved en the cruise; so returning to my hotel, I prepared my baggage, and made ready to quit the fair-city, which the inhabitants in their pride have christened *Genova la Superba*.

And truly they have not erred, for if ever city were worthy of the name, it is the Queen of the Mediterranean, which is built on the margin of the gulf of the same name in the form of a crescent.

The Appenines rise from the water's edge, giving the town the appearance of an amphitheatre, while the background is covered, even to the very summit of the hills, by the beautiful country houses of the Genoese nobility. Viewed from the harbour the *coup d'œil* is splendid, and much as I afterwards deplored putting myself on board so wretched a craft, I shall not soon forget the impression produced upon me as we sailed out of the harbour, the wind blowing fresh from the north-west. My *compagnons du voyage* were, Mr. B., the son of a Northumbrian banker; a red-hot son of Erin, in the person of Mr. C. and Jean Gazzola, whose adventures I am about to relate, the whole of us meeting for the first time in a miserable craft, crank as a canoe, and unseaworthy as a washing tub. However, for our comfort, the wind was fair, and the vessel scudded through the sea, casting the blue waves from her bows in wreaths of snowy whiteness, and we were just congratulating ourselves on a quick run and speedy deliverance, when the hitherto smiling aspect of the heavens began to change and look threatening, while a thick mist, not unlike a wetting shower, came on. We had certainly not made ten miles, and the prospect was anything but cheering, an open boat in such a night holding out few temptations, when our worthy captain, who had neither compass nor chronometer, soon cut the matter short; in spite of all our remonstrances to the contrary, the vessel was put about, and in an hour we found ourselves re-entering the harbour of Genoa.

In the meantime night had come on, but bad, as we considered our situation to be, worse remained behind, for *Il Capitano* refused to allow our baggage to be landed until we had first deposited half our passage money, such being, according to his version, the custom of the port of Genoa. As we had quite, abandoned the idea of proceeding by sea, we naturally enough declined paying for a passage we did not intend to take; high words ensued, neither party quite comprehending the language of the other, but the expressive language of the eyes, pretty well understood in all countries, gave sufficient notice that matters were becoming serious, the Irishman proposing to knock the captain into the sea, a determination which I had great difficulty in preventing being adopted. Our grey-headed friend at last stepped forward, and professed his willingness to arbitrate between us, for since he had determined to wait till the weather cleared up, and the vessel sailed again, it could make no difference to him which party succeeded.

It were useless here to relate how we were bandied about from the officers of the customs to the commissary of police, and thence to the consul of the marine. Our own consul was from home, and from him, therefore, we could receive no assistance, so we were obliged to put off the subject till the following day, and weary enough we became on arriving at our hotel, to which Gazzola accompanied us.

Next morning at ten we all assembled in the office of the marine consul, and were not long in discovering of how little avail were all our endeavours, for after we had stated our case, to which the captain replied, dwelling strongly on the state of the weather, the consul decided that he was in the right, and that if he were prevented by the rain and the fog from performing his part of the contract—*"Madre di dio"*—who could blame Providence; we must be content to pay, and to deduct the sum paid from the amount of our passage-money whenever the weather should clear up and allow us to pursue our voyage. In vain our advocate protested that there was no occasion for our return—that we might have proceeded without any tempting of Providence, had not the cowardly fears of the captain prevented us—in vain we asserted that this verdict was contrary to law, justice, reason, or common sense: the case had been decided before we had been heard, and we were at a loss to determine which was the greater villain of the three, the captain, the witness, who had declared what we considered a fair wind had amounted to a hurricane, or the consul, who had followed the Devonshire maxim of "Lydford law; first hang and draw, then hear the cause." They all seemed much on a par, so uttering curses, not loud but deep, we paid the money and quitted the office of the unjust judge.

Thus ended our voyage, and here, in all probability, would have ended our acquaintance, but that feeling annoyed at our defeat, we determined to have done with our worthy captain, and to proceed by land; so hiring a carriage, we offered our interpreter the vacant seat, free of all cost and charge, and once more bidding adieu to Genoa, we took the maritime road to Pisa.

Of the three strangers, I was the only one with whom the Piedmontese could hold converse, for Mr. B—knew no living language save that of the country in which he was born, and Mr. C—had scarcely the advantage of him, his knowledge extending no farther than a few Irish oaths picked up from his nurse; Gazzola and I were therefore left to ourselves, and after a tedious and dreary journey of three days, during the whole of which time it rained in torrents, we arrived at Pisa, where we separated—he taking the road to Florence, while we pursued that to Leghorn. In a few days, however, we all re-assembled in the former city, and be then offered himself as a master to perfect me in Italian, with which language I was as yet but little acquainted.

Thus our intercourse commenced and was continued, and as he had no other employment and his means were scanty, he became a constant visitor at my lodgings—a frequent and welcome guest at my table; and after two or three such bursts as that with which I commenced this chapter, I succeeded in getting him to relate some passages in his history, the more prominent parts of which I was accustomed immediately to commit to paper.

Poor fellow!—fortune bad indeed frowned upon him; and yet, although his hair had become almost silvery white, and the moustache had lost the ebon hue upon which he had prided himself in times gone by, that perfect *gaité de cœur*—that devil-may-carishness which he had acquired from his long service in the French army, had never deserted him, and he seemed as light-hearted and volatile as in his most palmy days, never, during our acquaintance, giving way to low spirits.

Of his subsequent career I know nothing, and as many years have elapsed since we parted, during which I have never heard anything of him, I presume he has passed to that bourne whence no traveller returns. Of the reasons why these reminiscences have not before been given to the world, or why they are now published, I may perhaps speak hereafter; at present I shall content myself with saying, in the language of the poet,

I know not how the truth may be,
I say the tale as 'twas said to me.

CHAPTER 2

La Ballerina

It would matter little, *said Gazzola, one evening,* when or where I drew my breath, or who were my parents; the children of misfortune need never boast of their ancestry; but as my first essay, and subsequent appearance as an actor in the hustling scenes of this world were entirely the effect of my own imprudence, I must say a few words on the early days of my youth.

I was born in the north of Piedmont, but my family had removed to Turin, and being the eldest son of a widowed mother, who was left by her husband in tolerably easy circumstances, I became her favourite; indeed, with such indulgence had she treated me, and deferred for so long a period my departure from home, to which she could never make up her mind, that I had attained the age of sixteen years before any profession had been thought of for me, or any fixed mode of life determined upon. I had been scantily educated, for the revolutionary troubles of France had extended to our own country, the people were fraternizing, and matters appeared in much too unsettled a state to allow of my being sent far from home, while, taking advantage of the too great partiality of my parent, I had little ambition for the character of a studious young man.

Poor dear mother! When I look back upon these times and recall your great anxiety that I should become a gentleman of the world—your charge that I should bear myself as became a man—and the pains you took with my dress and appearance, I cannot but smile at your too partial pride, and wonder what you would have said had you witnessed some of the scenes of after-life through which your ungrateful child was fated to pass. Oh! what can equal the untiring devotion of a mother's affection? and yet, fool that I was, I valued it not while I possessed it, and now that the loss is irreparable, I become sensible of its extent. It is the polestar of our destiny—the never-varying compass on the stormy ocean of life—an oasis in the desert of man's existence, to which, with undying feelings of love, we recur again and again when all besides is forgotten, and the remembrance of which expires but with our latest sigh. Through all my wanderings—in the stillness of solitude or amid the bustle and turmoil of the camp—in the wearying night march, the dreary bivouac, the hour of victory and the moment of repulse, memory has exerted her power, and the remembrance of my mother's deep devotion and unceasing affection has stolen over me, filling my bosom with sad and mournful thoughts, and dimming the eye of the rough soldier with unhidden tears. I may with truth affirm, that however bitter have been my disappointments, I have had but one unavailing regret, and that has been caused by my conduct to my mother. I do deeply, passionately regret that I parted from her without bidding her adieu, and that another's bosom pillowed her head while her last sigh was breathed in a prayer for the welfare of her child.

I am becoming sentimental: it is a fault of grey hairs into which I shall not readily fall again, but at sixteen years we think differently to what we do at sixty; and at the former period I was the beau of Turin—for such in her pride my fond parent declared me to be. Caressed and flattered by the women, smiled at and noticed by the men, who can be surprised that, although my stature scarcely allowed me to rank with the latter, I had ceased to consider myself "in simplicity a child." My time was entirely my own; I was free to come and go as I listed, with a purse amply supplied. And as dancing and fencing were considered accomplishments indispensable to the education of a gentleman, my only study was to render myself completely master of them, and I flatter myself I became a tolerable proficient, leaving no stone unturned in their acquisition, and spending the greater portion of every morning in the *Salle d'Armes* or the *Ecole de danse*.

Fatal attendance! hence arose all my misfortunes! Attached

to each of the principal theatres of Italy is a school of dancing, in part supported by the government; and at that of Turin the young men of the city were accustomed to assemble to take lessons from the ballet-master, while the whole *corps de ballet* also attended for the purpose of learning some new piece, or perfecting themselves in an old one. Their attendance was compulsory, while ours being voluntary, gave us an opportunity of becoming acquainted with all the dancers of the theatre, an acquaintance at once the most fascinating and dangerous. Happy, happy boyhood; how many hours were idled away ostensibly in taking lessons in this delightful amusement, but really in whispering soft nonsense into the ears of the ballerinas, most of whom were chosen for their personal grace and beauty.

It has been well said, "*Le sage n'a ni amour ni haine,*" but I was a boy of sixteen, and not a wise man; so I took the earliest opportunity to fall desperately in love, or at least to fancy I was, much the same thing to a young imagination; for though, as one of your poets has declared, "the cold in clime are cold in blood," and in your more frigid atmosphere the idea of a boy of sixteen being in love would appear ridiculous, it is not the same with us—in the sunny south the passions are more precocious; and Adela, or, as she was more generally termed, "*La Bella,*" lit up a flame in my bosom that somewhat interfered with my devotions to the foil and the valse. I made her acquaintance in the Salon during my attendance on the Ballet Master, from whom she was receiving the instructions necessary to qualify her for the part of Prima Ballerina; and seeing she was beautiful, I believed she was good, and had therefore no hesitation about her.

When the business of the morning was concluded I generally accompanied her home, spending hours in that soft dalliance which takes place between those who love and believe themselves beloved. I loved her with all the ardour of a first passion; and there is a purity in the first love of a boy, ere the lip is clothed with the early down of manhood, or the heart seared by contact with a rude and unfeeling world, which elevates our nature above itself, robbing it of all its baser passions—and this once lost is never regained. The purity of first love never again returns to us—the early freshness of our thoughts once sullied, is sullied for ever; and we grovel on, cherishing a mixture of admiration and passion, and endeavouring, but in vain, to cheat ourselves into the belief that it is love. Such has ever been the case with me: "other arms have pressed me, other forms caressed me;" but this, my early passion, was indulged without one thought of the future, one dream of its termination. And yet, while hugging myself with its continuance, it suddenly received a shock—the illusive veil was rudely torn aside—the whole current of my love was checked, and my feelings were stunned by a blow, the remembrance of which has never passed away.

Weeks of this pure intercourse had passed, during which my love burnt with an intensity none the less that it was unopposed. I loved and was beloved, enchanting thought. What was the world to me, no feeling of doubt or jealousy had crossed my mind, until she earnestly entreated me to abstain from attending her from the rehearsal, preferring to go home alone, and to receive my visits on such evenings as she was not engaged at the Ballet. Fell dissembler! So well did she conceal her real motives, so plausibly did she gloss over the true cause, that, jealous as it made me, I was fain to consent, little thinking that all her love was pretence, and that even at that moment she had accepted the protection of another, who was in the habit of visiting her every day on her return from the theatre.

This I afterwards discovered to be the case, and hearing by accident, that, occasionally in an evening, when she had professed to be too ill to entertain me, some one else had been admitted, rage and jealousy took possession of me, and, though I knew not the name of my rival, I determined on being revenged.

This resolution filled up the whole current of my thoughts, I was restless and unhappy, never still nor satisfied;

For, oh, what damned moments tells lie o'er,
Who dotes, yet doubts, suspects, yet strongly loves.

And I was bent on being convinced, to which end I laid a plot, which succeeded but too well, for, alas! to its success the whole of my misfortunes in after life may be attributed.

CHAPTER 3

The Confirmation

I have said I was resolved to satisfy my doubts, and to enable me to do this, one evening, when she was not to be engaged at the theatre, I sent word that I was ill, and waiting till night came on, I threw my cloak around me, and repaired to her residence. This was situated in an old palace, long since abandoned by its noble possessors, and now degraded by being let in floors as lodgings, a fate to which many of the noblest edifices in this country have been obliged to submit. Passing through the outer door, you ascended a flight of steps into a long corridor, very feebly lighted by a single window placed near the entrance, and at the other extremity was a door leading to my lady's apartments, towards which I stealthily advanced, completely concealed by the gloom by which I was surrounded; I heard voices in the room, one of which I plainly perceived was that of a man, and all the demoniac passions of our nature rising in my bosom, I pictured to myself my rival occupying the place I had fondly believed reserved for me alone. These thoughts quickly gave place to others; "and now, said I, for revenge; yes, caitiff thief, that steals men's mistresses, here you shall meet your reward." Drawing my sword, a weapon without which, even at that early age, I never left my home, I retired a little from the door, while the advancing hour of night rendered my concealment the more secure; in a short time the door was cautiously opened, and some one prepared to go forth; but having taken the precaution to conceal the light ere they parted, I could not distinguish who it was, though the weight of the footstep pronounced him to be a man. I have often wondered what restrained my hand—why I did not rush forward and immolate both on the spot; perhaps some feeling of tenderness kept me back, and it was not till she had wished him good night, accompanied as I thought by an audible mark of affection due only to myself, and the door was closed upon him, that I remembered the errand upon which I had set out. He paused a moment ere he turned to quit the place, and in less time than I have taken to relate it, I cautiously advanced, pricking the opposite wall with the point of my weapon.

Little dreaming of what was in store for him, my rival had made one step in advance, when I struck something which I knew was much too soft to be the wall; he immediately drew his sword, but before he could defend himself I made a lunge, and, throwing my whole force upon the blow, drove the weapon through his body, before I had time to repeat the attack, he uttered a loud cry, and thoroughly affrighted at what I had done, I turned and fled the road I had come, and was not many minutes in regaining my mother's abode: here my worst fears were confirmed by observing blood upon my sword, and I began to contemplate myself in the character of a murderer, a feeling not lessened by the intelligence of my brother, who, coming in soon after, told us that General—had been stabbed near the Pallazzo of the Ballerina, and that the police were in search of his assailant.

Though my rage had in some measure cooled, I can well remember the effect of this announcement. One moment I resolved to give myself up to the police, denouncing the general as the destroyer of my peace; the next I determined to seek the faithless fair one, and immolate her upon the spot, a just sacrifice to my outraged affections, By degrees, however, this tempest subsided, and fear got the better of all other feelings; for knowing how powerfully my adversary was connected, I abandoned all thoughts of revenge, and began to consider what was necessary to be done for my own safety, not doubting that her ladyship would suspect me, and feel little pain in denouncing the delinquent; and I must thus inevitably fall a victim to my own impetuosity.

Alarm, or perhaps shame, prevented my consulting my friends;

and my mother being absent from home, and knowing nothing of my attachment, I decided on flight; collecting a small bundle of clothes and such superfluous cash as I could lay my hands upon, I threw myself on the bed, determined to quit the city with the earliest dawn.

Great, I was aware, was the sacrifice I was about to make, but I thought it my wisest course; for as every kind of duel was at this period forbidden on pain of death, I had little hope of being forgiven for this encounter, which the malice of my enemies might have' construed into an attempt at assassination; and the police had recently so much improved in efficiency, that there was little chance of concealment by remaining in Turin.

"*Ce n'est que le premier pas qui coute,*" says the proverb; and on the morrow morning, at break of day, I sallied forth from the city, a fishing rod in my hand, the better to conceal my object, and passing through the *Porta d' Italia,* I took the road to Milan, my heart more heavily oppressed with care than my pockets with coin. Still I trudged on without a passport or paper of any kind, with my knapsack at my back; and the greater the distance I placed between my late abode and myself, the more buoyant my spirits became; until on arriving at Novara without pursuit, I stopped to refresh myself, and reached the city of Milan on the second day, taking up my abode at the Hotel of the Two Fountains.

I was now my own master, lord of that barren heritage, myself—launched on the wide world without compass or rudder—free to come and go as I pleased—and this I miscalled liberty—yet was I still a slave—slave to a passion for a dishonoured woman. But I had visions of a life of pleasure, and true it is that "*la volupté sacrifié l'avenir au present,*" for I entered into all the amusements of this enchanting city without thinking what was to be my future destiny, or how my purse was to be refilled when its contents had disappeared. From the café to the theatre—from the theatre to the *bal-masqué,* for it was the time of the carnival, and masquerades were not then the poor tame things they have since become, one half of the company government spies, and the other half their victims—I wandered on till enjoyment produced satiety, and I began to long again for my quiet home; when one morning, while standing on the steps of the hotel, musing as to what might be my future fate, a carriage drove into the court yard, out of which stepped the cause of all my misfortunes. Yes, here in truth she was, and, quickly recognizing her victim, she uttered a loud cry and threw herself into my arms. Fool that I was—the situation was too embarrassing, so instead of depositing her on the steps, and coolly wishing her good morning, I found my whole heart yearn towards her, and forgetting all the past drew her gently into my room, and laid her on the couch.

The fountains of her eyes were opened, and after a passionate flood of tears, her faint, for such it was in every sense of the word, went off, and she poured forth a volley of congratulations at my recovery—of her poignant regrets at my departure, assuring me that however appearances might be against her, they were entirely false, and she was, as she had ever been, wholly and solely mine. To my enquiries about the General she replied, that he had been seriously wounded but was likely to recover; and that having no suspicion by whom he had been attacked, no search had been made for me, nor any proceedings commenced against me. I was therefore free to return; and my mother, who was inconsolable at my absence, had spared no pains to discover the place of my retreat; "but," added the temptress, "what was her loss compared to mine; the instinct of true love guided my footsteps, and I have happily succeeded in a search which would have ended only with my life." Oh! thou invincible spirit of mischief, woman, though thou be'est a very devil, yet do we love thee still. In truth, she had no more idea of seeking me than had our holy father, the Pope, but had come to Milan to fulfil an engagement at one of the theatres, for, as the Carnival terminates a week sooner at Turin than at the former city, it was no unusual thing for the performers to come over there to finish the season. I knew not this, so I listened to all she said; and blinded by my passion believed her asseverations of purity, and was persuaded that to leave her was to sacrifice a faithful heart that lived only in my smiles; and this pretty tale, told with the most inimitable grace, would have had its effect on a less susceptible nature than mine. I was not the first the sex had betrayed, I cannot flatter myself with the hope that I shall be the last; and with her, success was certain, for how could I doubt the sacrifice she boasted of having made to follow me—her protestations of unalterable love—or her fixed determination to devote her whole life to obliterate the traces of her apparent inconstancy. The train was too well laid; the snare too carefully prepared; can you wonder I was caught, and that I but faintly opposed her proposition that we should consider ourselves as married, and while she pursued her vocation at the Theatre Carcano, I should continue to attend the school of dancing, leading, for the rest of the day, that "*dolce far niente*" kind of life into which I had fallen, and which seemed only likely to be cloying with too much sweet.

CHAPTER 4

The Flight

Unfortunate as was the termination of my short sojourn in Milan, I never recur to it with feelings of regret; for if amid the scenes of gaiety and pleasure the heart does sometimes forget its former cherished affections, and, abandoning itself to the present, cease to feel for the past, we are as supremely happy as we can hope to be under any circumstances. You, signor, who in sober manhood have visited this enchanting city, and beheld the scenes I will not endeavour to describe, can well believe the feelings of awe and delight with which I contemplated the glittering pinnacles of the Duomo, glowing in the warm sunset of an autumnal evening, or in the bright effulgence of the glorious orb of night. They thrill through the frame with a delight we strive in vain to account for, and leave an impression which a constant friction through after scenes may lessen, but cannot wholly obliterate. If, after having beheld the Cathedrals of St. Paul and Notre Dame, you could say that it was the first architectural pile you had seen in which the reality far exceeded the expectation, how much more intense must have been the sensations produced on one who had never looked on any thing superior to the Cathedral of St. John, at Turin. Viewed in the silvery light of the moon, the thousand statues casting their long shadows over the adjoining piazza; the effect was enchanting, and but for an incident that occurred the first evening I so contemplated it, the effect would have been one of unmixed pleasure. On that occasion the moon was at the full, and as I stood with my back towards the palace in which the Archduke now resides, a solitary wanderer passed near me, whose receding figure was quickly lost in the shade of the building; a bustling of feet and a sharp cry succeeded, and hastening to the spot, I found that an assassin had just plunged his stiletto into the bosom of the passer-by. Alas! that man, under the very image of the Saviour, and shadowed by the temple raised to his glory, should thus brand himself with the mark of Cain, and yet, how nearly had I escaped a similar infliction. It was a lesson I have never forgotten.

I wandered through the marble aisles of this noble pile, and sad but salutary were my reflections. The murderer had escaped but his victim was taken up by the police, and conveyed to the *Ospedale Maggiore*, where in a few hours he breathed his last, and no search was ever made after his destroyer. To those who live in countries where the supremacy of the law is maintained, and crimes of any magnitude seldom go undetected and unpunished, it no doubt appears strange that in Italy we set little store by human life, and yet the penalty of death would have followed his discovery, but no efforts were made, and in the course of a few days the event was forgotten. Near to the spot where I saw this poor fellow meet his early doom, I once encountered a man who begged piteously and abjectly for alms. Surprised at the unusual occurrence, I enquired into his case, and found that his brother, in an accidental affray with the police, had had the misfortune to kill one of them. He was taken, and thrown into prison, from which there was no chance of escape, save by the scaffold, unless he could raise money enough to purchase a substitute, who, by filling the dead man's place in the ranks, would relieve the government from the embarrassment caused by the loss of their officer. Strange justice thought I, fully carrying out the opinion I have long entertained, that hanging is the worst use you can make of a man.

I never passed the Duomo afterwards without offering up a prayer of gratitude and thanksgiving to the Giver of all Good, that my conscience was spared the maddening blot, and such was the effect produced upon me that on returning home at night from the theatre, I constantly made a long detour rather than pass through the *Piazza del Duomo*.

I know not how long the kind of life I was at this time leading might have lasted, had its termination depended upon myself, for every day I seemed more and more satisfied with it. It was however suddenly brought to a close, for one night, on our return home from the theatre, my *cara sposa,* for such I considered her, asked permission to be absent for three days, for the purpose of visiting a sister then lying at the point of death at Brescia, to the theatre of which town she was attached as a Ballerina.

Little suspecting the real motive, I could not refuse so reasonable a request, and as the conveyance by which she proposed to go started at a very early hour in the morning, I retired to rest while she busied herself with preparations for the journey. The morrow came, and she arose and dressed herself, taking care to disturb me as little as possible, and wishing her safe back again, I turned drowsily in my bed and once more resigned myself to the influence of the place. Since we had lived together I had exercised little authority over the purse, and our common stock, composed of the remainder of the money I had brought from home, and a trifling sum saved from her salary, was deposited in an old secretaire which occupied a prominent place among the scanty furniture of our sitting room. When I arose, you may judge my surprise at finding that the whole had been abstracted, and though it was some time before I could satisfy myself of the fact, I became at last convinced that the illness of her sister was a ruse, that she had again played me false and abandoned me, having possessed herself of every farthing I had in the world, together with such articles of my wardrobe as she could lay her hands on. Money, clothes, and watch were gone, and as I stood by the empty secretaire, at last fully alive to my own helpless situation, I gnashed my teeth, and tore my hair for very vexation at finding how I had been duped. Here was I in the very position I had sometimes dreaded, but never contemplated. I was a beggar in a strange place, far from relief by my friends. But my rage was of little avail. I could not return to Turin; pride forbad an application to my mother, so I sallied forth to beg or steal as I best could, wherewith to break my fast, and bending my steps to the theatre, luckily found that two nights salary to my betrayer still remained unpaid, and having obtained possession of it, I adjourned with one of .the performers to a coffee-house, and there deliberated on my future prospects. My credulity had been fairly but severely punished, and I was rather an object of ridicule than of commiseration. My own exertions were my only resources, and they, Heaven knows, were feeble enough, since I had been brought up to no profession, and had no ostensible means of earning a subsistence.

There was, however, no use in praying to Hercules, so addressing myself to a theatrical agent, I received an offer of a situation at the theatre at Crema, a little town about twenty miles from Milan, and if to my connection with the stage I ascribed all my misfortunes, I was in the end dependent on it for support. Necessity overcame pride, and hunger, the most powerful of impulses, induced me again to shoulder my knapsack, most grievously lessened in weight by my sojourn in Milan, and once more to betake myself to the road.

Hitherto I had danced for my own gratification, I was now about to do so for the amusement of others; and, I must confess, that at first the novelty of my position in some measure impeded my efforts; by degrees, however, this wore off, and I soon became sensibly alive to the wretchedness of my situation, to which, as there was no relief, I submitted with as good a grace as I could.

From the theatre at Crema I went to that of Lodi, and from thence to *Alexandrie de la Paille.*

I must confess, that on re-entering my native country I felt some qualms of fear lest I should be discovered, and for the first time I dropped my patronymic, and appeared under an alias, assuming the name by which I am now known.

My mind may lose its force, my blood its fire, but never, while memory exists, shall I forget my first appearance on this stage, for there in form as tangible as form could be, I saw, on the first representation, the very woman who had been my ruin. My first impulse was to seize her on the stage and hurl her over the foot-lights into the orchestra, but reflection convinced me that her position here was much more favourable than my own, and consequently I must go to the wall, I therefore mastered my passion, and was compelled, in spite of my disgust, not only to dance in the same ballet with her, but even to take her hand.

On the morrow morning she sent for me, and attempted an explanation, begging me to return to our former intercourse, but her arts were of no avail, I resolutely declined any further intimacy with her, and heartily rejoiced when the termination of my engagement enabled me to depart, and commence another at Verona.

Chapter 5

The Discovery

Notwithstanding my hard fate, my spirits were not much depressed, and I once more turned my back upon my native country and the faithless woman who had been the cause of all my misfortunes, and journeyed on to Verona, a city celebrated by your immortal poet as the residence of that pair of hapless lovers, Romeo and Juliet.

At this period it was occupied by the Austrian troops, part of the army of General Wurmser, who was fast advancing to the relief of Mantua, then closely besieged by the French.

In the ranks of the Austrians were many of my compatriots, who hastened to join the only nation that seemed likely to make head against the overwhelming power of France; and though I ran some little risk of discovery, I considered my change of appearance, added to the alteration of my name, a sufficient safeguard. Such, as will be seen in the sequel, did not prove to be the fact.

Sometime before I left Turin, I had been intimate with, and received repeated acts of kindness from, an officer in the Piedmontese cavalry, and had given him a magnificent French poodle dog, bred by myself, and much petted for the tricks he had learnt, and his great devotion to his master. It was the latter cause indeed which induced me to part with him, for from his constant habit of following me, he occasionally gave more information of my whereabouts than was altogether agreeable.

On my making my bow to the audience, the first night of my appearance, who should I behold in the stage-box, staring me full in the face, as if it were a countenance of which he had a confused recollection, but that, memory had not fully decided that he had seen me before, but the identical officer to whom I had given the dog, and though I was considerably embarrassed by the recognition, which was instant on my part, yet his apparent uncertainty gave me hopes that I should still be able to preserve my *incognito*. To this end, I shrunk back from the foot-lights; and when abroad in the city, avoided every opportunity of meeting him, and although he came frequently to the theatre, and discovered, and called at my lodgings, I had ever the good fortune to miss him. Things went on in this way for some time, when my friend, somewhat nettled at my pertinacious avoidance of him, and becoming more and more convinced of my identity, resolved to satisfy himself, and as I seemed insensible of human feelings, he called to his aid those of his dog Bruno. Ensconcing himself in the rear of the box, the front seats of which were filled by some of his comrades, who were unknown to me, he patiently waited till the end of the ballet, in which I fancied I had acquitted myself with more than my usual success, having been vociferously applauded by the officers; I was therefore not greatly surprised at receiving an invitation to their box, a circumstance by no means uncommon when they wished to express to an actor, in person, the satisfaction they felt at his performance. Little suspecting that this was but part and parcel of a plan, or the scene that was prepared in which I was to play such prominent figure, I hurried forward to receive the compliments I flattered myself were my due, and the moment I entered the loge, Bruno, who till then had been lying on the floor at the foot of my friend, uttered a low whine, and springing upon me, satisfied his owner that his suspicions were correct. "Down, Bruno," completed the discovery; for how, if I were a stranger, as I asserted I was, had I become acquainted with the name of the animal?

Further disguise was useless, and I at once accompanied my friend to his lodgings, where I threw myself on his generosity, and in spite of all his offers and entreaties to the contrary, I determined to persevere in the line I had chalked out for myself.

In this I was confirmed by the tidings he gave me of my family. My poor mother had taken my loss so much to heart that it had brought her grey hairs with sorrow to the grave; whilst my uncle, a cold, austere man, who always disliked me, and, as dislikes are apt to be reciprocal, to whom I bore no good will, had taken possession of our patrimony, and sent my brothers and sisters to school. In vain did my friend represent to me the degradation of my situation—in vain did he paint in glowing colours the happiness and gaiety of a soldier's life—my hour was not yet come; and in a few days we parted, he to follow his fortunes in the service of Mars, while I still remained servitor of Terpsichore.

Wurmser, who had lately been defeated in a general engagement, now hazarded a second, which was attended by a like result; and Alvinzi, who succeeded to the command, immediately broke up his quarters at Verona, and the army prepared to advance. Thus my friend and I were parted, never to meet again; and thus another of the ties that bound me to my country was severed.

During my residence in Verona I had the felicity to acquire the friendship of the Marchese Giustiniana, a worthy scion of that noble stock from which, in former years, the ducal chair at Venice was frequently filled, with equal honour to the occupant and advantage to the country. This young nobleman had been married to a beautiful countrywoman about two years previous to the period of which I speak, and a little boy had been born to them—a pledge of love quite idolized by his parents. One morning, as I was standing at my window in Veronetta (the name given to the smaller portion of the city, which is divided into two unequal portions by the Adige), contemplating that rapid river, now much swollen by the late rains, I beheld a nurse-maid standing on the steps of the Palazzo Giustiniana, dangling in her arms the infant heir of that noble house—a fine, lively boy, apparently about nine months old. The laughing efforts of the child, and pleased appearance of his nurse, particularly attracted my attention, till at last I heard a loud scream, and saw the hapless infant floating down the stream. To doff my upper garments and plunge into the water was but the work of an instant, and I rose to the surface to battle with a current that every moment seemed to threaten me with annihilation; but I struggled on manfully, and, by giving way to it in some degree, I succeeded in grasping the terrified infant, and, bearing him in my hand as I best could, made for the shore with my prize.

How little did I think at that moment of the parents, how little heed what rank they bore whose unconscious offspring I had thus rescued from the jaws of death. The impulse was one of humanity, sudden as impulses generally are. And after changing my clothes, and arraying my recovered treasure in some dry things belonging to a child of my landlady, I stepped into a boat and crossed the river to the palace.

The scene that here met my view was one of the most heart-rending I had ever witnessed; for the Marchesa, sensible only of the loss of her child, had been in strong hysterics ever since, while her lord, the mute image of despair, was bending over her, endeavouring to look the consolation his lips denied him the power to utter. The servant girl, who had left the steps the moment the accident occurred in the hope of finding some one who could rescue her darling, stood with uplifted eyes, and hands convulsively clasped together, a fitting representation of the bereaved mother, whose statue in the Gallery at Florence has enchanted half the world. I entered almost unnoticed until my little burden uttered a scream of joy, and held out its tiny hands towards his unconscious parents. It was like the convent bell to the weary pilgrim—the sound of peace and hope; and clasping the boy to her bosom, the Marchesa seemed at once restored to reason.

From that hour I became an especial favourite with both father and mother; the former insisting on being acquainted with my history, the latter lavishing on me every kindness that a grateful heart could dictate.

Till then I had never felt the degradation of my situation, though I had long been fully alive to its miseries; none other offered itself, and I was forced to finish my engagement in Verona without having determined to abandon the stage, or formed any settled plan for the future.

At last it was concluded, the theatre closed, and my kind friends, with solid remembrances and fervent prayers for my happiness, bade me adieu, and I went to Ravenna.

During the last few months the aspect of affairs had changed. Wurmser and Alvinzi, foiled in their attempts to relieve Mantua, which was still closely invested by the French, had again retired upon the Adige. The winter had commenced. Unabated vigour was displayed by both armies, and so unsettled was the whole north of Italy, that on my arrival at Ravenna I found the director had abandoned the speculation as hopeless, and that the theatre had been prematurely closed.

I was again without employment, and turning my steps northward, I by chance fell in with an officer of the French army, and by him was persuaded to join its ranks. With the same recklessness and precipitation I had before displayed, I accepted his offer, and took service in his regiment as a volunteer. Here a new career was opened me. I had abandoned the mimic stage to occupy a part on the grand theatre of war, and hastening with my companion to join the division of the army to which he was attached, in a few days I found myself in the environs of Mantua, forming part of the force by which it had been so long invested, and the commander of which declared he would leave behind him in the trenches ere he would raise the siege.

And truly he kept his word, for though day after day as many men fell from fatigue as from the fire of the enemy, he never for one instant relented; others supplied their places, and the work of destruction proceeded as before. But let me not anticipate.

CHAPTER 5

The Siege of Mantua

Henceforth my career was to be one of glory, for although I may have been said to be in arms against my native country, I considered that I had abandoned her and become cosmopolitan. As a citizen of the world, I entered the ranks of the army of France, and although so young, I considered myself the soldier of liberty, and felt a love of glory mount in my bosom, a feeling to which it had hitherto been a stranger. I was now under the command of the "Little Corporal" and formed part and parcel of that army which had already won for itself the admiration of the world—I was a portion of that living machine which, once set in motion by the master-mind of Napoleon, overcame all obstacles, and engaged but to conquer.

I had taken an irrevocable step—one from which there was no retreat—and was now a renegade, not indeed to my religion, for our holy father, the Pope, having long since declared all connected with the stage as without the pale of the church, we, on our parts, had made no efforts to remove the interdiction, but by our conduct proclaimed that we had nothing whatever to do with religion. In truth, I professed none; I despised alike all sects and denominations; and lived on in this world, as if all were to end here and there were no hereafter.

But if our own faults alone ought to make us unhappy, I was conscious of none, and therefore felt no remorse, for however the vain boaster may affect to despise what he calls the trammels of religion and the faith which other men profess; if the foundations of education be based upon it, the edifice may totter, but it never falls prostrate: the early lessons return upon us when we least expect them, proving that although the impression may be defaced, it is not wholly obliterated. This, however, was not my case; and in the dreary solitude of a prison I have since become acquainted with a merciful Creator, and learned to adore that Benevolence whose right hand is stretched out to protect the meanest of His creatures; yet at this period of my career I lived as if none such existed. My spiritual education had been neglected even more than my temporal one; and thus, without one feeling of compunction, I became a renegade to my country, a traitor to my fatherland, and joining the ranks of her enemies, employed those arms against her which should have been wielded in her defence.

Yet conscience, that doth make cowards of us all, exerted no influence on me, my step was firm and elastic, my laugh joyous and free, and I entered on the duties of a soldier, with all the ardour of a young mind pursuing its first passion, and though at times the memory of the green fields I saw destroyed, the trees and shrubs uprooted, and all the ornaments and beauties of the earth trampled upon and reduced to ruin, exhibiting a prospect naked and bare, and presenting to the eye mud and stones and sand; came across me and saddened my heart: when I beheld the country as it was, and remembered what it had been, vivified by nature—clad as it were in a nuptial garment, and unfolding to our gaze a scene of which the eye was never weary—the heart never sick—I did at times shudder, and, despising the gaudy trappings of the soldier, sigh again for peace.

There are few—however happy may have been their youth, however glorious their career—who would willingly live over again all their early scenes; for, although the brilliancy of success may in some measure compensate for the misery it entails, yet would we not wish it repeated. How few are there who have stood in the deadly breach, waiting for the word to advance, who have not recalled to their minds the desolate hearths they have witnessed—the many martyrs they have seen fall before the shrine of glory.

Although the details of the siege of Mantua belong more properly to the historian, I must, with the view of rendering myself better understood, say a few words relative to the position of the contending armies prior to the time at which I joined that of the French.

Mantua had been invested as early as May in the preceding year, but the advance of Wurmser had in part been crowned with success, for although he had been twice defeated, and a new general, in the person of Alvinzi, had succeeded to the command, yet the siege had been raised on the 23rd of July.

Scarcely had the ravages of the enemy been repaired, and the place re-provisioned, than Wurmser, who had beaten Murat and Pijeou, at Corea, on the 12th of September, and by the merest accident failed in the capture of Napoleon, now pressed on, and, foiled in his attempt to unite his forces with Alvinzi, cut to pieces a body of French horse by which he was opposed, and threw himself into the suburb of S. Giorgio. By this he hoped to be able to maintain his communication with the surrounding country, and thus supply himself with provisions and forage.

His position was, however, much too favourable to allow of his retaining it undisturbed; and after a severe and bloody struggle, in which many men fell on both sides, he was compelled to retire within the walls of Mantua.

In the character of the veteran Austrian there was a sufficient guarantee that the reduction of this stronghold would be no easy affair; and all that human ingenuity could suggest, or human efforts effect, had been done to prolong the struggle. Sortie after sortie had been made and repulsed, every attempt at relief had been frustrated, yet still the heroic Wurmser held out, declaring that he would bury himself in the ruins rather than capitulate.

Matters were in this state when I joined the blockading force, then under the command of Serrurier, and notwithstanding the nights were cold and frosty, and a light covering of snow obscured the face of nature, the men were employed in the trenches without intermission; and as party after party relieved each other, the work went steadily on, while each battery, as soon as it was completed, opened upon the devoted city.

Provera, who had attempted its relief, and failed, managed to communicate with Wurmser, and together they planned measures for his assistance, when suddenly Napoleon, who had just won the bloody field of Rivoli, arrived at Roverbella, a few miles from Mantua. He attacked Provera, drove the garrison, which had sallied out to his assistance, again within the walls, and prepared to prosecute the siege with redoubled ardour.

As yet I had played no part in the game of war, for, steadily employed in acquiring my drill, my position as a volunteer prevented my accompanying the troops to work in the trenches. And thus a month passed on.

Mantua is situated on an islet at the extremity of a small lake, which seems to have been formed by the sudden widening of the banks of the Mincio, that river flowing through the town and dividing it into two nearly equal parts. These were connected by five or six bridges, the principal one, the *Ponte di Molini*, being defended by the two citadels, and the *Ponte di S. Giorgio* strongly fortified at either end. Both portions of the town were surrounded by a wide and deep fosse, filled by the waters of the Mincio, and lined on the inner side by a high and massive wall, from the embrasures of which projected the brazen mouths of hundreds of cannon, which hurled destruction on many of our men as they pursued their work in the trenches.

Still the work went bravely on—our batteries answering the challenge, and the heavy boom of the cannon, now and then interrupted by a sharp fire of musketry, was ringing constantly in our ears; but our leader persevered, and as parallel after parallel was completed, till at last our nearest work approached within point blank range, none doubted the result, and we kept hammering away at the massive wall without intermission. Occasionally shells and rockets were thrown into the town, but these seemed only an episode in the grand drama; for, with the dogged perseverance for which our commander afterwards became so celebrated, we kept battering away, nothing seeming to divert him from the main point—that of effecting a breach.

At length we succeeded, and as stone after stone came tumbling down from the effects of our shot, we began to make up our minds that it would soon be fit to be stormed, and nature having already provided us with an icy bridge over the ditch, every thing was prepared for the dreaded moment.

At last it came, the engineers reported the breach practicable, and the storming party was selected, and I have often felt surprised that it was composed principally of recruits—volunteers like myself—determined to earn their first laurels in the most dangerous of enterprizes. We were to be led by an old veteran from the 10th regiment of the line, one who had before performed prodigies of valour, and whose coolness and courage on more than one similar occasion, were taken as the prestige of success.

How I envied the gallant fellow the medal that hung on his breast, and resolved to win such an one or perish in the attempt; but these feelings gave place to others, as taking my position on the right of the leading file, I marched slowly down to the edge of the ice. No word was spoken, no sound broke the stillness of the night, save the hurried breathing and audible beating of the heart in many a bosom where, in a few short hours, it would be still for ever, and the slow and measured tread of our devoted band as it advanced. It was dark as night could well be, when the ground is covered with snow, and all around seemed still and calm as that death to which so many of us were hurrying.

We were already on the ice when the guns from the walls opened their fire; and as rocket after rocket illumined the sky, and rendered our position apparent, a withering fire of musketry mowed down our ranks, and the leading files hesitated to advance, when a deep, full voice, whose tones I had never before heard, but which afterwards became familiar as household words to my ear, arrested my attention. "*Courage, soldats, tenez ferme,*" were the words it uttered, and confidence seemed suddenly restored. He, the child of Victory, was there directing our movements, and as our batteries replied to the thunder of our enemies, the word forward was again given, and rushing madly across the moat, we dashed at the breach. Still at times the music of that deep, full voice, now hushed in death, comes over my memory, and recalls to my mind the electric shock that seemed to thrill through every muscle, on my becoming aware of the presence of him whom I believed miles off, snugly ensconced in his tent; every man seemed animated by the same thought that, as he stood upon the edge of the moat, his eagle eye could pierce the ranks of strife, and mark the road we took. We fought like incarnate devils, and though a murdering fire of musketry mowed down our ranks, and despatched many a gallant fellow to his last account, others quickly supplied his place; no thought of retreat came across our minds, we were pledged to death or victory.

Our path was impeded by the dead and the dying, and as volley after volley added to the carnage, I, as yet unscathed, pressed forward, urged on by those in the rear, all equally eager to be first in the town. At last as my foot rested upon the breach, the discharge of one of the guns lighting for an instant the surrounding gloom, discovered to my eyes the open space beyond the wall, defended by the bristling bayonets of the enemy, whose front seemed firm and unbroken, and whom we had pressed forward thus far to conquer or to die. "Forward!" was still the cry; the crash of musketry and the heavy booming of the great guns were lulled into temporary repose, when as I made good my footing in the street, surrounded by my comrades, all equally anxious, a well directed fire of grape swept away the force before us, wounding many of our own men, and scattering death and destruction around. Many of our best men here bit the dust, but still we advanced, till driving the enemy before us, we made good our position, and the place was won.

In the confusion that followed, as regiment after regiment poured in through the breach our gallantry had won, I remember little that occurred. The conflict continued hand to hand in the streets, every inch being hotly contested, but it was all to no purpose, we made good our position, and the Austrians retired to the citadel, while our troops, satisfied with what they had acquired, set about providing themselves with quarters, and when the day broke I was quietly sleeping, dreaming over again the scenes through which I had passed; the noise and din still echoed in my ears, but with the exception of two or three slight bruises, I had passed through the thickest of the fray unhurt.

Chapter 7

The Place of Mantua

Glory, thou unsubstantial vision of the mind—thou word of power which hast caused young hearts to beat with high ambition and hope, what art thou, after all, but an *ignis fatuus* which distracteth the youth, misleadeth the middle-aged, and tempteth the veteran to the very verge of the grave, luring them onward by thy flickering rays?

Ask the young soldier, as for the first time he dons his glittering uniform and girds around him the sword as yet unsheathed, even on parade, while his eye with conscious pride keeps wandering over the lettered page on which his name appears as gazetted to the —th, what is glory, and he will reply, the undying record of some brave action. Turn ye to the veteran of a hundred fights, and to him glory has brought a wooden leg and a pension. And yet we still pursue the phantom, though the down-hill journey of life has robbed it of its first bewildering halo, and, regardless of the fate of the heroes of Marathon, hope that our names may be preserved to posterity.

Out upon thee, empty bauble! the glory of Napoleon terminated on a barren island; who, then, would covet thee?

The morning after the attack broke cold and bright, for a clear frost prevailed, and the sun, after many ineffectual attempts to break through the icy clouds that surrounded him, at last shone forth, covering the crisp earth with myriads of glittering icicles. It was early in the month of February, and nature seemed prematurely awakened to welcome the first gleams of the forthcoming spring.

I know not how long I may have slept, when the sharp ringing notes of the bugle, as they sounded the *reveillé* broke upon my ear, and quickly donning my uniform, none the brighter in appearance for the scenes it had gone through on the preceding night, I slowly proceeded to the place of muster, and joined my regiment on parade.

The men were resting on their arms, all eyes directed towards a young officer in plain military undress, who, surrounded by a brilliant staff, was silently contemplating the scene before him, and although his presence had been recognized by many of the older soldiers who had shared his successes, and followed him to victory, no sound of welcome escaped from their lips. He appeared to wish to pass unnoticed, and with all who knew him, his slightest wish was law. There was something in his appearance that at once struck you he was no common man, and when the sound of his voice, which I had never heard but once before, came in well-remembered tones upon my ear, I immediately recognized the spectator of the last night's attack; the man whose slightest sentence had re-animated the spirits of our faltering band. In the buzz of conversation that went round, I soon became acquainted with his name, but my own being called over by an orderly among a number of others, we stepped from the ranks in front of that brilliant throng, and each received from the hands of Serrurier, a musket ornamented with trophies in silver. It was the policy of Napoleon to reward those in the ranks with some mark of his esteem, a policy which afterwards suggested and matured into the Legion of Honour. Ere we were dismissed to our several regiments, Napoleon addressed a few words to us. "Remember," said he, "that you are now admitted into the ranks of brave men, and let your after-conduct be a proof that you are worthy of the distinction conferred upon you." The words were few, but the tones were kind; it was an admonition I shall never forget. As I returned to my regiment I felt that the distinction had been well-deserved, and that I had great reason to be proud, since it was won the first time I had ever faced the foe, in an enterprise the most dangerous in which a soldier can find himself engaged; that in fact I had a right to be included amongst those who had "earned an eternal title to the gratitude of the country."[1]

After we had been dismissed, I was slowly sauntering to see the breaches we had won last night, when I was passed by a flag of truce borne by an aide-de-camp of the Austrian general, and retracing my steps I followed him to head-quarters, where I learnt that, finding further resistance of no avail, and every hope of relief having disappeared, Wurmser, with true courage, had embraced the only alternative left to him, and had dispatched this officer to our camp with an offer to capitulate on certain conditions. "We have yet," said he, "plenty of provisions, and although your guns and disease have made great havoc in our ranks, twenty thousand men will not lay down their arms, unless they can receive such treatment as gallant men should accord to an enemy who have done all that human art could effect."

"No," said Serrurier, "this may not be; let Wurmser lay down his arms, and surrender himself and his troops as prisoners of war, and every clemency shall be exercised towards them, failing this we will carry the citadel by assault, as we have the suburbs, and every man shall be put to the sword."

The aide-de-camp turned slowly to depart, when again a deep voice spoke "*Arrete*," and a figure muffled in the cloak of a dragoon approached the table, and, taking a pen, wrote a few sentences on a sheet of paper which he handed to the Austrian, "Give this," said he, "to your general, say that we can respect his situation and appreciate his bravery, let him, if he chooses, make another effort to redeem his fortune, and should he be unsuccessful, I pledge my word there shall be no difference in the terms—to-morrow I advance."

It has been the fashion in England to ridicule this scene, as a mere clap-trap affair on the part of Napoleon, the effect upon those who were aware of his presence was the very reverse, and it was regarded as a proof of delicacy in a young, towards a grey-headed, but less fortunate antagonist, as a further proof of which

1. Proclamation of Buonaparte after the capitulation of Mantua.

I will quote a passage from his letter to the Directory, announcing our success, in which he says:

> I have taken upon myself to exercise the generosity of the French nation towards Wurmser, a veteran of sixty-six years, who, in this campaign, although deserted by good fortune, has never ceased to display a constancy and courage that posterity will do justice to. Shut up in the town, he headed three sorties, in each of which he was repulsed, for, besides the obstacles which our victorious troops threw in his way, his men were enfeebled by disease and discouraged by defeat.

Wurmser had, in fact, excited the admiration not only of our general, but of the whole army, having, in this most protracted struggle, lost upwards of 20,000 men, and held out until famine had begun to stare the inhabitants in the face. He had anticipated the effects of a long siege, and endeavoured to prepare for it by salting the horses of his cavalry, on which food even, his troops had been for some time on short allowance; as a prolongation of the struggle, therefore, offered no prospect of success, he wisely accepted the offered terms, which were, in reality, much better than he had any reason to expect; for, to console him, Napoleon had directed that himself and 500 men of his choice should not be comprised in the number of prisoners, besides which he presented him with four pieces of cannon and four covered carriages, with which he prepared to quit a place where he had been shut up for nearly six months, and defended with a skill and courage worthy of his well-earned reputation.

At ten o'clock next morning the troops were under arms, and Wurmser, at the head of twenty thousand men, not above one-half of whom were effective, marched out of the citadel, and crossing the *Ponte di S. Giorgio*, quitted the city. Advancing to Serrurier, who had conducted the siege, he presented him with his sword, and as every eye was turned upon him, we could see the tear steal down the cheek of the old warrior, as if he deeply felt the parting with a well-tried friend. It was accepted by our commander, for Napoleon, actuated by the same feelings of respect which had dictated the terms of his surrender, declined to be present when the veteran resigned his sword, and as the slowly receding line of the Austrians faded from our sight, there was not a man amongst us who did not feel pity and respect for their leader.

Thus fell Mantua, which we immediately occupied, and fully alive to the importance of the position, our engineers set to work without delay to repair the damages our long protracted siege had caused, and threw up additional defences, our general making this his head quarters.

I was now fairly a soldier launched in that career which afterwards raised so many brave men from the ranks of our army to be generals of division, and was made corporal in a regiment of *chasseurs à cheval* which formed a part of the garrison.

I confess that the routine of garrison duty did not well accord with the activity of my natural spirits, and that although we were occasionally employed on foraging parties, confinement to the walls of a barrack was not to my taste. I sighed for more stirring scenes, and envied such of my former comrades as were under the more immediate command of Napoleon, that mighty master in the art of war, now over-running the centre of Italy, and advancing fast upon Rome, to the no small consternation of his Holiness the Pope, and a whole host of emigrant clergy, who had fled from the revolutionary troubles of France, to seek the protection of the successor of St. Peter.

Balls and masquerades, the theatre and the *salon de jeu,* were quickly set afloat, and feasting and dissipation occupied moat of our time. For my own part, though utterly devoid of religion, I was not innately vicious, and I often turned away from the orgies of my companions to wander in solitude in the environs of the city, or spent hours in sailing on the lake, and thus the days passed on till the regiment to which I was attached received orders to hold itself in readiness to join the main body of the army, then taking up a position in the north of Italy, preparatory to its advance into Austria by the Tyrol.

CHAPTER 8

The Advance

The Archduke Charles had succeeded to the command of the Austrian army, and his great success in Germany pointed him out as the most fit person to oppose the torrent which threatened to issue through the passes of the Tyrol and overwhelm the capital of Austria. Young, active, brave, well versed in the art of war, as well as a successful commander, Prince Charles re-animated the drooping hopes of his nation, and he was at the same time aware that in the conqueror of Beaulieu, Wurmser, and Alvinzi, he had to meet talent of no common order.

Our troops occupied Vicenza and Padua, extending along the left bank of the Arisio to its junction with the Adige, and on the right bank of the Piave to the Adriatic. The enemy was in position on the opposite banks, having his centre placed behind the Cordevale, while his right, defended by the Adige, extended as far as Belluno.

Although reinforced by two divisions only, drawn from the army of the North, and amounting together to 18,000 or 20,000 men, Buonaparte determined to abandon the scenes of his triumphs, and quitting the soil of Italy, to make the dominions of the Emperor the theatre of his exploits; but to execute this project, it became necessary to cross many considerable rivers, to traverse long defiles covered with snow and ice; in fact, to march on Vienna, if the Emperor still refused the peace offered to him on the most moderate conditions. Great as were the obstacles which nature and the enemy opposed to this plan, they were not insurmountable; his vast genius, fertile resources, and valiant troops, were not likely to fail, and he determined that it should be at the gates of the capital that he would finally demand that peace which the people of the whole continent of Europe so ardently desired.

Such was the position of affairs when at the latter end of February, 1797. Buonaparte assembled four divisions in the Marsh of Trevisane, and while Joubert endeavoured to effect a junction with the army of the Rhine, under Moreau, defending on his left the passage of the Tyrol, advanced on Prince Charles, then in position as before described.

We passed the Piave on the 13th of March, and, falling on the Austrian rear, obliged the Archduke to retreat; leaving in our hands a general, several field officers, and 1,200 men. It was in vain he attempted to defend the passage of the Tagliamento, it opposed no barrier to the conquerers of Italy. Nevertheless the position was a strong one, and not to be abandoned without a struggle; entrenchments were thrown up to defend his communication with the Tyrol, whence all his supplies were drawn. The French divisions were hardly concentrated at Valvasone than Buonaparte disposed them for the attack. The infantry, formed into two columns under the orders of Generals Guieux and Bernadotte, was destined to attack the right and left of the entrenchments, and each column was covered by a strong advanced guard of grenadiers, with twenty-four guns, these in turn supported by Espinasse's artillery on the right, and by that of Dommartin on the left, while the cavalry, and several batteries, formed the reserve, and were under the orders of General Dugua.

At noon all was ready. The advanced guards, led by Duphot and Murat, received orders to pass the river, and as they gallantry threw themselves into the stream, the enemy opened a galling fire from his field guns, supported here and there by the cannon in the entrenchments. Before the whole had passed, the fire became so devastating that Murat ordered the troops to form as they emerged from the stream, and nobly was the order obeyed. The 5th were first on the opposite bank, and rushing boldly at the guns, they carried them at the point of the bayonet, the artillerymen fell fighting sword in hand with the greatest coolness and determination. The infantry, by whom the guns were supported, turned and fled, re-forming in front of the entrenchments, from which they were again driven, after a sharp struggle. On the left the enemy had slightly given way, retiring with an unbroken front, till our men, in the pursuit, came within range of his batteries, from which they were saluted with a plentiful shower of grape and chain shot, which committed fearful havoc in our ranks, sending many a gallant fellow to his last account; but forward was still the cry, and the men pressed bravely on. Between the bank of the river and the entrenchments, a little on the right, was a house, the walls of which the enemy had loop-holed for musketry, and this being defended by the guns in the battery, proved a strong position, from which it was necessary to dislodge him. The building was carried at the point of the bayonet, and notwithstanding that the Austrians fought like very fiends, the veteran troops of France were not to be withstood. Man to man, hand to hand, was the conflict carried on; the Colonel of the 5th falling by a ball through the head, while leading the advance, Legros was bayoneted, and Mirabel shot through the leg; nevertheless they made good their entrance, the defenders, not one of whom escaped the bayonet, falling on all sides, our own loss being proportionably great, scarce one in ten of the party employed escaping without a wound.

In the meanwhile the whole line was in motion, each half brigade moving by *echellon,* in close masses, on its second battalion, the cavalry drawn up in squadrons in the rear of the intervals.

Nothing had been neglected by Prince Charles to prevent our passage, but his efforts had been unavailing; notwithstanding the most determined bravery, he must submit to be repulsed, though as yet he had not been beaten. He had calculated on overwhelming our right by his cavalry, and our left by his infantry.

During the engagement the division of Serrurier arrived, and Napoleon determined to advance the whole of his cavalry and artillery. We who had as yet been anxious spectators, were now to take our turn in the affray. As our guns passed the river and took up their position they opened upon the entrenchments, and, after two hours hard fighting, nothing remained but to carry the works by assault. Again the advance was sounded, once more the infantry was in motion; a withering fire of grape and musketry mowed down rank after rank—nothing could exceed the coolness of the Austrians—but the bayonet prevailed, and notwithstanding the loss was great still we pressed onwards, driving the enemy out and retaining possession of their works.

As our regiment gained the opposite bank of the river we wheeled into line, and, putting our horses to the gallop, charged the now retiring masses of the Austrians, mowing them down or riding over them, till the nature of the ground obliged us to abandon the pursuit. Here and there our advance was impeded by squadrons of the enemy's cavalry, and on one occasion a hand to hand encounter was the consequence, and comparatively trifling as was our loss otherwise, in this affair it was severe. In my own troop seven were killed and sixteen wounded, enough to show the determined resistance of the enemy, as his infantry was broken and in flight before we received the order to charge.

Nothing conduced so much to our success as the rapidity of our manœuvres and the superiority of our artillery.

Night had come on, and we were not sorry to hear the bugles sound the recall, for, although we had not been fighting all day yet three hours is enough to give a man an appetite, and many of us had not tasted food since breakfast, and even then the meal was not the most substantial of its kind.

Having been foiled in his attempt to resist us on the banks of the Tagliamento, the Archduke retired on the Torre, where he again endeavoured to maintain his position. He was driven thence by two divisions which occupied Palma Nuova, while a third manœuvred to turn his right flank and thus cut off Willach, which served as the point of communication between the different divisions of the army; this endeavour proved unsuccessful.

He again retired on the Lisongo, hoping that this rapid river would prove an obstacle to our progress; it was, however, passed at a ford, and the garrison of Gradisca capitulated.

The consequence of these operations were 1,000 prisoners—the élite of the Austrian army—the capture of many guns and colours, and the fall of Goritz, at which place Napoleon established his head quarters. My own immediate gain was a step up the ladder I had determined to climb, having been appointed serjeant-major in place of my comrade, who fell at the passage of the Tagliamento.

One evening, after a short brush with a squadron of the enemy's cavalry, I received orders to join a foraging party, about to be despatched from the camp, both men and horses standing in great need of refreshments, of which they had not partaken since morning.

The rain fell in torrents, accompanied by a sort of drizzling sleet, more benumbing to the senses than snow, and this, added to the comfort of an empty stomach, and the prospect of a night, with the heavens only for a coverlid, made the men grumble. We mounted and were off, taking 30 men of the 4th squadron of the regiment who had only been partially engaged, and, after groping our way some half a dozen miles, came in sight of a hamlet, the lights in which flickering here and there gave token that the inhabitants were astir.

What we took for a hamlet was in fact a small town, so galloping through the street we reined up at a large building, which proved to be the town-hall, and demanded everything that was eatable and drinkable, as well as forage for our horses and waggons, &c, wherewith to convey the same to our camp. All was in a state of bustle and confusion, the inhabitants declaring they had nothing for themselves, and we on our side threatening what should be the consequence unless our demands were complied with, and that right speedily. A truant disposition led me from the detachment, and straying into a house where I saw some pretty young Tyrolese, I soon discovered that an Austrian detachment was then in the village, but that being alarmed at our numbers, (believing in fact that we were a regiment), they were concealed by two's and three's at the different houses, for, as our trumpeter had sounded the charge as we galloped up the street, they never for a moment supposed a mere handful of men would be guilty of such temerity. I returned to the officer in command and communicated my discovery; threats and persuasions drew their numbers and whereabouts from the burgomaster, and we started in pursuit. Having searched the houses unsuccessfully, we entered a stable for the purpose of taking off the horses, and seeing a pair of spurs sticking out from under the straw, I naturally concluded the boots must be somewhere near.

A stab or two with the point of my sabre was replied to most lustily, and in a short time out turned my friend, the German master of the boots.

A repetition of this plan at each succeeding house was attended with a like success, and we thus became masters of sixteen Austrians and their horses without firing a shot or striking a blow. The provisions mounted and the detachment on the march, my pockets pretty well garnished with florins, levied as a contribution from a portly tradesman of the place, we were not long on our return. The first man I met was the Colonel. "Gazzola, what cheer?" "Bravely, bravely, *mon officier*," said I; "we have obtained the wherewith to sup and make merry, in addition to which we have got sixteen well-mounted recruits."

He was quite a matter-of-fact person, and when I said recruits, muttered over to himself, "Recruits! recruits! where the devil do they come from?" I let him chew the cud for a bit, and then related the particulars. The trumpets sounded the distribution, and the prisoners were properly secured and taken care of; and, notwithstanding the unfavourableness of the season, we laid ourselves down to rest in the best manner we could.

The activity of Buonaparte deranged all the calculations of the Austrian Prince, who had been accustomed to the slow and timid tactics of Moreau. He retreated precipitately, and dividing his army into two columns; the one covered the road to Vienna, while the other, under the orders of Gontreuil and Bazalitsch, with the artillery, turned upon the Lisongo and the Nation, and debouched by the defiles of Over-Preet, Tarvis, and Caporetto.

The discernment of Napoleon enabled him to penetrate the designs of Prince Charles and to take advantage of the mistake he had committed in the division of his army. While one of our divisions followed the Prince, another marched upon Tarvis, overthrowing everything in its route, and a third having beaten Bazalitsch at Pufera, occupied the gorges of Caporetto, to which place Napoleon himself came by way of Canale. In vain Ocsh and Gontreuil advanced to retake Tarvis, the progress of our victorious troops could not be restrained. Twenty days had sufficed, and in that short time the First Consul had overcome the whole power of Austria, beaten her favourite general, and destroyed or taken prisoners 20,000 men, with trifling loss on our side. So well planned had been his movements—so well executed his combinations, that we had encountered no obstacle that was not easily overcome. One by one the generals had succumbed, until the rapidity of our progress had reached the Imperial ears, spreading inquietude and alarm in the Austrian Court. Still our leader pressed on, the capital was menaced, when the Emperor demanded a suspension of hostilities, which being agreed upon, preliminaries of peace were signed at Leoben, where the army was assembled, and whence, at the first order of its mighty chief, it might easily have been launched upon the plains of Austria.

A portion of the army now retrograded, to chastise the insolence of the Venetian Republic, while the division to which our regiment was attached received orders to return to France.

The treaty of Campo Formio was ratified by the Austrian Emperor, and might be considered the termination of the Italian campaign. It results were 100,000 men killed in action, 150,000 made prisoners, 166 standards, 4,000 pieces of cannon, parks of artillery, consisting of 650 pieces, all the vessels of war belonging to the Venetian Republic, the arsenals, the *chefs-d'œuvre* of the most celebrated artists of Italy, both ancient and modern, and all these, with loads of plunder unaccounted for, were the glorious trophies gained by the genius of Napoleon and the courage of his troops.

When we for a moment reflect on the well-digested plans and astonishing success of the army of Italy, under its invincible chief—on the apparently insurmountable obstacles which it had overcome—when we see it invading a country where the people were led on by a fanatical priesthood and ferocious demagogues, having before it numerous and well appointed troops, commanded by the most celebrated generals in Europe—when we see it destroy army after army, without itself receiving a check, we may well believe ourselves transported from the realms of fact to the regions of imagination, but certainty succeeds the moment of illusion; a sentiment of admiration springs up in the breast of the citizen, he would fain partake of the enthusiasm which is aroused, identify himself with the heroes of Italy, and be pleased with the idea that his turn may come to follow so brilliant and glorious a career.

   Such indeed appeared to be the case in the places where we did garrison duty, the losses we had sustained being quickly made up by the conscription, and here we remained the latter part of the year 1797 and and the commencement of 1798, until the active mind of our leader again called us forth for another harvest in the field of glory.

Chapter 9

The Voyage

The subjection of Egypt, a project of Buonaparte, was submitted to the Directory, who now, in perfect accord with him, ordered the ministers to second it by all the means which the Republic possessed. He seems to have meditated on this project for some time, since he had desired a part of his force to rendezvous at Corfu, from whence it sailed to Toulon. During the passage the corps were exercised at the guns with the sailors and marines of the fleet.

It appears now an odd way of forwarding his greatest desire—that of crippling and destroying the influence of England by the annihilation of her commerce, but be that as it may, he superintended, with the greatest care and anxiety, the preparations for the embarkation of the army, by which such great designs were to be achieved. On the 19th of May, 1798, we sailed from Toulon, and having, according to the language of the order of the day, "made war on the mountains and in the plains," nothing now remained but to make it on the sea.

The sun shone brightly on the clear blue waters of the Mediterranean—fair presage of our success—and the numerous line of battle ships and transports of which the fleet was composed, as they let fall their sails and quitted the harbour, seemed to compose an armament equal to the conquest of the world. The fleet was further augmented by a division of transports, containing the troops under the command of Desaix, and making up a disposable force of 40,000 men, and after a tedious passage of three weeks we cast anchor before Malta, then occupied by the Knights of St. John of Jerusalem.

The reduction of this island was not only necessary to the prosperity of our commerce with the Levant as a principal depôt, but also as being an intermediate station between France and Egypt. To avoid the effusion of blood, our general demanded that the port should be opened to him, but the Grand Master, confiding in the valour of his Knights (who however proved unworthy successors of the men who had, with unparalleled bravery, held this almost impregnable island against the Turks in ages gone by), rejected the proposition, and it being found necessary to employ force, orders were given to Admiral Bruyes to make preparations for the attack. The next day our troops landed upon every point of the island, and before night the whole had submitted, and the town was invested on all sides. After a few discharges of cannon the garrison made a feeble attempt at sortie that was easily repulsed; the Grand Master demanded a suspension of hostilities, which being acceded to, on the evening of the 12th of June, a convention was signed, and we became masters of the place.

The inhabitants generally had reason to congratulate themselves on the generosity of their conquerors, who obtained possession of two vessels of war, many pieces of cannon, small arms, ammunition, and other necessaries of war, half of which were left behind for the use of the garrison. Buonaparte remained some days on the island, in order to organise it according to the principles of the Republic. He abolished slavery, proclaimed equality, obliged the inhabitants to adopt our institutions and laws; he removed the fetters of the Turkish and Arab slaves, whom he dismissed to their respective countries, restoring these unhappy beings to that liberty which they fancied they had been for ever deprived of, and such were their transports of gratitude that they would have kissed the feet of their benefactor; he was, however, too truly great to permit such humiliation on the part of his fellow-creatures, and thus, one of the objects of the expedition being obtained, we were in some measure repaid for the sacrifice it cost.

General Vaubois, with 4,500 men, was left in garrison, and on the 19th of June the fleet again set sail for the coast of Africa, where, after a quick passage, we arrived, the English fleet having left the roadstead at Alexandria about three days before; in fact, it was thought by many that we should have a naval engagement before we quitted the ships; the presence of Nelson in these seas being known to our commander. This was, however, spared us, and we disembarked at Marabout, about a league from Alexandria, at four o'clock in the morning of the 30th of June.

This was the first time I had ever been at sea, and long before the conclusion of the voyage I had fervently prayed it might be the last. We were crowded on board a wretched vessel—twice as many human beings as she was ever intended to carry; and here, in addition to the miseries of sea sickness, I experienced all the horrors that were ever accumulated on the heads of those who go down to the sea in ships, and have their business on the great waters. Truly, if there were ever a correct representation of that place which is never named to ears polite, it was the transport in which I made the passage from Toulon to Egypt. The filth and abomination arising from the too-crowded state of the vessel, increased a hundred fold by the powerful action of the sun, thoroughly disgusted us; and there was not a soldier on board who would not willingly have exchanged his situation for one in front of the most forlorn storming party that ever stepped forth from the ranks of the army. But the wished-for release came at last—we received the order to disembark, a service of difficulty and danger, for some of the boats were swamped by the surf, and many of the men perished. Our vessel was one of the first that made the land, and the regiment to which I belonged the earliest on shore, and as soon as the rest of the division had landed, we formed on the sands and marched towards our position.

The division was reviewed by Napoleon, who divided it into three columns, commanded by Kleber, Bon, and Menou. We advanced rapidly on the town, Kleber's division occupying the centre, moving by Pompey's Pillar to escalade the walls, which were fast crumbling to decay; that of Bon preserving the right, to which was entrusted the attack on the port of Rosetta; whilst the left, under Menou, advanced against the castle. The attack took place at break of day, and although we had no artillery landed, the town was carried by assault, in spite of the vigorous resistance of the inhabitants, at whose hands we sustained some loss, a wound in the leg falling to my share. During the assault the artillery and the rest of the cavalry were disembarked, but not in time to join in the attack.

Of the subsequent sack and plunder, I can give little account save by report, though I could not stop my ears to what was going on; however a few days confinement in the hospital soon set me right again, and I once more resumed my duties in the field.

Who but those who have passed through the same circumstances can picture to themselves the intense enjoyment which thrilled through every vein, as I lay at the door of my tent enjoying the first sunset after my recovery? Who but those who have passed days and weeks "cribbed, cabined, and confined" in a filthy transport, can call to mind their first extacies on passing a night of peace and comfort on shore? Never while memory holds her own shall I forget my sensations. Very little time was lost at Alexandria, which was garrisoned, a provisional government organised, the fortifications repaired and put in order, under Kleber, who, being wounded at the attack, was unable to follow the army in its advance, and was therefore installed as commandant of the town.

I am not going to relate the history of the campaign, all the world is familiar with it—but if such were not the case, I am incapable of giving it. I am content to relate some of those scenes in which I was engaged—some of those trifling incidents which, make up the sum of a soldier's existence when not actually engaged in the field, adding only such general details as may serve to make my narrative better understood, or to give it a more connected form.

We left Alexandria on the 7th of July; some proceeding in boats up the Nile, others advancing along the banks, but each of us pressing forward with all the rapidity possible towards that El Dorado which many had promised themselves, though the less sanguine considered that we were much more likely to fall in with the Mamelukes who then occupied Cairo.

We took the route by Demanhour—the shortest but the most painful, as it traversed the desert. Unaccustomed to march over burning sands, our troops threw away the provisions which were served out to them when they started, and in a short time began to experience all the horrors of famine and thirst. Discontent and disappointment soon prevailed amongst us, especially in those regiments that had formed part of the army of Italy; nor were these confined to the ranks, even our commanding officer Murat partook of it, a feeling in which he was joined by Lannes. Harassed by the Arabs, who hovered continually on the flanks of the columns, entailing certain destruction on whoever strayed from the ranks; discontent continued to increase as we advanced through the sandy and barren country, so unlike our own fertile plains, and after a forced march, and fatigue unheard of, we arrived at the village of Chabriesse, where Mourad Bey awaited us at the head of his troops, the sight of whom caused every murmur to be hushed, every voice to be stilled.

I had, hitherto, been engaged against men wielding the same weapons, and using the same exercise as ourselves, but, with the change of country, we had also changed our enemies, the tactics of the Arabs no more resembling those of the Europeans than did their arid and sterile soil, the fertile plains of Italy. The whole country seemed studded with horsemen, who acted independently of each other, and whose charges were rapid, as their retreat was instantaneous. Our regiment being the only cavalry attached to the division, we formed the advanced guard, and it was no uncommon thing to see them hovering on our flanks, charging even to the very heads of our horses, and suddenly rein up, wheel short round, and retire. Many were the encounters we had, and severe the loss we sustained, for every straggler was sure to be cut off; but we were successful in our turn, and much valuable booty fell to our share, for their arms were of the highest and most exquisite finish, and numbers of them carried considerable sums of money about their persons.

This sort of warfare continued as we advanced, the Mamelukes threatening many times to charge, without ever making up their minds to do so, and after resting some part of the day within the range of our guns, which once opened upon them, scattering death among them, they retired, and we took up our position none the better pleased that we were within reach of such active enemies.

Chapter 10
Boulak

We were early under arms and continued to advance, notwithstanding the excessive heat, and soon came in sight of the Pyramids. When within six leagues of Cairo, Buonaparte received Information that the Beys, with all their force, were entrenched at Embabè, a village opposite to Boulak, and that their position was defended by sixty pieces of cannon.

The division to which I belonged, consisted of four regiments of infantry and one of cavalry, under that dashing soldier of fortune, Murat, and we were destined to lead the attack. The village of Boulak was not fortified, the main body of the Egyptians being posted between it and the Pyramids; drawn up on the plain, in front of the village, was an imposing force of Arab infantry, supported on the right by a body of Mameluke cavalry. "Soldiers!" cried Napoleon, "you are about to engage in battle to-day with the rulers of Egypt; remember that from the height of those monuments forty centuries look down upon us." The enthusiasm of the general was communicated to the troops; the bugles sounded the advance, and putting our horses to the gallop, we charged the main body, and then, wheeling suddenly to right and left, retired through the intervals between the regiments of infantry, by whom we were supported, and formed again in the rear. In this manner, charge after charge was made, our troops sustaining but little loss, as the enemy were principally armed with matchlocks, until the main body arrived within musket shot, when pouring in a murderous volley along the whole length of the line, our men advanced, and settled the matter with the bayonet.

The battle now became general, the other divisions of the army being engaged. In the meanwhile we had plenty of work on our hands, for the body of Mamelukes whom we had observed on the right of the Arab infantry, with which we had been engaged, and who had seemed to look on unconcerned during our attack, now put themselves in motion, and crossing the plain at full gallop, reined suddenly up before our regiment had time to get into line, and charging us independently, many of our men bit the dust, and the conflict became hand to hand. The Mamelukes, to the amount of 12,000, were now engaged, their whole force being concentrated on the right. In vain they penetrated even to the very squares, charging up to the point of the bayonet, the most daring bravery availed them not, and the field was soon covered with the slain.

It was here that my early devotion to the foil stood me in some stead, for in the *melée* that ensued, I found myself opposed to one of these turbaned gentry, who, in addition to a quick eye and ready hand, united great personal strength to dexterity in the management of his horse. Twice had my sabre drawn blood from his arm, and twice had he escaped a blow I intended should be fatal; the event was still uncertain, I had an antagonist who was not so easily subdued; I who had seldom met my match in the salle, was here foiled by an untutored son of the desert. I was beginning to lose my temper—a loss that would in all probability have been soon followed by that of my life—when a stray ball struck my antagonist's horse, causing him to stumble, before he could recover himself my sword cleft his skull, and I drew from his pockets many a glittering piece of gold, besides acquiring a rich sabre and a magnificent pair of pistols.

In the mean while the other divisions advanced and carried the entrenchments at Embabè at the point of the bayonet, after great carnage on the enemy, who fled on all sides, abandoning their dead and wounded, together with their artillery, 400 camels, and a great quantity of baggage, and horses richly caparisoned.

The other portion of the Mamelukes were defeated by Dessaix in an attempt to carry Bilkil by a *coup-de-main*. The route was complete, and on my returning to the village, of Boulak, which had been given up to the troops, I beheld scenes which made the carnage of the battle field pleasureable when compared with them, and well nigh disgusted me with the men with whom I had so long associated.

I had witnessed carnage enough, Heaven knows, in my time; had seen sufficient of the horrors of a siege, at Mantua; but my wound had spared me the sack at Alexandria, and happy should I have been to escape seeing one here. No imagination can picture, no pen describe the state of a place abandoned to the mercies of an infuriated soldiery; and surely no soldiery in the world can equal the French in the brutality of their actions; the atrocities of their cruelty. Rapine and plunder go hand in hand; the most brutal passions are inflamed; the most demoniacal desires gratified; no age nor sex was spared. The night had far advanced before the bugles sounded the recall, and the village had been fired in twenty places, ere the work of carnage had ceased in Boulak.

Throughout the whole of my military career, varied and chequered as it has been, I cannot call to mind anything to compare with the horrors of that night; and I have thousands of times inwardly cursed Murat for following the diabolical policy of Napoleon.

Order was in some measure restored, and the troops recalled to their duty, when it became necessary to seek the means of subsistence, the commissariat having failed to supply us with rations, and a night of starvation promising to succeed a day of action. This appeared anything but pleasant, so, calling two or three of my comrades around me, we sallied forth in the hope of finding some house which, having escaped the general sack, might provide us with the means of satisfying our hunger. I had traversed the greater portion of the place without success, nothing but desolation staring me in the face, and the flames fast consuming that which the violence of man had left, till, on approaching the most distant suburb, I perceived a house surrounded by trees, bearing apparently fewer marks of devastation than any I had previously witnessed, and promising success in an attempt that was beginning to appear hopeless. Putting our horses to the trot we soon reached the gate, where I dismounted and passed through, to the no small consternation of a young creature apparently about fifteen, who, in the same habiliments which nature had bestowed upon her when she entered the world, was endeavouring to conceal herself from the rude gaze of one who, from his dress and unceremonious manner of entering, she instinctively felt must be an enemy. Finding the attempt ineffectual, and that I advanced towards her, she burst into tears, and, casting herself on the ground, raised her hands to Heaven, and in accents the most piteous besought, as I supposed, my compassion. What her words were I knew not; for Arabic or Egyptian were as unknown to me, as French, of which she had probably never heard, was to her; but the language of her eyes was not to be mistaken, and now the experience of the stage stood me in great service; I commenced the most expressive pantomime to reassure her, and by degrees succeeded.

I have already described her dress, or rather her want of it, but of the strangeness of her appearance she seemed quite unconscious, for there is an innate sense of purity in the untutored children of the desert which would put to shame the more fastidious, but in reality less scrupulous inhabitants of what are called highly civilised countries; for treasuring no impropriety in their own thoughts, they are slow to believe it is ever harboured in those of others. My captive had probably never before been in the company of a man, at all events she seemed quite unconscious of what appeared to me the strangeness of her situation. Her skin, dark as the olive of my own land, seemed covered by a soft and glossy down, while her raven hair, unrestrained by band or comb, fell gracefully around her, forming an imperfect veil, that heightened rather than concealed the beauties of her figure, which was faultless as that of the Grecian marble to which with such enthusiasm we bow as the beau ideal of a woman. Although when raised, her step possessed the uncertainty of fear, it had all the elasticity of youth, forming altogether: an object that at once won its way to my heart, where an restrained compassion took immediate possession. But why should I dwell upon this picture of helpless innocence—my heart, seared by the blighting effects of its last passion, had not recovered itself sufficiently to make room for another, and I determined that in this case no baneful influence should interfere to rob my captive of her peace, and that I would be to her, in every sense of the word, the most disinterested of protectors.

I motioned for her to await my return, and quitted the house to communicate with my comrades, who could little appreciate the feelings by which I was actuated, and, amid their laughter and jeers, I unstrapped from my saddle the valise attached to it, and tumbling out a shirt, pantaloons, and stable dress, I re-entered the house, and having clothed my prize in these strange habiliments, and placed a forage cap upon her head, I mounted her behind me, *en-croupe* and prepared to continue our search.

In this and a neighbouring house, which we found abandoned, we were lucky enough to get plenty wherewith to satisfy our wants, and also two Arab horses, upon one of which I mounted my new recruit, and returned to the camp.

At an early period of life, we act first and reflect afterwards, and had I reversed the order of proceeding, in all probability, it would have induced me to have left this defenceless being to her fate—what that fate might have been, I shudder to contemplate—to the remarks of my comrades I turned a deaf ear, and deposited her in my tent, where no prying eye could disturb her avocation—no intruder annoy her by his presence, and bearing in mind that the fortune of war might sometime or other expose my own sisters to a like fate, I left no means untried to render her captivity as little irksome to her as possible.

Chapter 11

Cairo

On revisiting the field the morning after the battle, I passed on to that portion of it beyond the village of Boulak, in which I had not been employed, and if I had been struck before with the great military talent of our leader, how much more was I astonished at the perfect success of his plans against an enemy whose method of warfare was as novel as it was impetuous.

In advancing on the entrenchments occupied by Mourad Bey and the main body of the Mameluke force, Napoleon ordered the divisions of Dessaix and Regnier to take position to the right, between Dgyzech and Embabè, so as to cut off the communication with Upper Egypt, to which, in case of defeat, it would become necessary for the enemy to retreat. Mourad Bey, who was a much braver general than a skilful one, perceiving this movement, resolved to charge in two divisions. The infantry formed into squares, awaited the approach of his columns until the leading files had advanced within fifty paces, and then a murderous fire of artillery and musketry opening upon them, mowed them down by hundreds. Still they advanced, throwing themselves into the intervals between the squares, charging up to the very points of the bayonets, and all without avail; again and again the heavy roar of great and small guns saluted them till at last they gave way; Buonaparte watched this movement, and ordered the division of General Bon, then in position on the hill, to move up in such a manner as to take in the rear those who had issued out of the entrenchments, and to cut off their retreat, while it threatened the position of Mourad Bey on the left. He had impressed on all three generals the necessity (to ensure success to his plans) of observing well how far their movements were attended with success, on being assured of which they were each to advance on the entrenchments, forming the first and third division of each battalion into columns of attack, while the other divisions sustained the brunt of the battle.

The result of the battle of the Pyramids was the entire subjection of the Lower Province, while it opened the road into Upper Egypt. The conquest was completed, and the dispositions of our general were crowned with success, nevertheless the bravery of the enemy had been unparalleled, and his loss proportionably great.

Cairo was now evacuated, the flotilla and boats on the Nile being first destroyed; the enemy, dividing into two corps, one of which, commanded by Mourad Bey, retreated into Upper Egypt, the other, taking the road to Syria, under the orders of Ibrahim Fey.

We entered the city on the 22nd of July, and Napoleon, desirous of giving to the inhabitants a specimen of his power, ordered the preparations for a fête, which was to overwhelm them by its magnificence. To this he was impelled by another motive, for his soldiers had begun to turn their eyes towards a country, the recollection of which is so dear to a Frenchman, that nothing can efface it. In this feeling I participated, for, although not naturally a child of France, all my habits and thoughts had become French; but brave and generous as all the world admits them to be, none are more easily dazzled by their glories, and led away by events which immortalise them.

This was well known to Napoleon, who seemed to partake of their enthusiasm, and eager to augment it. This made him study to efface from their minds the fate of the fleet which Nelson had recently destroyed at Aboukir; he announced its destruction with face unmoved, in terms that led them to believe that he considered its loss a matter of little importance to the army. "We have no longer a fleet," said he, "ah! well, we must remain in these countries, or leave them gloriously, as did the warriors of old." The fête would lead their thoughts to other channels, offering a spectacle which, by awakening in their hearts the most lively emotions, might banish for a time the memory of that dear country to which they gloried to belong, and to which many were growing anxious to return.

At daybreak salvos of artillery announced the anniversary of the foundation of the Republic. The army, formed round a majestic pyramid raised in the *Place d'Esbetrier* to the memory of the brave men who had fallen in the preceding battles, awaited in silence the arrival of the General-in-Chief. He came, attended by a brilliant staff, the principal officers of the military administration, and the leading citizens of the town, and was received by the acclamations of the whole force, mingled with the roaring of cannon, loud blasts of trumpets, and rolling of drums. He seemed like a father in the midst of his children.

Taking his stand at the foot of the pyramid, and stilling all sounds by the simple motion of the hand, again the deep voice I had heard under the walls of Mantua, and in the Place, broke forth with an eloquence that at once carried persuasion and aroused enthusiasm. There, in words that thrilled through every one that heard him, he briefly recapitulated the services of those he addressed, winding up with an eulogium that none felt could be gainsayed. "From England, celebrated in arts and commerce, to the fierce and hideous Bedouin, we had fixed the attention of the world" Oh! how a little well-timed flattery will reward men for the perils and hardships of a campaign. Talk of ribbons, flattery is equally successful, and ever so much cheaper. Scarcely had he concluded than the air was rent with cries of "*Vive la Libertè, Vive la Republique.*" After going through a variety of manœuvres, the army passed in review before the General and his Staff, and accompanied the civil authorities to a banquet, where all ranks and sentiments were strangely mingled together. It was, indeed, the most singular sight the world ever beheld. Europeans, Africans, Asiatics, uniting together in the enjoyment of the moment.

Mounted *en cavalier,* on my Arab prize, clothed in the undress uniform of my corps, my captive accompanied me to witness the horse and foot races, for which prizes were given by the general, while an exhibition of fire-works, and a general illumination both of the town and the camp, closed this day of feasting and rejoicing.

I had taken upon me an arduous and a dangerous task, for in

becoming the protector of a woman, I also exposed myself to the danger of degenerating into her slave. Our relative ages were too young to afford much hope of escaping the temptations our situation afforded; but I reflect with gratitude to an all-wise Creator that we did escape, and that, instead of making her my mistress, she became my servant.

The recollection of the Ballerina had not passed away; and although time and reason had both exerted their influence upon me, still memory with tenacious fondness, clung to those hours when I knew her, and believed her all she ought to have been.

Poets and novelists agree that there is no second love, and I then believed them; passion had not as yet usurped its place, and my prize, clothed in a suit of uniform I provided for her, was so constantly at my side, that in a short time both my companions and myself became so accustomed to her that we ceased to remember her sex, and she escaped those importunities to which her natural habiliments would perhaps have subjected her. I was glad to have her by me, whether in the bivouac or the skirmish, and there I invariably found her; for though she carried no arms, she followed me in two or three little skirmishes in which we were engaged, providing herself with a bottle of brandy or *curaçoa* wherewith to sustain our courage, or reanimate our drooping spirits.

In one of these affairs a ball struck me in the back part of the neck, tumbling me from my horse, and there, in all probability, my earthly career would have been ended, but for the watchful care of the Arab maid. Quickly dismounting, she poured some brandy into my mouth, and dragging me from the *melée,* with some difficulty got me back to my quarters, and here I found a reward for having saved the life of my captive; here she amply repaid the care I had bestowed upon her. For some weeks I was confined to my room, during which time she waited upon me with that kindness and attention which only a woman can bestow, soothing, with a sister's care, the irritability caused by my wound, and anticipating every want with as much tenderness as if I had been a child.

At last, I was declared convalescent, and, although my wound had not healed, I returned to duty, but the incessant occupation of the saddle brought on a relapse, and I was ordered to the rear.

My campaigns in Egypt were, however, closed, for I lingered on for some time without recovering my strength, till an order from our commander sent us home, and I quitted my captive and the soil of the pyramids, to endeavour to re-establish my health by the invigorating breeze of my native land.

I was thus constrained to leave my prize, and I confess I parted from her with feelings of the most lively regret. She had began to learn my language, and made herself interesting by the earnest endeavours she displayed to make herself understood. Presenting her with all the money I had been able to save from my pay, I warned her of the fate she might expect if she remained with the army, and begging her to return to Boulak and endeavour to discover if any of her family had survived our attack, I bade her farewell, and stepped on board the vessel which was to bear me from her for ever. I will not attempt to paint the despair which seemed to have taken possession of her; she begged to be allowed to accompany me, but this could not be; my rank in the service did not give me the privilege of keeping a servant, and the transport was too crowded to allow her to go as a passenger. The fates decreed that we should part, and part we did with feelings of poignant and unavailing regret.

We sailed from Egypt with a fresh breeze, and I was heartily glad when I entered the hospital, where I remained till my health was restored.

During my inactivity the French had attacked Acre, and had another affair at Aboukir. I fretted at the thought that I had not been there, and, like a chained animal, made myself unhappy that I could not break my bonds; no help remained, and at last I resigned myself to my fate, until I heard of the arrival of Napoleon, who landed at Frejus on the 30th of September, 1799.

This event decided me to return once more to the army, which I had almost resolved to leave; but the circumstance of my youth prevented my seeking other employment, while the death of my mother and the unkindness of my uncle was an effectual bar to my returning to my country. Chance had made me a soldier, and a soldier I must continue.

CHAPTER 12

The Passage of Mont St. Bernard

After the affair of the 18th Brumaire (10th of February, 1800,) the army was assembled in camp at Dijon, and thither I hastened; for as it was composed mostly of conscripts, a small number only of the troops having seen service, I made sure that one who had had the good fortune to belong to the army of Italy, as well as to have formed part of the expedition to Egypt, would be well received, and that my old rank would be preserved to me, even if I failed to get promotion.

On my arrival I presented myself to General Berthier, then in command, who appointed me to a vacant sub-lieutenancy in the Grenadiers à Cheval of the Consular Guard—that guard which, by its untiring attachment to Napoleon, and its unceasing devotion to his cause, became so celebrated in after years. It was composed of the *élite* of the army—picked men- in the very vigour of their existence, and from its steady and unflinching conduct in the field soon acquired the name of the "Wall of Granite."

If, during my career as a soldier, I had at times felt disgust or dissatisfaction—if on the wearying night march, the picket guard, or the bivouac, I had contrasted my present situation with what it might have been, to the evident disadvantage of the former—if the harsh words of a commander or the irksomeness of obedience had sometimes chafed my spirit, or ruffled my temper—all was forgotten, and I mounted my first guard at Dijon with heart as elate, and spirits as buoyant, as when I stepped from the ranks in the square at Mantua to receive my reward as a survivor of the storming party.

I had taken upon myself to be the architect of my own fortune, the foundation of which I had laid before the walls of Mantua; and insignificant as I felt my position, compared with that of the thousands of gallant fellows of which the army was composed, still it had attracted the attention of one whose all-pervading eye could pierce even the remotest ranks, and make him condescend to notice the humble efforts of a corporal-major of chasseurs.

Our division marched by the Jura, on Geneva, at which place we were reviewed by the First Consul himself, and received the astounding intelligence that instead of proceeding by Chamberi and the Mont Cenis, our commander had the hardihood to conceive, and the head to execute, a project never dreamt of since the days of the Romans, and that in imitation of the Carthagenian General, to whom, both in the rapidity of his movements and the boldness of his conceptions, he bore no inconsiderable resemblance, he had determined to brave nature herself in her stronghold, and to carry the army into the north of Italy by the almost inaccessible pass of the Saint Bernard.

The idea of invading Italy by this route emanated exclusively from the First Consul. Having stood the brunt of battle in Europe and in Africa, the cannon of the battery, the bayonet of the infantry, the mail-clad warriors of Austria, the turbaned followers, of Mahomet, the incredible difficulties that now presented themselves did not daunt the courage of his troops. With conscious reliance on the generals who had been accustomed to brave fatigue and danger, and on the men who had never failed to respond to his call, he resolved to attack the icy barrier, and in spite of difficulties appalling even to the simple traveller, who can choose his time and opportunity; to attempt to pass an army by a route, covered in part by eternal snows, destitute of herbage, of shelter, or of habitation, the snow-crowned summits of the pass being approached by a path strewn with barren and rugged rocks; a path where even the practised foot of the goatherd is obliged to proceed with caution, and where on the one hand masses of snow suspended above threaten to break in avalanches and sweep the traveller away in their descent, and on the other a false step would be followed by certain death.

It was to be attempted, however, and none dreamt of failure; the halo of success hung over the brow of Napoleon, and to doubt was treason; so on the 7th of May we were once more in motion, and marched to Martigny, a small town in the Valais, situated about six leagues from the mountain, the General-in-Chief having selected this place, by reason of its proximity to the pass, in which to prepare for the work he had determined to execute. Here we remained, quartered in the *Maison de Convalescence du Mont St. Bernard*, a house belonging to the order to which the older brethren retire to end their days, and the valetudinarians to re-establish their health

The advanced guard, consisting of the 6th Light Brigade, the 28th and 44th regiments of the line, the 11th and 12th Hussars, and the 21st regiment of Chasseurs, under the command of General Lannes, was pushed forward to St. Pierre, at the foot of the pass; but the hamlet was quickly deserted by the inhabitants, who, alarmed by the number of troops which arrived, concealed themselves among the rocks, which were still covered by frost and snow. It contained only forty houses, or, as they might with more truth be called, huts; but for two months it became the depôt for the artillery, and here were excuted the various works necessary for our transit. By degrees the people returned to their habitations, which they soon repented ever to have quitted, as many of them were afterwards employed as guides, or as porters to carry the baggage of the officers, by which means they acquired handsome wages, that were in all cases punctually discharged.

The advanced guard having surmounted every difficulty, and crossed the mountain, were followed by the first division, under General Watrin, who fell in with the enemy at Saint Remy—about six leagues from the Convent—an enemy of whom we never again lost sight until victory crowned our arms on the plains of Marengo. Although inferior in numbers, they awaited the attack, believing that only a few regiments had passed, and being protected by the nature of the country. A hand to hand encounter was the consequence, nor did they retire until they perceived one of our corps descending the little St. Bernard and menacing their rear—threatening to cut off their retreat to Aoste.

The First Consul had arrived at Martigny on the 20th of May, and took up his abode at the Convent. Here he remained three days, expecting the surrender of the Fort of Bard, situated beyond the mountain on the road to Yvrée; but, although we received the news of the attack of the advanced guard, and the surrender of the town, still the fort held out, and our General began to chafe at its non-reduction. As yet neither artillery nor any of the munitions of a siege had passed—all was heaped together at St. Pierre. To transport this branch of the army by the pass of the St. Bernard appeared impossible; but what was an army without it? Its wants were imperative. In vain were obstacles started to alarm the imaginations of the desponding, or damp the ardour of the most sanguine—everything had been arranged by the genius that had planned and superintended the execution of this gigantic enterprise of the modern Hannibal.

The establishment of the convent on the mountain, for the purpose of affording assistance to the few solitary travellers who pursue this route, is sufficient evidence of the dangers to which they are exposed in these stormy regions; but the present array, consisting of infantry, cavalry, baggage, cassoons, artillery, &c. &c, bore little resemblance to the few straggling parties for whose use it was founded. The passage, however, was to be attempted; so the artillerymen proceeded to dismount the guns, waggons, forges, &c; piece by piece was every thing dismantled, while the engineers, under the direction of the Inspector-General of Artillery, Gassendrie, prepared troughs from the excavated trunks of trees, in which the guns were placed, and to which were attached five or six hundred men, according to the size of the piece, who dragged this heavy burden from the foot of the pass to the convent. Sledges had been provided at Auxonne on which to carry the axles; the wheels were placed upon poles, and borne on the shoulders of men who were relieved at every 100 paces, while the ammunition, enclosed in deal boxes, was placed on the backs of mules. By way of encouragement, Marmont, who commanded the artillery, offered a premium of 500 francs for each gun mounted and attended by its ammunition waggon which should reach the other side. An entire battalion was necessary for the transport of the two objects—one half being obliged to drag the troughs, sledges, &c, while the remainder conveyed their comrades' muskets, camp utensils, and provisions for five days, which in bread, meat, and salt, was served out previous to our departure from Martigny. Each of these men was, therefore, provided with a burden weighing from 70 to 100 lbs, the baggage waggons returning to Lausaune, every soldier, even to the First Consul, being obliged to content himself with the most simple necessaries.

What will not determined courage, when directed aright, accomplish? The morning broke clearly but coldly as we assembled at-St. Pierre, and put ourselves in motion, to follow the path of our comrades. Arrived at the foot of the mountain, we fell into single file, mounting one by one, no person being allowed to pass the one in advance, and where this command was disobeyed, the inevitable result of its infringement was the disappearance of the offender, who was soon buried in the snow, and fortunate indeed were they who had the good luck to be dug out again.

The leading files were often obliged to halt, and those in the rear profited by these frequent stoppages, taking care to slake their thirst, which would otherwise have been insupportable, by soaking their biscuit in the melted snow, a delicacy which none can appreciate, save those who, like us, have crossed the St. Bernard, ere the summer has set in.

There can be no doubt that the firmness of the snow, as we advanced, smoothed many obstructions, the path being more difficult than dangerous; however, after five hours excessive labour, the convent appeared in sight, and in a short time we were at the gates.

The First Consul, who was mounted on a mule led by a guide, was often stopped by those carrying the ammunition, or by the soldiers who were employed dragging the cannon up this miserable road. Was there more than the usual difficulty his presence reanimated their drooping courage, his advice encouraged them to attempt its overthrow; wherever he found those in advance brought to a stand still, his directions were attended to with the most imposing silence, and followed by an execution more prompt than the most unsparing distribution of gold by any other hand could have produced.

During the ascent I had the good fortune to attend the Prior of the Convent, who, mounted on a mule, followed in the suite of the Consul. He was a fat jolly old fellow, who had passed many years in his mountain home, and related many tales of the travellers that had been rescued from destruction by the dogs of the convent. He pointed out to me the dangers which beset those who attempted the pass without the assistance of a guide, and beguiled the long and tedious route with anecdotes of himself and his order. On our arrival at the Hospice, tables were laid out in front, and each soldier as he passed received a piece of bread and cheese and a glass of wine; and this welcome liquor, although almost frozen, proved of the utmost service, in the warmth it conveyed to the body, and the assistance it rendered in recruiting the strength. I will venture to say that there was scarcely a man in the army who would have exchanged his glass of wine for all the glittering wealth of Peru.

Here were we then at the summit of the Saint Bernard, where the Drave and the Doria take their source, and where the cold is excessive even in the middle of summer. Not a solitary shrub or stunted bush announced the presence of vegetation; not a herb or leaf afforded to the eye the presence of soft verdure; never do the birds make this their resting place. Nature appears to have determined that it shall be abandoned in its most savage state. A vast extent of dark and monotonous grey rocks of ice heaped together; an immense perspective of a mountain chain always white; a frightful silence, disturbed only by the thundering avalanche; clouds which sometimes seem to precipitate themselves to the foot of the mountains, and sometimes to envelope them on all sides; such are the startling features which offer themselves to the notice of the traveller who seeks these elevated points of our hemisphere.

And yet even among these savage and dreary places men are to be found, whose principal occupation is to afford relief to those unfortunate persons whose business leads them this way, and who are frequently menaced with danger, and in some cases absolutely lost in these unfrequented passes. The monastery of Bernardins is like a vast inn or eastern caravanserais, while two other buildings of smaller dimensions are near to, and dependent on it. When these good monks have a summer of three months, and only three hours of fine weather each day of this hasty season, they consider themselves highly favoured by Providence.

About a hundred paces distant from the Convent on the left, is Mount Veland, the highest of the chain, and, at the time when I passed the sun shone out upon its crest, covering it with myriads of sparkles which dazzled the sight. Its crest is 3,600 metres above the level of the sea, and it takes two days to attain the summit, not so much on account of its height, as by the numerous fields of ice which surround it.

The naturalists, who travel in these mountains, arm themselves with a pole, an axe, and climbing irons. The pole assists them to ascend and leap over the chasms, the axe to cut stairs or steps in the ice, and the sharp irons prevent their sliding. Provisions and guides are equally necessary, for in summer as well as in winter, many persons are lost among these almost inaccessible rocks, and the bodies of such as are recovered by the dogs are carried to the chapel, where they are deposited, the coldness of the climate preserving them from decay.

With what pleasure did I bestow my caresses on these dogs, so useful to the belated traveller! Who could calmly speak of their charitable instinct, ordained by a bountiful Providence to rescue suffering humanity from danger, and even death? Who could fail to admire and respect the good monks whose lives are devoted to this cause? Notwithstanding the scarcity of provisions, there was scarcely a French soldier who did not offer to these noble dogs a portion of the bread supplied to him. Morning and night these fine animals start for their tasks, and if in the course of their undirected track, echo carry to their attentive ears the miserable cries of some unfortunate nigh upon perishing, they run towards him, lavish their caresses upon him, and seem to bid him take courage till they can return with assistance. Then they course back to the convent, and with sad and and plaintive cries announce to the brethren what they have seen. These append to their necks a basket of such viands as are proper to re-animate the sufferer, and, following their humane messenger, in many instances rescue the unhappy wanderer from impending death.

What a contrast between these godly men, who employ the most ingenious methods to preserve the life of a single individual, and that destructive spirit which unhappily at this period seemed to have taken possession of the earth, blotting its fair face with oceans of human blood, and destroying in very wantonness the image of the Creator. The reflection was anything but complimentary to the soldier, but was as evanescent as the sunshine on Mont Veland.

In the winter season, when the winds, the rain, hail, or snow have swept away and destroyed the path, the guides come with their mules, and these sagacious animals quickly discover it if any trace be left, and, by passing and repassing frequently, render it once more practicable. This is often a work of time, occupying three or four days, and, whenever the frost becomes a little more severe than usual, the monks seize the favourable opportunity to re-provision the monastery.

Singular as it may appear, the passage offers greater difficulties in summer than in winter; the rain penetrating through the cracks in the snow, causes it to melt underneath in a manner not easily perceptible. It there forms cavities, on which the traveller steps, unaware of the treacherous gulf beneath, when suddenly the surface gives way and he disappears in an instant. A severe frost is therefore always to be preferred, because then the transit is attended by greater security.

At 200 paces below the convent is a lake, the depth of which has never been ascertained, as it but rarely thawed, and often times the snow is so deep upon its frozen surface, that persons pass over without noticing it.

And here, in these unhospitable regions, did 124 men of the 28th demi-brigade of the line pass the winter, having to guard the passes of the St. Bernard. I leave you to guess how pleasant the sojourn must have been, especially to those who had just spent three years in garrison in the gay city of Paris.

Each man having received his refreshment commenced the descent. There were still six leagues to go, but six leagues which the extreme rapidity of the descent rendered terrible. At every step we were met by immense chasms, formed by the melting snow. In vain the cavalry held their horses firmly by the bridle, they could not prevent them slipping; the men themselves, in spite of every precaution, often fell, and unless they were quickly on their legs again, they ran the risk of being dragged off the path, and of perishing in the yawning gulfs that opened on every side around them.

The First Consul, accompanied by the Prior of the Maison du Convalescence, and attended by Duroc, Le Marai, Merlin, and others, entered the Convent, and visited the Chapel and the libraries. We attended his return in the great hall of the Convent, conversing with the monks on the vastness of their habitation. Napoleon wore his grey great-coat, and seemed to suffer a little from fatigue, which, however, gave place to disappointment at not meeting any one to inform him of the surrender of the fort of Bard. He remained here about an hour, and when he departed, exhorted the brethren to persevere in a course which so well accorded with the dictates of humanity. His horses and mules followed us. On reaching the summit of the pass, Napoleon, desirous no doubt of rejoining the army by the shortest route, followed a path which had been used by some of the infantry, but had not proceeded far before he was obliged to dismount. His attendants followed his example, and the descent becoming exceedingly rapid, he seated himself on the snow, and slid down a height of 200 feet. The rest of the journey was continued on foot, sometimes sliding and sometimes walking, but the chasms into which we were at each moment slipping, rendered the descent much more fatiguing than the ascent. We had marched at midnight, and the clock had struck the hour of nine ere we arrived, having come 14 leagues, almost without stopping, and but scantily supplied with food. Few there were, however, who complained of hunger, the fatigue and the want of rest made us easily forget the scantiness of supper.

Chapter 13

The Fort of Bard

A few hours of rest afforded our wearied troops an opportunity of recovering from the fatigues of the preceding day, and we marched on Aoste, a town of Piedmont, which the advanced guard had occupied the previous evening. We arrived there early in the morning, and were met outside the town by a deputation of the inhabitants, who came forth to compliment the First Consul on his success, and to conduct him to the residence of the Bishop.

Although ill-built, wretchedly paved, and filled with the poorest inhabitants, it proved of the greatest utility to us, for from the neighbouring vallies were drawn the supplies served out to the troops for the passage of the St. Bernard.

The First Consul remained here five days, while the General-in-Chief, Berthier, with his staff, followed the movements of the advanced guard, and fixed his head-quarters at a convent about a league distant from the celebrated fort of Bard.

Mine, at this period, was no life of indolence, for a courier charged with despatches from the occupant of a tottering throne to his powerful ally, could not have been hurried backwards and forwards with greater haste than were myself and two or three other officers of our corps.

In vain Napoleon waited for the news of the surrender of the fort of Bard, for although the town had been carried on the 25th of May, the fort as yet held out.

I had galloped up to the quarters of the First Consul at Aoste one morning, with despatches, when I unexpectedly received a summons to attend him, and, following the messenger, I was not long in finding myself in the presence of the conqueror of Italy.

Standing with his back to the fire, enveloped in the same grey frock in which he had crossed the mountain, with a short riding whip in his hand, with which he occasionally tapped his boot, he appeared waiting in moody silence the return of the messenger sent for me. Near him were Lannes, Duroc, De Marai, and others, and as I passed into the chamber, his restless grey eye caught sight of me, and he beckoned me to approach.

"Ah!" said the First Consul; "my brave comrade of the forlorn hope of Mantua, what news from Bard?"

I was pleased with the recognition, and felt myself fast swelling to a level with the brilliant staff around me. A repetition of the question, however, recalled me to myself, and I replied that as yet there appeared no chance of its surrender.

Turning on his heel to General Lannes, he launched into complaints against Berthier. "I am weary," said he, "of staying here; those fools will never take Bard; I must go myself and see what can be done. How vexatious to be tormented by so contemptible an affair." The brave comrade of Mantua was forgotten, and as I slowly left the room, I could not help thinking how different would have been the case had my news been of a more pleasing character.

The division of Lannes was now pushed forward towards Chatillon, where he found the enemy drawn up ready to oppose the passage of a bridge over a ravine, which our infantry could not descend. Without a moment's hesitation the Chief of Brigade, Tournier, charged them with the 12th Hussars, and overwhelming all who opposed his passage, took forty hussars and two hundred infantry prisoners, together with a three-pounder, which composed the whole of their artillery, and pursuing the fugitives even to the very walls of the fort, hardly allowed them time to enter and raise the drawbridge.

The fort of Bard commands the road, bounded on the left by Mount Alvaredo, and on the right by a torrent called the Doria Baltea, by which it is separated from the town; and this fort, or rather rock, suddenly arrested the army, and shut it up in a gorge, where four days sufficed to consume the whole of the resources which the difficult passage of the Saint Bernard had allowed us to accumulate. This delay afforded an opportunity to the Austrian General, Melas, to oppose our passage. To his misfortune he fancied that he had discovered the plans of Napoleon, and doubted not that he should be able to prevent their execution; but the slow movements of the Austrians were no match for the rapidity of the French, for though nature had formed the rock in the shape of a sugar loaf, and art had rendered it almost impregnable, still the feeble assistance rendered to the garrison prevented their doing all that should have been done.

As I have before said, the road lies at the foot of the rock, watered on the right by the Doria Baltea, now a deep, rapid, and dangerous river, the opposite bank of which was rugged and inaccessible, serving as a harbour for rats and owls. On the left were other rocks, as high as these but less precipitous; and these latter were covered with vines, to attain which the miserable inhabitants of these places are obliged to cut staircases in the rock. We had but the choice of two alternatives—either to take the fort by assault, or to find another route which, by avoiding it, might enable us to pursue our march. But the genius of Napoleon directed us, and it was on this occasion especially that he proved that what is necessity to him who struggles is but choice to him that is willing, and that nothing is impossible to the man who is determined.

Of all the miserable beings it had been my lot to fall in with, none could bear comparison with the inhabitants of these regions. Their skin bears resemblance to nothing so much as a piece of soiled old parchment, while their features are disfigured by horrible wens. They have naked feet, and their legs are so burnt by the sun that they appear at first sight to be covered with black stockings, while their clothes are the colour of soot. They make their bread at Christmas for the whole year, and are obliged to hammer it to pieces when they want to consume it.

Like the owls, whose hideous features they resemble, they choose the most elevated points on which to erect their miserable habitations. They seldom frequent any town, having no wants save such as are supplied by their cows and their goats. We had plenty of time to become acquainted with them, for they came to Aoste, carrying on their heads bundles of forage weighing from 200 to 300 pounds, and, in spite of these heavy weights, they were always running, even in the most dangerous paths.

And vast service they rendered the army at the siege of the Fort of Bard, for, in the absence of horses and mules, they carried the supplies to the troops, performing all their services willingly and with pleasure, for which they were always punctually rewarded.

Three companies of Tirailleurs had taken possession of the town of Bard, and made good their position. During the day they were obliged to screen themselves from the fire of the fort, but, nevertheless, they annoyed the besieged considerably, by picking off such men as showed themselves, at the embrasures or loopholes.

I have already said nature had done much for the strength of the fort. Twenty-two pieces of cannon, five hundred men, many mortars and outworks defending the road to it, had been the contribution of art, and together had rendered it difficult of approach. The first means tried, however, were to be the assault, and about eleven o'clock at night, lighted by the rays of a brilliant moon, the chief of brigade of the brave 58th, at the head of many companies of grenadiers, marched in silence among the thickly strewn rocks and boulders, until they approached the palisades, where they were saluted with a shower of balls, which, however, did not check their advance; and, following the enemy from outwork to outwork, they compelled him to retire at the point of the bayonet, and to re-enter the castle. Notwithstanding our heavy fire of grape and musketry, the enemy replied as warmly; great guns, grenades, howitzers, were all put in requisition, and these succeeded at last in arresting the impetuosity of the French. Large stones piled on the walls were thrown down on the assailants, beating many of them to the ground; the gallant leader fell mortally wounded, and further advance being impossible the retreat was sounded. It was obeyed with as much steadiness as if the troops were on parade, although we had to regret the fate of many a brave fellow killed or seriously wounded, amongst the rest, General Dufour, who distinguished himself greatly, and was dangerously hurt.

Chapter 14

The Repulse

Although a small portion only of the army had been engaged, the loss had been serious; and as the fort if well defended was announced impregnable, and if Melas took advantage of our position, it was likely to be a critical one, the other alternative was mow to be tried, and a reconnoitering party was despatched to endeavour to discover some route by which the fort might be evaded.

They reported that by using the steps made by the peasants, Mount Albaredo might be crossed, and we should fall into the road on the other side of the rock. This was now to be essayed; but in mounting the ladder-like ascent, we had to pass over a certain portion that was commanded by one of the guns of the battery, which soon opened on the passers by. It, therefore, became necessary to show as small a mark to the enemy as need be, and on arriving at this spot, we took care to make the interval as much as ten paces between each soldier. But this did not content us; so by dint of vast efforts we managed to haul a four pound gun up a portion of the passage, and placing it in a cleft of the rock, we found we could return their fire, and as it completely commanded their battery, we kept firing away without intermission.

The advanced guard only took this dangerous route, and great difficulty they had in accomplishing it; to the men, however, who had carried a part of the artillery over the St. Bernard, the little sugar-loaf hill in our front was an obstacle of small account, but they were constrained to pass by single files, and to bivouac on the top. The infantry got safe to the road at the foot of the hill, and now commenced the difficulty of carrying over the cavalry, for the poor horses were obliged to follow the example of the goats of the country, and leap from rock to rock, a feat which the most bungling soon learned to perform with precision, for instinct, which in them serves the place of reason, showed them how to avoid rolling over the precipices by which, they are surrounded; nevertheless, several horses and mules were lost.

The advanced guard had passed, but though we had carried the guns over the Alps, they could by no means be dragged up these stair-like passages, and some other means had yet to be discovered, and however exposed the route through the town might be, by that and no other could they be conveyed. The genius of Napoleon was again in the ascendant, and in the dead of night, dark and cheerless as the thickest November sky could have made it, the troops commenced strewing the street of Bard with straw and dung, and the whole of the artillery, carriages, and caissons, were drawn over them, by thirty men harnessed in single file to each gun and carriage, having first taken the precaution to bind the wheels with hay bands to deaden the noise. Seizing the favourable moment, the *cortege* began its march, but the enemy being on the look out, soon discovered that something unusual was going on, and from time to time a dropping fire of musketry saluted us, killing a few men, and wounding others. Yet the work went steadily on, gun after gun was carried by, and when all had passed, the last was turned upon the outwork of the fort, and, being within point blank range, soon demolished it, when the troops by which it was defended, finding themselves short of provisions, and fearing an assault, surrendered as prisoners of war.

The First Consul frequently visited the works in company with General Berthier, and other members of his staff. He ascended the rock on foot, and rested some time on the summit, from whence the eye could easily command a view of the fort. Fatigued with his exertions—for the path was very rugged and the day hot—he on one occasion lay down upon the grass, and was soon wrapped in slumber, while each soldier as he passed contemplated him with feelings of interest, and took especial care not to disturb him. Yes, here the conqueror of Italy reposed upon the green sod, with no other canopy than the blue vault of Heaven, and no doubt enjoyed a sounder and sweeter sleep than ever fell to his lot under the gilded domes of the Palace of the Tuileries.

The Austrians were at St. Martin. To attack them, drive them back upon Yvreé, took only as much time as was necessary to traverse the distance by which we were separated. In the citadel of Yvreé we found fourteen pieces of cannon, which being unable to carry away, they had spiked, some munitions of war, and two hundred prisoners. Here the First Consul remained four days, making it the head-quarters of the army, a rest which proved of as much service to it as a reinforcement would have done, although the supplies which were issued to the troops were very dear.

All the ovens and bake-houses of the town were put in requisition, and were employed night and pay to produce bread, of which the army stood in need, none having been served out for the last eight days. Here, too, the plan of the campaign was determined upon, and each general of division got ready for the start. The troops under their command deployed, and menaced the whole north of Italy; the beauty of which country, as seen lying at our feet, and the mildness of the climate, contrasted strangely with that of the land we were about to leave.

And here occurred one of those laughable affairs which sometimes fall out, and serve to render the monotony of a guard room, less irksome than it would otherwise be.

The enemy was not far distant, and although I had been employed as orderly, conveying instructions to the different corps, it fell to my lot to form part of the picket on duty that night. The grenadiers of the guard, both horse and foot, had bivouacked in the garden of the mansion in which the First Consul and his staff were lodged. The night was dark and cold, no star illumined the dreary expanse above us, no sound was heard, save the low moaning of the wind as it blew in fitful gusts among the trees, or the distant cry of the sentinel on guard as he passed the word; sounds which had become too familiar to the ears of the troops to disturb their rest The influence of the hour had prevailed on all save those on watch, one by one the voices of the talkers had ceased, all the world seemed wrapped in profound repose, when suddenly I was aroused from a reverie that would have soon become a slumber, and astonished by the report of several muskets, which the balls of which came whistling through the trees above our heads, making strange havoc with the branches. To turn out the guard was the work of a moment, all was in commotion on the instant. "The Austrians, the Austrians," ran from mouth to mouth, though no one could tell where the alarm commenced, or whether any portion of the troops were engaged. Here one was met with his knapsack on his back, prepared to fall back or advance, as the word should be given; there was a dragoon hastily saddling his charger; without drum or trumpet we were soon under arms, while an orderly was despatched to awaken the General, and a man from each troop ran off to summon the officers. Before they came we were drawn up in line, each trooper as he arrived falling into his place; all the division seemed at once restored to life, and only to be waiting for the order to move, when a chasseur, who had got ready sooner than his comrades, came galloping up with the news that a neighbouring barrack-room had taken fire, and that in their hurry and alarm the inmates had discharged their muskets, and thus aroused the camp. The fire had been easily subdued, and we soon returned to our duties; the slumberers not in the most amiable humour at the accident which had deprived them of some hours of rest. However, the surprise of Yvreé proved a fruitful topic of conversation, and afforded us many a laugh long after the annoyance had been forgotten.

 I was once again upon my native soil, and still in the ranks of those who were called the enemies of my country. I had imbibed the latitudinarian notions of revolutionary France, and having held no communication with my kindred, had ceased to regard them as such, or myself as a citizen of Piedmont.

 Fortune had smiled upon me, and should she prove as propitious as she had hitherto done, I should have no cause tor repentance. I was now about to revisit some of the towns in which I had enacted a part on the mimic stage, then the despised of mankind, shunned by the good, scoffed at by the wicked; now I was an actor in the great drama of life, the world the audience, the heroes of France the players; now was I the companion of the brave, who had earned their reputations on the battle field, and esteemed me as a friend and a brother.

By the captain of my troop, Barbanegre, an officer who on several occasions had greatly distinguished himself, I had been treated with marked partiality. He had recommended me to the notice of General Berthier, and my own conduct had proved that I was not unworthy of the recommendation; added to this, I had attracted the attention of our chief, who, though not many years my senior in age, had already stamped his name on the imperishable records of fame: that tide in the affairs of men which taken at the flood leads on to fortune, had set in auspiciously for me; and ambition, the polar star of the brave, now led me on; I determined whenever the opportunity occurred to do or die; and though the routine of a soldier's duty was occasionally a little irksome, a few cheering words from my superiors soon set all right again, and I looked forward to the time when I should become—I knew not what.

Years have passed away since then, yet still can memory recall these feelings as vividly as when they first came over me. The dream of ambition is broken, yet can I now repaint the scenes I shadowed forth during the earlier periods of my employment as a soldier; the impression, like the writing with invisible ink, wants but the revivifying influence of the spirit to become as legible as when it was first imprinted there.

Chapter 15

The Passage of the Tessin

Four or five thousand men drawn hastily from Turin and the neighbouring garrisons, were united to those whom we had beaten previously, and had taken position at Romano, where they threw up some entrenchments. The Chinsella, a deep and rapid river, covered their right, but they had neglected to destroy the bridge, an omission which I attributed to their ignorance of our position and force. They declared haughtily that Napoleon did not command us in person, but that our leader was an adventurer who resembled him; that his troops were a mass of Italian refugees, without artillery or cavalry, which had been detached from the army to amuse the enemy, whilst Napoleon occupied himself against Genoa; and, buoyed up by this opinion, they flattered themselves that they had nothing to do but to attack us, and then, by feigning a retreat, to draw us out into the plains, where we should easily fall before their matchless prowess.

Poor deluded wretches! Too soon did they find their mistake; for early in the morning the advanced guard, under Lannes, commenced the attack, and two hours sufficed to destroy their vain hopes and enlighten their blind ignorance. In that short time the mountains were in our rear, Romano was carried at the point of the bayonet, and the bridge and the redoubt were swept away, while their loss in killed and wounded was frightful, giving them terrible proof of the bravery of the French, who, after putting them to the route, pursued them on the road to Turin, to which they seemed disposed to retreat.

Thus since our descent of the mountain, the army had taken

Aoste, Chatillon, St. Martin, Yvreé, Sûsa, and Labrunette, to which was now added Romano, which lay open before us, notwithstanding that the bridges and boats on the Oreo had been destroyed.

Profiting by the nature of the ground as he retreated, the enemy rallied in a large plain, where a strong body of cavalry formed, and charging our infantry, whose impetuosity in the pursuit had outstripped their prudence, many were ridden over or cut down before they could be thrown into squares. Happily, however, the 11th and 12th regiments of hussars and the 21st chasseurs were near, and these, with the 6th light infantry, and the 28th and 44th regiments of the line being quickly brought up—charged the advancing squadrons, and threw them into disorder. I had just ridden up with orders for the general, and witnessed the charge of the 21st, and never on the most brilliant field-day did I see one executed with more coolness and precision-

The main body of the army having passed Mount Albaredo defiled by Yvreé, where it was supplied with provisions, which restored vigour to the frame of many a famishing soldier, and soon, in spite of the privations they had undergone, the abundance which began to manifest itself, effaced the remembrance of the distress we had left behind.

Buonaparte, desirous of concealing his plans, ordered two divisions to march on Turin, to support Lannes, who had driven the enemy to Chivasao, on the Po. Attacked there, he retired on Casal where he burnt the bridge. We made a feint to pass the river, and many of the men threw themselves into the stream to take the floating bridge, but while the enemy believed that we were menacing Turin, a division of cavalry entered Verceil, where were considerable magazines and forage.

Thus had all the divisions passed into the open country, and so well had their movements been combined that their success was great.

The division of cavalry which had taken the route to Verceil now moved forward under Murat, and the main body entered that town without firing a gun; but while we were employed throwing a bridge of boats over the Sesia, the advanced guard perceived the enemy on the opposite bank of the Tessin.

The rapidity of the river Tessin, without a bridge, or boats to construct one, offered an obstacle to troops less ardent than the French, but four or five little shallops, which the inhabitants of the little village of Galiate had concealed from the enemy, were soon taken possession of. Into these the soldiers quickly threw themselves, under a murdering fire from the enemy's right. The carabineers of the 6th light were the first afloat, protected in some manner by a well-directed fire of musketry and some cannon, and were speedily followed by the grenadiers of the 28th. The opposite bank was soon gained, and as quickly mounted. The enemy being better provided with cavalry than infantry were obliged to abandon a marsh covered with osiers, and a small wood which incommoded them as soon as they failed to protect it. Our men then threw themselves among the trees, and the Voltigeurs made strange havoc in the ranks of the Austrians.

I had been sent with an order to the officer in command of the Voltigeurs, who held possession of the extreme point of the wood nearest the enemy, when a ball struck my horse in the chest, and we both rolled over. The poor animal was dead; and as I with difficulty raised myself from the ground, a ball took my shoulder, carrying away my epaulette, and another passed through the crown of my shako. Happily, neither had touched my flesh, but my proximity being too great to be pleasant, I fairly took to my heels and ran for my life; and notwithstanding that the rifles of the Voltigeurs would have brought to the ground any one who had the temerity to pursue me, I had been for some moments under the shelter of the wood before I had recovered sufficient equanimity to discover the whole extent of my loss.

Here was I in truth a dismounted dragoon, anxious to return to my post whence I had been despatched in the absence of the regular officer of ordonnance, yet unable to guess where that post might be, and still more unable to attain it even if I had known where it was. The bugles soon sounded the recall, and I accompanied my new companions to the rear, where I procured a fresh horse and directions to my regiment.

The principal point to which our efforts were directed was

Buffalora; and the passage of the river took place about a league lower down the liver. Our troops menaced the rear of the enemy, but a party of Grenadiers, too ardent in the pursuit, entered the town, and the width of the streets permitting cavalry to act with advantage, General Landon, who had just arrived from Genoa, either discovering the weakness of our force, or willing to ascertain its strength, put his horse to the gallop, and returning at least two leagues, brought up two divisions of cavalry of Bussy's Legion, fell on the Grenadiers, re-took the town, and made a company prisoners. The remainder, rallying quickly at the entrance of the marsh, kept the enemy in check, and, with the assistance of others who kept pouring in from the boats, forced him to retreat; and when the night came on we had a considerable force on the other side the river.

In his anxiety to be among the first in the melee, Duroc, senior aide-de-camp of the First Consul, threw himself into a boat, carrying over a full complement of grenadiers. The boat, from its crowded state, became unsteady, and Duroc was thrown into the stream. Here, in all probability, his campaigns would have ended, had not Harmand, a grenadier of the 28th, precipitated himself into the river, and thus saved him from a watery grave.

The passage of the river being accomplished, the enemy retired, and on the morrow the head quarters of the French army occupied Novara. Already many of the divisions waited with impatience on the borders of the river the signal to cross. It was an interesting spectacle to witness the general enthusiasm which pervaded all ranks. All the world seemed desirous of following in the suite of the First Consul. Cavalry, oxen, mules, baggage waggons, carriages of all kinds crowded to the bridge, each interval filled up by a crowd of foot soldiers. Hardly were we on the opposite shore than the hope of occupying Milan seemed to give us wings—we fancied we were hurrying to the land of promise.

Nevertheless our entrance into Milan was delayed for some hours, for the enemy, undecided as to whether he would shut himself up in the citadel, or willing to employ the time in augmenting the provisions, for four hours harassed the advanced guard. At this time many of the inhabitants fell victims to their desire for the entrance of the French, being killed or wounded by the guns from the citadel. To avoid them we took a different route, by the bye paths, which conducted us to the Porta Ticinisa, on the road to Pavia, before attaining which the First Consul and his staff were obliged to take refuge at a farm-house by the road side, to avoid a terrific storm, which wetted those who were not so fortunate to the skin. Besides the unpleasantness of the storm, we were in some danger from the enemy, numbers of whom paraded the neighbouring roads, and the advanced guard had not arrived, when an aide-de-camp rode up, and hastened the march of the Horse Grenadiers of the Guard.

As they came up the enemy disappeared, and we followed in the rear of the brilliant cortege, which presented itself at the gate of the capital of Lombardy.

CHAPTER 16

Milan

Notwithstanding the unfavourable state of the weather the staff of the army formed a large and brilliant throng, which the Milanese came forth in crowds to meet, while the ladies, equally well-dressed as those of Paris, mingled with the groups of citizens, repeating with enthusiasm, "*Vive Buonaparte! Vivent les Francais.*" The farther we advanced, the thicker became the crowd, till at last the street seemed filled with one dense mass of human beings.

Some time had elapsed since I had last entered Milan—time which was not to be measured by the ordinary rule of computation, but by the events that had crowded one upon another; for how often do we find that we live more in one short hour of excitement, than in days or even weeks measured by the monotonous hands of the dial! The common current of existence, when it runs smoothly on, takes little note of its advance towards the ocean of eternity; and noiseless as may be the tread of the destroyer when it falls upon the verdant paths of pleasure, his tramp is more sounding than that of the war-horse, when the route is chequered by misfortune, or overstrewn with the thorns of remorse.

Few, very few years had elapsed, a short span only of the usual number vouchsafed unto man, yet had my existence appeared, to exceed that of a whole generation. Then, a fugitive boy, anxious only to escape from well-merited punishment, with a little coin in my pocket, and a knapsack on my back, reflection had not yet established her empire in my mind, and I was careless alike of the future and the past. Now, with a name unstained, with fame and fortune in my grasp—the equal of the brave, the companion of the courted—with head erect as that of the war-horse when he first scents the far-off odours of the battle field, I followed in the train of our martial leader, as different a being from my former self as were the occupants of these serried ranks from those with whom I formerly trod the boards of the theatre.

Then was I the shunned and guilty outcast of society, seeking the bye-ways and hidden corners of a great city, to find concealment even from my nearest and dearest friends; and now, clothed in the glittering panoply of a soldier, courting the admiration of the fair sex, and exciting the envy of the men, the raw unbearded boy no more resembled his present self than does the caterpillar, before he has thrown off his disfiguring slough, the gay and glittering butterfly which floats away from flower to flower.

Few there are, I trust, and fewer I hope they may yet become, who like myself have gone through a transition so dangerous, but I believe that many of the number would have withstood the test. Few there are who have gone through the purifying cauldron of the world, that have not come out brighter metal, worthless as may have been the ore when first cast into it, for there are few who have received the early attentions of a mother, whose lessons, though forgotten in the strife of battle, recur forcibly in the solitude of a watch, but will acknowledge that as they were the earliest imprinted on their mind, so are they with the most difficulty eradicated.

No, I shall not readily forget our entrance into Milan. The windows were thronged with well-dressed women, every open space was crowded with spectators, while the shops, tricked out in their gayest manner as if to attract the gaze of customers, gave evidence of the confidence the Milanese reposed in the French. But the *coup d'œil* the most striking—the moment the most flattering—was when we arrived in the *Piazza del Duomo*, when the hero who commanded us beheld the transport with which he was received by the immense concourse of people there collected; the reiterated applause, the universal cry of "*Vive Napoleon! Vive l'armee Francais!*" penetrated our souls, and added not a little consequence to those who followed in the wake of the conqueror, giving us that gentle pride which sits so well upon the victors.

Murat followed with his division of cavalry, and with the infantry and advanced guard surrounded the citadel, where 4000 Austrian troops had shut themselves up. The troops were bivouacked on the ground they had taken, while we of the guard were billetted in quarters round the palace of the Viceroy, in which Napoleon took up his residence, though it would hardly be believed that even there we could not find as much as a faggot wherewith to dry our dripping habiliments. Truly his Serene Highness the Archduke, in his hurry to vacate the palace, did not leave much behind to comfort his successor.

After the guard had been set, and I had looked at my horses, I was slowly sauntering down the Corso, musing on my change of fortune—the near proximity of the theatre Carcano not adding to the pleasures of my reminiscence—when a gentleman passed, and as I raised my eyes from the ground and caught a transient view of his face, the thought struck me that it was not unknown. It was one of those we often meet with casually, without at the moment being able to recall to our recollection when and where we last beheld it; and while I was turning over in my mind such persons as I fancied it might be, a well known voice exclaimed—"Excuse my freedom, sir, but unless I am much mistaken, you and I should be acquainted."

"The Marchese, by all that's wonderful," said I; "pardon me, my benefactor, that amid the varying scenes through which I have passed, so many faces have been stamped upon my memory, that she has for one moment ceased to recognise you."

"Ah! indeed, Gazzola, the gay uniform of the soldier, which well becomes you, at first deceived me, added to which you are much older, and more manly-looking; but for once the old proverb is reversed, and I, who am greatly your debtor, was more ready to recognise you than you were to know me. Come, come, man, no apologies; I am dying to bear of your changed fortunes, added to which there is one as greatly your debtor as myself, and we cannot do better than seek her."

The warmth of my friend did away with any little scruples I might have had in re-commencing an intimacy with one so much my superior, but then I hoped to be a general of division in the course of time, and knew that he would not despise me for the scenes through which I had been obliged to pass.

I would at this moment gladly have declined the proposed visit until I had thrown off my stable dress and clothed myself in a garb more fitting the presence of a lady; this the Marchese would by no means allow. "Come, man," said he; "come at once; Adela will be none the less glad to see you that you are not decked out in your gayest uniform. 'Tis not the glittering tinsel that she values; so come at once!" As he would take no denial, I passed my arm through his, and accompanied him to the Palazzo Cusani, where he had been residing for the last twelve months.

Entering the boudoir of the Marchesa, who was sitting with her back towards the door, playing with her little boy, whose lucky rescue first led me to their acquaintance, he exclaimed, "Adela, I bring you an old friend, and not the less welcome that he is totally unexpected." If I had little reason to complain of the warmth of her husband's manner towards me, still less was there to find fault with in that of the Marchesa. He plied me with questions until I had given him the history of my doings since we parted at Verona; and when the relation was complete, nothing would do but that I must make their house my abode during my stay in Milan, which he prognosticated would be but short; so, notwithstanding my remonstrances to the contrary, a servant was despatched for my baggage, and in a few hours I found myself domesticated in his hospitable mansion, and an honoured guest at his board.

How I blessed the change which enabled me to feel that, although I could not aspire to be the equal of the noble, not a blush of shame need cross his cheek at making me his companion; and proud indeed did I feel, that I could now be the escort of the high-born dame, and no sense of degradation enter like iron into my soul. The little fellow I had saved, had grown, and now, a sprightly child, would play with some article of my uniform, or ride on my sword to the evident delight of his parents.

On the day after our arrival in Milan, a grand ball was given at the Seals Theatre, and to which Marchese insisted I should accompany him. It was the first entertainment of the kind I had witnessed since I had left the stage, and the recollection of my former avocation conveyed too little pleasure to induce me to do anything to recall it; but the lady added her entreaties to those of her lord, and as she would need a cavalier, I was fain to comply.

Giustiniana had been induced to leave Verona soon after the occupation of Venice by the French, and had removed to Milan without mixing at all in political matters. Looked at with distrust by those in authority, and not too well loved by the rulers of the city in which he had taken up his abode, he lived in retirement, mixing little in society, but like many of the young nobles of Italy, he had imbibed some notions of liberty, and though born an aristocrat, and descended from a long line of ancestors, who had formerly occupied the ducal chair in Venice, he wanted but the intimacy of a few French officers to become a thorough republican. But for his attachment to his wife and child, he would doubtless have joined the French army; but be that as it may, he welcomed its entrance into Milan, the more so as during the former campaign he had made the acquaintance of Generals Berthier and Lannes.

He had renewed his acquaintance, and as I was slightly known to each, (the former indeed had offered me an appointment on his staff) he hoped by affording me his countenance at the ball to do me some service. It was kindly meant, for although the slight insight I had received of the duties of officer of ordonnance, had made me decline an appointment I thought hardly equal to that of a courier, I was in daily expectation of receiving my promotion, and my ambition was at this moment limited to a lieutenancy in the guard.

As I returned from the Piazza after morning parade, a note, without signature or address, was put into my hands by a boy who immediately mixed with the crowd, and was lost to sight ere I had time to ask from whence it came. It contained these words:—"If you are the same person who was discovered by a dog in the theatre at Alessandria, meet me in the passage leading out of the Duorno this evening at ten, while the world is at the Scala."

Who could by possibility know me now? "Who had seen me

in the situation to which the note referred? I puzzled my brain, and returned to the palazzo to dress without having come to any satisfactory conclusion. That no harm was meant me, I felt certain; and at last I made up my mind that the only person who could know any thing of me must be a former companion on the stage, who, used to the varied changes of the scene, had less difficulty in recognising me.

I determined, therefore, to accompany my friends to the ball, and, desiring my servant to attend at the theatre at the stated hour with my pistols, to take an opportunity to steal out unobserved, and give my mysterious acquaintance the meeting.

CHAPTER 17

The Ball

Dressed in my gayest uniform, I entered the carriage which contained the Marchesa and her spouse, and away we rattled to the Scala, the street in front of which was already thronged with carriages, bearing the lovely belles of Milan to the ball.

All the beauty and fashion of the city was present, for though the notice was short, still in this abode of the goddess Terpsichore there was no difficulty in getting up an impromptu affair of this kind; and as we entered the pit, converted for this occasion into a *salle de danse,* I found myself the observed of all observers, for the rank of the party I accompanied was a sufficient passport to any society. Generals of division, gay colonels of regiments, subalterns of both cavalry and infantry regiments—horse, foot, and dragoons—all were there, and though last not least, he who had led these various officers to victory was also present, dressed in the uniform of the Guides, a corps for which he bore great partiality, and whose plain and simple garb he often assumed. No medal nor epaulette adorned him, the small gold arrow on the collar being the only decoration he wore.

Berthier, Lannes, Murat, the soldier of fortune, Duroc, first aide-de-camp, Le Marai, Bourrienne, and a host of others whose names were then familiar, but have since escaped my recollection, moved in the brilliant throng, and as we pressed on towards the stage few passed without exchanging a word with the Marchesa, and fewer still to whom I was known, but wondered how I became the companion of the handsome woman then hanging on my arm.

Shall I confess that I felt much less at my ease than if I had been charging the enemy at the head of my troop. The recollection of how I had last trod, the stage of a theatre came ever and anon to remind me of what I had been, and made me but a sorry companion. However the kindness of the Marchesa, who honored me with her hand in the waltz, in some measure re-assured me, and I was just beginning to throw off the gloom that enshrouded me, when the warning note of time reminded me of my appointment, and whispering in the ear of the Marchesa that I should shortly return, I hurried into the street, donning the cloak my servant had provided me, I seized my pistols and sought the Piazza del Duomo. I was thinking of the unfortunate being who had met his fate here as I passed some years since, when I saw a man near the same spot, who, from his loitering pace, and studious desire of concealment under the shade of the building, I fancied ought to be my correspondent. Pistol in hand I passed and re-passed him, and the second time he exclaimed, "Your pardon, *signor*, but are you not Jean Baptiste Gazzola?"

"The same," was my reply, "but you have somewhat the best of me; and what may be your business with one to whom you are unknown?"

"Not so; but time that has made some change in your features, although I immediately recognised them, may have totally obliterated mine from your memory, especially as the night is none of the brightest, still you and I were once well known to each other. I was engaged with you at the theatre of Crema, and afterwards at Alessandria, and was on the stage the evening that your dog Bruno discovered your *incognito*. I remember you well, as also the affair of the Ballerina; and although circumstances have since led me into other pursuits, and induced me now to bear a name you would fail to recognise, I am still in a situation to do a friend some service, if the desire should be reciprocal. I am under a pressing necessity to see the First Consul, but as certain death would follow were I known to be here, I have sought to make him aware of my presence through the medium of some third party. In this I have hitherto failed, two or three of my old acquaintances having been absent when I sent to them; time pressed, and recognizing you in the street, I watched your footsteps, and sought this interview. Take this ring to the First

Consul, and tell him the wearer seeks an audience; he is now at the ball, to which you may return and watch your opportunity, but fail me not, as you would rise in the service you have embraced."

Truly this was no pleasant task to be undertaken for one whose acquaintance I would rather not have renewed, as it bore too many reminiscences of the past, but the more I demurred, the more earnest became his entreaties, till at last, on his pledging himself that no possible evil could result to me, I consented to be his messenger, and taking the ring returned to the theatre.

Luckily, on my entrance, I saw the object of my mission in close conversation with the Marchese; so, assuming a nonchalance I was very far from feeling, I strolled past them, when my friend exclaimed, "The very man I spoke of; this, general, is the officer I mentioned to you; allow me to present to you my friend Gazzola." "He is already favourably known to me," was his reply, and was about to pass on, when I requested a few minutes conversation.

Notwithstanding that my request was immediately complied with, his countenance betrayed his surprise, and when I showed him the ring, he eagerly demanded where and how I became possessed of it. On my affording him the requisite information, he desired me to return to the person who sent me, and to accompany him, in an hour, to his private cabinet. "I will," continued he, "make your excuses to the Marchese, and say that in all probability I may detain you for some time."

Little dreaming the purpose of my former acquaintance, I hurried back, and found him waiting my return; we crossed the piazza to the palace, and passing in by a private entrance, entered the waiting room. In a short time my name was called by an attendant, and we were shown into the private cabinet, where Napoleon was sitting, dictating to his secretary. "Wait outside the door," said the former, "and let no man enter, but be ready when I call;" so making him a bow, I retired leaving the door slightly ajar. I had no wish to overhear the conversation, and retired to the farther part of the room, which was untenanted, save by myself; but though unwilling to play the eaves-dropper, I could not get beyond the sound of their voices.

"What!" said the First Consul, to the man I had introduced, "you here; have they not shot you yet?"

"No, general," was the reply; "not yet: you were absent in Egypt when the war re-commenced, and I determined to abandon an occupation that was never much to my taste; but no man can control his destiny. I had not made enough to keep me; let me once succeed in that, and I will give it up—till then I must take my chance. I determined to serve the Austrians in your absence, and have been sent by General Melas; but I can give you an exact account of his force, the names of their commanders, and their position. From me you may learn the present situation of Alessandria, and you know me too well to believe I would deceive you; but I must have some information to carry back to the general, and you need not fear giving me some true particulars, which I can report to him."

"As to that," replied the First Consul, "the enemy is welcome to know my force and position, provided I know his, and can keep him in ignorance of my plans. You shall be satisfied: serve me well, and I will reward you; but if you deceive me, vengeance shall overtake you when you least expect it. Your reward shall be a thousand louis;—but beware!"

It was a spy, then, I had been instrumental in bringing here, and however much they may profit by the treason, few feel any respect for the traitor. A silence ensued, and the secretary wrote down, from the dictation of the spy, the names of the corps, their force, position, and by whom they were commanded. I was called into the room, and observed Napoleon sticking pins into a map, on which he marked his plans, respecting which the spy had enlightened him. "Call General Berthier," said he to me, "and return here; but mark, sir, I forgot your proximity, beware how you divulge what you have overheard."

I hastened to the quarters of the general, with whom I returned to the cabinet. The spy repeated what he had said, and added, that Alessandria was ill-provisioned, and Melas little dreamt of our besieging it, that many of his troops were on the sick list, and were short of medicines, and other necessaries. Berthier was ordered to draw up a nearly accurate statement of our position, and this being given to the spy, we departed. On quitting him, I bade him farewell, I trusted for ever, for a loathing of his infamous profession came over me, making me disgusted with the duty that obliged me to consort with him, even for so short a period.

Towards the end of the campaign, we met again by accident, and he then told me that Buonaparte, finding his information very accurate and useful, had paid him the thousand louis, while Melas was so delighted with the manner in which he had served him, that he, too, had paid him handsomely. "I am now content," added he, "and will abandon the odious occupation, and return again to the stage."

The First Consul, with his guard, remained seven days at Milan. Enjoyment of every kind was offered to those who could take advantage of it, and the time went merrily on. The troops, of whom the distribution was well regulated, and who desired nothing but to be well fed and lodged, were content; but more greedy of glory than pleasure, they envied not those whose pleasures were greater than their own.

Under Buonaparte, however, Milan was not destined to be long our resting place. General Melas was not far from us, while a large force was concentrated before Genoa, which, under the command of Massena, still held out. Either Melas was deceived as to our strength, or else he awaited orders from Vienna, the Emperor desiring to render himself master of that city, no matter at what cost, General Orello was, therefore, despatched to Plaisance and General Ott on the Tessin; in fact, he hoped to cause a diversion, and pushed forward six thousand men on the Po to Chivasso, the advanced posts extending even as far as Verceil, one of which was cut off, three hundred men falling into our hands.

I must confess I parted from my kind friends with regret, but more stirring duties soon served to obliterate them, and to these I again addressed myself. My position was elevated by my sojourn in Milan, many of the officers who had rather shunned my acquaintance now seeking it. This stimulated me the more, and I looked forward to the hour when promotion should enable me to hold my head with the highest, determined, as the war proceeded, to leave no stone unturned to satisfy my commander.

Chapter 18

Passage of the Po

Without taking credit to himself as an astute politician, able geographer, or great tactitian, there were certain signs by which even the least instructed soldier could see that the battle so much desired by both armies was necessary to decide the fate of Italy. None but a Frenchman, and one, too, inspired by the confidence which success so justly engenders, could shut his eyes to the dangers which seemed to surround us on every side.

There can be no doubt that the Austrian General Melas had deceived himself with the belief that the French army consisted only of five or six thousand men, who were intended to make an incursion into the north of Italy to relieve Massena, then shut up in Genoa. Nevertheless, alarmed at the progress of this small force, or what is more probable, better acquainted with its strength, he decided on quitting Turin and concentrating his forces on the strong places in Piedmont, with the double intention of holding the French in check and of effecting a junction with General Elnitz, who was returning from France, whither he had been despatched.

For this purpose his troops were in position as described in the last chapter, and in this state of affairs our army prepared for the encounter.

On the 7th of May, Murat, at the head of his division, marched upon Plaisance. In spite of 600 men, supported by a well-served battery, he carried the outworks at the bridge, but the enemy had time to destroy the latter, and seemed determined to defend the passage with the greatest obstinacy, so Murat amused them there, while the 9th light infantry and 59th regiment of the line seized some shallops at Noretto, with which they crossed, and, attacking Plaisance on the other side, took six hundred prisoners. Cavalry, infantry, commissaries, surgeons, apothecaries, guns, caissons, baggage wagons, entered pell-mell into the citadel, whence they kept up a devastating fire, until at last they were forced to surrender one hour only before General Melas informed them of the convention made at Alessandria, they were in consequence prisoners of war.

However, the advanced guard, together with the main body of the army, took up a position on the Po, which at this point is joined by the Tessin, and becomes a wide and rapid river. Our next meeting was not to be an affair of outposts, or a combat of soldiers scattered and re-assembled in haste as formerly, for the advanced guard of the Austrian army consisted of 15,000 or 18,000 men, picked troops, who had been told that we were nothing but recruits, and who, inflamed by their former successes under General Schérer, awaited us on the opposite bank of the river. The former affairs had been of little importance in comparison with that which was about to begin, and men looked to the result with the most intense interest.

Buonaparte now issued one of those spirit-stirring proclamations which he knew so well accorded with the vanity of the French, concluding in these words:

> But shall any one with impunity violate the territory of France? Will you suffer to return to their hearths the men who have carried alarm into the bosom of your families? No! Fly to arms, march to the encounter, oppose yourselves to their retreat, snatch from them the laurels with which they have covered themselves, and so show to the world that the frowns of destiny are sure to fall on those who have the folly to insult the territory of the Great People. The result of all our efforts will be glory without a cloud—peace—lasting peace!

Such were the means used by the First Consul to stimulate his men; meanwhile our force increased every day. A strong division of the army of the Rhine had marched from Ulm, and having traversed the Grisons and crossed the St. Gothard, had, like us, overcome all the difficulties of such a passage, hunger not the least of the number, and arrived just in time to share our dangers and our triumphs. They had been obliged to leave their artillery behind.

The grenadiers and carabineers of the advanced guard solicited the honour to be first across the Po, while the rest of the battalions burned with impatience as these brave fellows crowded into the boats. The enemy seemed struck with their daring, and suffered them to land unmolested; but their numbers increased at each moment, and their courage sustained them on the bank of the river. Now flying bridges were quickly established, the whole of the advanced guard passed over, and cheering each other, commenced the attack which the Austrians sustained with firmness.

Then General Lannes ordered the charge, and his courage and coolness made us redouble our efforts. The 6th light infantry, the 22nd, 28th, and 44th regiments of the line, bayonet in hand, threw themselves on the enemy, whom they drove back into a morass, pursuing them as far as Stradella, on the road from Plaisance to Tortona. Here prudence checked their impetuosity, and suggested the recall; night came on, and each man retired to his post in the hope that the combat would recommence on the morrow.

The sun had scarcely illumined the horizon, when the advanced posts began to bestir themselves. The artillery opened the attack, while the battalions moved into position. Our light artillery, together with that of the Consular Guard, were soon in motion. Montebello, which gave the name to this bloody day, was taken and retaken, the resistance was equally obstinate on both sides, although the numbers were not alike. Our advanced guard consisting of six thousand infantry, and one thousand cavalry, had as yet borne the whole brunt of the battle, but Watrin's division advanced, determined to force a passage. While these things were doing, six battalions of the enemy, and several fresh squadrons, threw themselves on our advanced guard. Their numerous cavalry, profiting by the advantages of the ground, charged the 11th and 12th hussars, and the shock was terrible, the carnage awful, nevertheless they held their own, during two hours, carrying San Diletto at the point of the bayonet, and marching on Casteggio, which was bravely defended.

Just then Watrin's division came up, and in the twinkling of an eye the aspect of affairs was changed; the whole corps engaged seemed animated by a fresh impulse. Again the charge was sounded; the enemy hesitated, wavered, and fled as if engulphed in a torrent. The wheat and rye were so tall as to impede the view. Austrians and French pursued each other without being certain of their respective forces; the terrible bayonets were crossed, carrying on all sides certain death. The impetuous courage of the French prevailed; the Austrians, broken at all points, gave way, while the mitraille, dealing destruction at every point, augmented the confusion. The rout became complete, and the enemy retired precipitately on Voghera, abandoning the field more quickly than happens in a simple retreat.

Six thousand prisoners, five pieces of cannon, many general and field-officers killed or wounded, the earth covered with the bodies of the dead and the dying, attested the obstinacy of the fight, and must have satisfied Melas that they were veteran troops instead of raw recruits to whom he had been opposed.

The First Consul, willing to manage all himself, had left Milan early in the morning; he stayed one hour only in Pavia, and passing the Po, came up with the advanced guard in the moment of victory.

Considering the number of troops that were engaged, this was one of the most obstinate and bloody engagements it had ever been my fate to witness. I had two horses shot under me, and received a slight wound from a sabre cut, while fifteen of my troop fell to rise no more.

The conflict was so terrible, that our general, in describing it a few days afterwards, said, "Bones were cracking like a shower of hail falling on a skylight;" and so highly did he esteem the honour of the victory, that when in after years, the policy of the Emperor bestowed on him the baton and a title, he chose that of the Duc de Montebello.

From the prisoners we learnt the fall of Genoa, and the honorable capitulation of Massena. This unhappy event caused a great sensation in the army, although our success, in some measure, soothed the bitterness of the misfortune. It was, for the moment, a great calamity, which two days afterwards served to augment our triumph, having the glory to engage the whole Austrian force, and to achieve one of the most memorable victories on record.

Spite of the reduction of Genoa, General Melas had taken up an extraordinary position previous to the affair of Montebello, and this became much worse afterwards, because, in evacuating Stradella, he had lost the means of securing his retreat.

General Dessaix, who was a great favourite of the First Consul, had lately arrived at Paris from Egypt, and been ordered to join the army of Italy, without delay. Though not in time to share the glories of the field, he was soon enough to witness the effects, and the whole army was overjoyed to possess a general as brave and beloved as he was. It is well said, that one happiness never arrives but it is followed by another, and what could exceed ours on the advent of victory, to receive into our ranks this model of a hero? He was immediately appointed lieutenant-general.

Ours was not the only regiment that suffered severely in the affair at Montebello. The 12th regiment of *Chasseurs à Cheval*, of the army of the Rhine, had marched from Memmingen to Milan in 19 days, and mustered on the evening before about 220 horses. Lieutenant-General Victor ordered them to take up a position on his left flank, which they immediately proceeded to occupy. Opposed to them were 1,500 of the enemy's cavalry, supported by a brigade of artillery, under the command of an Austrian General, who was charged with the siege of Tortona. At the moment when they were ordered to rejoin General Victor, they were attacked in full force, lost three-fourths of their men in killed, wounded, or taken prisoners, but succeeded in keeping the enemy in check, and regaining the head quarters, and were so happy as to have interrupted the advance of this strong column of the Austrians. It was in this corps that Murat made his first campaign; they were now under the command of Colonel De Franc, and had covered themselves with glory, in thus withstanding a corps eight times more numerous than themselves.

Head-quarters were at Voghera the morrow after the battle of Montebello, through which town the whole army marched in its advance on Tortona. In passing under the windows of the First Consul, we saw General Dessaix and an officer who had come in with a flag of truce. The joy that revelled in our hearts was expressed in our countenances, and loud cries of "*Vive Buonaparte*" were repeated from all sides. With bands playing and colours flying, regiment after regiment passed on, and when it came to the turn of the grenadiers of the Guards, their band struck up the burlesque air which answers to the words, "We attacked them in the flank;" and I remarked that this allusion caused a blush on the cheek of the Austrian officer. The army took up a position before Tortona in column by divisions. The advanced guard surrounded the place, and the day passed on without any remarkable occurrence; the only thing we made sure of was, that the Austrian army had retired on the road to Genoa, establishing its head-quarters at Alessandria.

CHAPTER 19

Marengo

On the 13th of June the army abandoned its position before Tortona, taking the route to Alessandria. The advanced guard halted at San Juliano, a hamlet of three farms, about a league from Tortona, and just at the entrance of the plain of Marengo. The First Consul and a thousand of the guard, together with the staff of the army, took up their quarters here. When the main body came, they were formed in order of battle, and marched on to the plain. The enemy appeared at the bridge over the Bormida, from which a feeble attempt was made to dislodge him; but although our disposition announced our intention to give battle, General Melas seemed to decline it, either that his reinforcement from Genoa had not come up, or else that he was deceived in the strength of our force.

The First Consul, accompanied by the guard à *cheval* and a light field piece, passed over every portion of the plain. He rode about 40 yards in advance, examining attentively the nature of the ground, frequently giving way to fits of abstraction, which were interrupted by a succession of orders. Evening crept on and we were still on horseback; still our leader seemed lost in thought, when a dripping rain came on, wetting every man, even the First Consul, to the skin, he, like the rest of us, having forgotten his cloak—and so chilling our limbs that we were obliged to dismount to re-animate the circulation.

Some chasseurs brought two or three fagots to dry the garments of the Consul, and those of the other chiefs. And there, seated before a fire, his chin resting on the back of a chair placed in the middle of the plain, and ankle-deep in mud, surrounded by the èlite of his generals, sat the First Magistrate of the French, he who one little month before walked the marble halls of the National Palace of the Tuilleries.

Here were brought many deserters from the Austrian force, and some prisoners, among the rest an officer from Bussy's legion, wearing the cross of St. Louis. Buonaparte questioned them with great interest, nor were they a little surprised when they were informed that he in the grey frock to whom they had been talking was the First Consul.

We lay down to rest at San Juliano at eleven o'clock, the troops who had been under arms all day bivouacking on the ground, and the army soon appeared wrapped in profound repose, little thinking of the morrow.

The morning of the 14th commenced, the heavy firing of cannon soon aroused us from our repose, and breakfast was dispatched with as much rapidity as the supper of the preceding night. The army was formed in double *echelon* in two lines. As for me, I was in attendance on the First Consul, a post that afforded me an opportunity of witnessing the conduct of that extraordinary man.

At eight a.m., the enemy had not displayed any extraordinary vigour. He attacked some weak points, and made his dispositions accordingly. We had no notion of his intentions till towards noon, when he advanced in three columns, and the action became general.

Berthier was despatched to the field, and the *aides-de-camp* quickly followed each other with accounts of the progress of the battle. The front of the Austrian force now exceeded two leagues, extending to the bridge over the Bormida, San Stephano being the principal point of attack, his hope being to take Voghera, and cut off our retreat. By and by the wounded began to arrive, and from them we learnt that the Austrians were in force; and those who had made some campaigns were aware that if the enemy did not possess the fury of the French, they were not deficient in perseverance.

At eleven the Consul was in the saddle, and cantered off to

the field of battle, ordering up the troops in the rear, but Dessaix, who was in command of the reserve, was still far distant. The incessant booming of cannon and rattling of small arms, told that the field was hotly contested, while the number of wounded carried to the rear was immense. Seeing them pass, Napoleon said, "One cannot but regret not to have shared their dangers and to have been wounded." But the obstinacy of the Austrians prevailed, and our troops began to give way. Napoleon perceiving this, placed himself at the head of the division of Lannes, determined to lead them in person; he ordered different movements, hoping to take the enemy in flank, but a cry broke from the ranks, "We are unwilling that the First Consul should expose himself." Such was the generous devotion of the troops, who forgot their own danger in that of their chief, many of them preferring death where they stood to the disgrace of retiring before the enemy under the eyes of their general.

At noon all doubt ceased, and we became aware of the unwelcome truth that the whole Austrian force was engaged; they having accepted the battle which they yesterday declined.

The right wing, under General Victor, began to give ground, retiring under the fire of twenty-four pieces of cannon, which protected the advance of the enemy, raining on their devoted heads a shower of shot and shells, throwing the infantry into disorder, and mowing down the cavalry by whole troops. By and by the firing advanced towards us, a frightful cannonade was heard in the centre, while that near the Bormida suddenly ceased. We were in a state of inexpressible anxiety, hoping that our troops maintained their ground, a hope unfounded for the wounded who passed, declared that the right wing was giving way.

When the First Consul advanced, the courage of our troops seemed revived, and the Guard, as yet unemployed, prepared themselves for the attack. A cloud of Austrian cavalry debouched rapidly on the plain, and formed just before us, masking several pieces of light artillery, which were soon brought into action. Berthier, who was charged by them, was forced to retire on us, but Murat, at the head of his dragoons, took them in flank, covering the retreat of our infantry, and protecting the right flank of Victor's division.

The grenadiers of the Consular Guard came up at this moment at double quick time, and formed with as much coolness as if on parade, about one hundred yards in advance of the spot on which the First Consul was placed. Without being supported by artillery or cavalry, in number about five hundred only, they well deserved the epithet of the *Wall of Granite*, for they withstood the impetuous attack of the conquering army. Regardless of the force by whom they were opposed, again the enemy charged, beating down every thing in his passage; again the haughty black eagle hovered over their devoted ranks, threatening them with annihilation, while a single ball killed three grenadiers and a farrier. Charged three times by cavalry, riddled by the muskets of the infantry, discharged at fifty paces distance only, they formed square, and putting their colours and their wounded in the centre, their ammunition being exhausted, and further resistance useless, they retired slowly, and in good order, and rejoined the rearguard, who had been astonished at the coolness and discipline they had displayed.

Nevertheless, the whole army was in retreat, the centre giving way, while the enemy extended his front, and turned our wings. On the right, especially, his success was complete, and on the left he seemed advancing on our head-quarters, while the garrison of Tortona being apprized of our situation, made a sortie. Thus encompassed on all sides, our fate seemed certain.

The First Consul, who was always in the centre, cheered on the brave men who still defended the road and the defile through which it passed. It was bounded on one side by a wood, while the vines on the other were tall and luxuriant; the village of Marengo was to the left of this spot, so cruelly memorable. What rivers of blood flowed here! We had nothing to oppose to the constantly increasing number of our conquering foes but the discipline and long-tried courage of the troops. Our artillery was partly dismounted, and some few pieces were in the hands of the Austrians; while worse even than that, we had not ammunition enough to supply what were left.

Thirty pieces of cannon, well served, thundered away upon us, cutting in two, horses and men and trees, the branches of which increased our misfortunes, by crushing in their fall those unhappy beings who could not move out of the way.

At four, p.m., there were certainly not more than 6000 infantry, 1000 cavalry, and six pieces of cannon, within a circle of two miles, that could be called efficient. I may be accused of exaggeration in this statement, but I have no doubt of its being correct, and reflection will make its truth apparent. One third of our army was *hors de combat;* a want of proper vehicles to transport the wounded from the field, obliged another third to be occupied in this service. Whoever could furnish a plausible excuse took care to absent himself from his corps; thirst and famine drove many away, while the Tirailleurs had mostly lost the direction of their corps; but those who remained were so occupied in vigorously defending the defile, of which I have before spoken, that they had little time to think of what was going on in the rear.

In the advance of the guard, Jean Carlin, a *chasseur à pied,* received several wounds, and was left on the field for dead. When we retired he was surrounded by the soldiers of Bussy's legion, who proceeded to strip him. Having taken all his garments save his shirt they were beginning to tear that from him, when his cries attracted the notice of an Austrian colonel, who, coming up at the moment, laid about him with his cane, and dispersed the plunderers. "To what regiment do you belong?" said the colonel, addressing the prisoner whom he thought an officer. "I belong to the Consular Guard, now facing you," said the chasseur. "And a brave corps too," said the colonel; "come with me to the rear, and the surgeon of our regiment shall attend to your wounds." This the wounded man was unable to do, so the surgeon was brought to him, and he was conveyed to the rear on the ambulance. Some hours elapsed and the fortune of war changed; the Austrian did not lose sight of his prisoner, but offered his services to convey him to Alessandria, which the chasseur, hoping for his deliverance declined, with many thanks for the kindness he had already manifested towards him. In a short time our troops relieved him.

To return to the battle. It was now after four, and the day seemed lost, the star of Napoleon was about to sink before the veteran Austrian, and in this awful time, when the dead and dying covered the earth, Napoleon determined not to give way. In the midst of the balls which ploughed up the earth under the very feet of his charger, surrounded by troopers who were every instant falling round him, he gave his orders with as much coolness and *sang froid* as if he had been at a review, and appeared to contemplate the storm which approached without one atom of personal fear. Amongst those who saw him thus forgetful of the danger that menaced themselves, the cry was, "Does he seek death; why does he not retire?" and it is said that General Berthier entreated him to fall back. I had the curiosity to listen most attentively to his voice, and to examine his features with care; and although the bravest of men—the hero the most passionate for glory, might appear moved and not be accused of cowardice, he was not. liven at the moment when fortune seemed about to forsake him, he was still the Buonaparte of Arcola and Aboukir.

Who, then, under these circumstances, would have dreamt that in two hours time the fortune of war would have changed— that instead of being beaten we should have become the conquerers, having taken 10,000 prisoners, some generals, fifteen standards, and 40 pieces of cannon?—that the enemy would deliver up eleven fortified places, and evacuate the north of Italy? Who, while regiment after regiment poured down upon us, would have believed that in a few short hours an armistice would be concluded, giving lasting peace to the two countries? Had any one prognosticated such a state of things, we should have considered it an insult in our desperate situation, and yet all came to pass.

CHAPTER 20

Marengo II

General Berthier now approached the First Consul, and communicated the intelligence that the army was giving way, and the route beginning. Napoleon replied, "General, you do not make the announcement with calmness;" the firmness which had distinguished him, never abandoning him in the moment of danger. The 59th regiment of the line came up directly after, when the First Consul advanced towards them and said, "Come on, my brave fellows, display your standards; this is the moment to distinguish yourselves; I depend on your courage to avenge your comrades." The words had scarcely passed from his lips before a ball struck down the five foremost men; he turned again towards the enemy, and, with an air calm and undisturbed, exclaimed, "Come on, my frends, charge!"

The fortune of the day, however, appeared to be against us, for the enemy being unable to force the defile to which the whole of our troops that could make head had retreated, established a formidable line of artillery, under the protection of which he filled the wood and the vineyard on either side with infantry and sharpshooters. His cavalry, ranged in order of battle in the rear, waited but the moment when we should give way, to precipitate themselves on our broken ranks. If this misfortune had happened, everything would have been over: the First Consul would have been killed or a prisoner, although we would have been hacked to mince meat ere it happened.

When all appeared lost, the hour of victory struck; faithful to Napoleon, she smiled once more upon us, and again guided us to conquest. Already the divisions of Monnier and Dessaix began to appear, and in spite of a forced march of ten leagues, they arrived just in time, and forgetting their wants, seemed only animated with a desire to revenge our loss. The number of fugitives and wounded that these brave men encountered was enough to damp their ardour, but, with eyes fixed on Dessaix, they only thought with him of missing the danger, and not sharing in the glory of the field. Alas! they little thought that in one short hour they should no longer be commanded by the brave general. The grenadiers retreated covered with glory, but menacing with the bayonet the troops of Bussy's legion, who had collected the shakos of such of them as were killed or wounded, and placing them on the points of their weapons, shook them in derision at the survivors, who vowed vengeance on those who thus insulted them.

But the hour of victory approached, borne on the breeze that wafted sounds of the approach of Dessaix. Suddenly they fell upon the ear of Napoleon, and renewed confidence appeared on his countenance. "Frenchmen," said he, "we have moved too many steps in retreat, the moment has arrived when we should advance; remember, my practice is to sleep on the field of battle." The most enthusiastic shouts rent the air on the conclusion of this brief harangue, and every one found fresh courage mounting in his bosom.

Reinforcements continued to arrive—joy and hope re-entered our hearts—whilst the enemy, harassed and fatigued even by success, which had cost him dear, was still kept at bay by some brave troops, who, ignorant that relief had arrived, had resolved to perish on this new Thermopylæ rather than surrender.

General Melas, finding the resistance in the centre so dogged, thought that by extending each wing he should surround and cut us off entirely. This movement was executed at the same time, he thought without our perceiving it, his artillery still rattling away at our unflinching troops; but all had been foreseen, and he was equally deceived with respect to our reinforcements; in fact, always foremost in the post of honour, nothing escaped Buonaparte; he seized every occasion—directed every movement—giving orders for every portion of the army with the same coolness and decision that would have marked him at a review on the Champ de Mars.

As soon as the first battalion of Dessaix's division had mounted the height, it formed in close column. Each man was careful of his distance—each received his instructions. The First Consul, General Dessaix, Lieutenants-General, Staff Officers rode from rank to rank, cheering the men, and inspiring them with that confidence which heralds success. The hour consumed in this occupation was one of terrible length, for the Austrian artillery still thundered away at us, each discharge mowing down whole ranks,—men and horses fell before the devastating shower,—nevertheless they kept their ground, and, as each man fell, another stepped up to supply his place. During this time the cavalry in our van rallied, while a great many of the infantry belonging to different corps, encouraged by the appearance of Dessaix's division, returned once more to the field of battle.

All is ready—every calculation made—the battalions boil with impatience to advance; the drummer, his eye fixed on the cane of the drum-major, waits for the signal; the trumpeter, with uplifted arm, is prepared to sound the advance when the intrepid Dessaix places himself at the head of the column which had marched ten leagues without halting, and which evinced no dismay at the number of fugitives and wounded they had met. Napoleon gave the signal, the terrible *pas de charge* sounded, each corps advanced at the same moment; the fury of the French, like a torrent, tore down everything that opposed its advance; in the shortest possible space the defile was passed, the enemy overthrown at every point; dying, living, wounded, and dead, were trampled under foot.

Each chief having passed through the defile, and, being ready to enter on the plain, ranged his division in the order of battle, and our line soon began to present a formidable front. As each piece of artillery came up it was placed in battery, and dealt death and destruction upon the affrighted enemy. They wavered; their immense cavalry charged *en masse* with fury; but the musketry—the mitraille—the bayonet arrested their career; one of their caissons blew up, the confusion was redoubled; their disorder was increased by a thick cloud of smoke from the artillery;

the cries of the wounded augmented their terror; in short, the whole force was shaken—gave way—turned and fled.

At this moment the French cavalry entered the plain, concealing the paucity of their numbers by the boldness of their daring. They charged the enemy without fear of being cut off. On the right appeared the illustrious and virtuous Dessaix, at the head of his brave soldiers, and, like the thunder, he seemed to precede the lightning—everything gave way before him—he cleared all obstacles, overthrew whatever opposed his passage. The plain, unequal and difficult, was levelled with the same rapidity—the soldiers with their feet and hands filling up the ditches, and, triumphing over all obstacles, disputing even with their officers the glory of being first across. On the left, General Victor, with the same rapidity, carried the village of Marengo and threw himself on the Bormida, in spite of the efforts of a superior force of cavalry and artillery, which kept up a galling fire on his left flank.

The centre, though with fewer troops, especially cavalry, under the orders of General Murat, advanced boldly on the plain, charging to the very muzzles of the guns; they galled the enemy's centre, and by this movement held in check an immense force of cavalry, which could only manœuvre under the fire of three field pieces and one howitzer. Our infantry attacked them in flank, and having less distance to pass to arrive at the bridge, there cut off in their turn their means of retreat.

The intrepid Dessaix, by a quick flank movement, carried San Stephano on the right, cutting off the whole left wing of the Austrians, while General Kellerman, with eight hundred cavalry, collected from various regiments, obliged six thousand of the Hungarian Grenadiers to lay down their arms, taking General Zach prisoner, he falling to the lot of Riche, an officer of the 12th regiment.

In this charge every officer of the 4th squadron of the 20th Hussars fell, and the command devolved on Wilhem, the Quarter Master. Such was the decision and bravery he displayed that Kellerman promoted him to the command of the troop on the field, the most glorious reward the ambition of a French soldier could desire.

Alas! that the hour of triumph should be clouded by regret. After having saved the army, and in all probability preserved his country, the friend and model of the brave—General Dessaix—fell to rise no more. A ball terminated his career, which ended like that of Joubert and Marceau, and I had just galloped up with orders from Buonaparte, when I heard him exclaim to young Lebrun, "Say to the First Consul that my only regret is not to have done more for posterity." These were the last words he ever uttered, for on my dismounting to assist him, I found that the spirit which had animated one of the best and bravest of men had quitted its earthly tabernacle for ever.

His death redoubled the courage of his troops, who now added the desire for vengeance to their thirst for victory. They swore to avenge him; and, casting themselves on the Austrians, well did they keep their promise. The rest of the army seconded their generous efforts, while Melas strove in vain to rally his troops, who fled on all sides towards Alessandria.

I returned to the First Consul, and communicated the loss of the friend to whom he was tenderly attached. "Alas!" said he, "why is it forbidden me to weep?" but, making an effort to stifle his emotions, he questioned me again as to his fate, and turned towards the remains of the hero where he wept aloud.

Night came on while the disordered troops of the enemy—cavalry—infantry—artillery, crowded pell-mell on each other towards the centre, blocking up the road to the river. The artillery, which early in the battle they had taken from us, and sent to the rear for fear it should be re-taken, obstructed the passage; while General Murat, aware of the importance of augmenting the disorder, called on all around to follow him, advanced at the trot, charging a part of their infantry, which, unable to keep pace with the cavalry, were either cut in pieces or made prisoners. Our proximity augmented the confusion of the fugitives. The *grenadiers à cheval,* and chasseurs of the guard, took the right of the road, numbering about two hundred, and four or five hundred of the 1st, 6th, 8th, and 20th dragoons occupied the left, while the general rode, first at the head of one division, then at that of the other.

The decisive moment had arrived. The Colonel Bessiére, full of the ardour which animated each of us, bade us advance in language which was befitting the man who would lead troops to glory. We spurred our jaded horses to their best pace;—the desire to earn a name inflamed even the most indiffferent. Again the trumpets sounded the charge: the earth shook under our feet, and we fell upon the panting infantry. The Austrian cavalry, deciding to save the infantry, moved up in close columns with such rapidity that we were obliged to halt, changing front to the left. Only thirty paces and a deep ditch divided us. To leap the ditch, form line, sabre the enemy, and surround the two first squadrons, was but the work of five minutes; while, stunned by the suddenness of the shock, they defended themselves badly, and were cut to pieces. No quarter was asked or offered, but men and horses fell around, thick as the leaves in autumn; while another column of dragoons, taking the remaining squadrons in flank, dispersed them, after the most horrible carnage. They were pursued to the ravine, where the few that survived were made prisoners.

Reduced by the obstinacy of the battle to a very few effective troops—the country difficult, and the night approaching—the extreme fatigue of the horses, who had been all day without food—a numerous body of cavalry, under the eyes of whom the action had passed, and which might have been brought up against us—all these things weighed with the prudent and brave Murat, and prevented our following up, as the more ardent desired, the fruits of this glorious victory. As the infantry came up they were halted and formed; but had we persevered in the pursuit, and received a check, they were too distant, as well as too fatigued, to render us any support. The bugles therefore sounded the recall, and the drums beat to quarters. But where were those quarters to be found? The two armies had been engaged for sixteen hours, during which time few of the troops had been unemployed, and none had time to receive those succours of which exhausted nature stood so much in need: each man, therefore, prepared to rest where he stood—the infantry lying down with their knapsacks for pillows, their muskets placed between their legs—the cavalry holding the reins of the horses in their hands, wrapping themselves up in their cloaks;—their common mother earth their resting-place, the blue vault of heaven their canopy.

Austrians and Frenchmen had forgotten their feud and become brothers, occupying the same sod; they mutually helped each other, while the darkness of the evening prevented our rendering assistance to all the unhappy wounded, a great number of whom were left upon the field.

The clock of Marengo had sounded ten ere the First Consul prepared to quit the field on which he had spent so many eventful hours, and we returned slowly towards San Juliano. Many of our men, harrassed by fatigue, fell asleep on the backs of their horses, each instant disturbed either by the miserable cries of some unhappy wretch who was carried by on a rude litter, hastily constructed, oftentimes with the muskets of the infantry; or by those partially disabled, who, abandoned to their fate and scattered about the fields implored our assistance in harrowing tones, which went to the heart of many a gallant fellow, filling with melancholy those humane and feeling bosoms which are not unknown among a brave soldiery, and redound so much to their honour. Here and there horses tottering on three legs, recognised by their loud neighings the approach of those of our troop, while each step we took was obliged to be marked with caution, or turned aside to prevent our adding to the miseries of the wounded. At every pace the route was impeded by the dead or the dying, dismantled guns, caissons, ammunition wagons, the horses of the cavalry, or the equipages of the ambulances; while more distant, several houses in flames tottered to their foundations, destroying the inhabitants, who, previously half dead from fear, had concealed themselves in the cellars. The profound obscurity which surrounded us rendered the prospect still more dreary, and the prisoners not knowing where to go, wandered here and there in the hope of making their escape. If they chanced to be met by the troops, bending beneath the weight of their wounded comrades, they were forced to return, and the unhappy burden was transferred to their shoulders.

In time we arrived at the farm, now converted to the use of the wounded, and each man crept in among the dead and the dying, and disposed himself for the night as he best could, the cries of anguish by which he was surrounded seldom prevailing over the unconquerable desire for sleep. As for me, sick, hungry, fatigued, slightly wounded in the shoulder, and a prey to thirst, I asked but for rest, even though that rest should be eternal.

Thus ended this memorable day—a day which had stamped "Marengo" on the laurels of every man who had the good fortune to survive; for there was not a corps, not even a soldier, who had not earned a chaplet from the garland of fame; and surely never was battle struggled for with more determination—never was victory disputed with greater obstinacy.

CHAPTER 21

San Juliano

I awoke on the morning of the 15th of June with all the gnawing pangs of hunger which a thirty-six hours fast was likely to produce, and oppressed with sadness I entered the court of the farm where Napoleon had established his head-quarters, in the hope of finding something to relieve my own wants as well as those of my horse, who like myself had been forced to do without food. The most horrible spectacle met my view, for more than three thousand wounded Frenchmen and Austrians, heaped one upon another in the court-yard—the barns, the cow-houses, and stables—nay even in the granaries and cellars—were uttering the most frightful cries, swearing even at the surgeons who were unable to dress all their wounds at once. On all aides I heard the distressing cries of many of my comrades and fellow-troopers, who demanded food and drink, two articles of which I stood in so much need. All that I could procure was some water, which I fetched in a canteen that lay by, and forgetting my own wants and those of my steed, I remained more than two hours, fetching water and assisting the surgeons in the hospital, a duty imposed upon all who came in, that were able to perform it.

I had witnessed wounds on the battle field, death in the breach, but never had I contemplated the horrors of a military hospital after a bloody combat. My heart sickened at the indifference with which the surgeons seemed to perform their offices; a leg here, and an arm there, cut off and thrown carelessly by, as if it had never formed a part of that living being whom the Creator made in his own image. And yet these men had hearts—hearts to feel for the sufferings they endeavoured to alleviate, and pursued their irksome tasks all day and all night, denying to themselves that rest of which all stood so much in need, taking no note of time or the scarcity of provisions, of which all around complained, but labouring on in their vocation with an attention seemingly engrossed by their duties. Do not tell me that surgeons are callous to the feelings or sufferings of humanity; the head that can devote its best energies—the heart that supports men through difficulties and even dangers, for the ambulance on the battle field, is not always respected, by the fire of the enemy—the courage that can sustain men through affairs like these are things of no light stamp, and ought to command as much respect and admiration as the most determined bravery in the charge. With sleeves tucked up to their elbows, hands reeking with blood drawn from the hapless patients whose mangled limbs they had just removed, the surgeons pursued their way without let or hindrance, nor was I sorry when a summons removed me from the hospital.

On all sides the prisoners kept coming in, and these augmented the number of the famishing; and the day appeared to us of an insupportable length, when an event occurred which gave birth to all kinds of conjectures, and added not a little to our inquietude.

A flag of truce was announced from the Austrian camp, and a French aide-de-camp immediately started for Alessandria. No one was aware of his demands, and each man formed his own opinions. Thither also, at noon, General Berthier departed. All the world seemed at fault, none daring to hope that which on the morrow we found had been obtained.

On the morrow morning we were informed that an armistice had been concluded, which filled the French with joy, while the Austrian army, trembling with rage, defiled, on that and the following day, on the field of battle, which was still reeking with their blood and ours, and where the crowded carcases already began to fill the air with putrid exhalations.

At last the Commissariat succeeded in procuring provisions, and vehicles for the transport of such of the wounded as were able to be moved, and a separation took place between the victims of that sanguinary day. We saw, without inquietude or jealousy, the French and the Austrian side by side—those who two days previously would have cut each others throats—we saw them even receive from the same hands, under the same roof—nay, even in the same chamber, the necessary succours, and the careful attention, of ready humanity.

There can be little question that on the 14th we had from 40,000 to 45,000 men upon the field, of whom 3,000 only were cavalry, and from 25 to 30 pieces of cannon, and two companies of flying artillery. According to the report of the Austrian prisoners, their force numbered from 55,000 to 60,000 men, of whom 16,000 were cavalry. They had 48 pieces of cannon, 200 caissons, with an immense quantity of munitions of war, of which it is well known we were greatly deficient.

This victory, great as were its results, costs the Republic dear, for we lost some of its bravest defenders, and best Generals. Dessaix, and a brother of General Watrin were killed; Generals Chamberlac, Muller, Mainoni, Champeaux, and Rivaud were wounded.

The loss of the Consular Guard was considerable, especially in the infantry. Of five hundred men which they took into the field, two hundred and fifty-eight were killed or wounded. The cavalry of the guard lost about a tenth. The flying artillery was almost totally disabled, all the horses being killed, and the guns dismounted; by good luck, however, they had only one man killed, though several were severely wounded. When we consider the results, however, we must not estimate it as too dear, for in all probability we saved the south of France from invasion, and the horrors of a war at home. An armistice was concluded, which was the forerunner of a desirable and glorious peace, and this was sufficient to calm our regrets.

And yet these regrets were poignant, when we thought of one, who had been the friend—the model of every man who had served under him. I shall not readily forget the impression made upon me, when the morning after the battle, on going to head quarters, I beheld the carriage which contained the remains of General Dessaix, wrapped in a flag, and covered by his cloak. He had passed the First Consul, dressed all in blue, without lace or embroidery, no plume in his hat, and wearing common riding boots; in fact, nothing but the extreme simplicity and plainness of his dress distinguishing him from the common herd; but there was that in his countenance at the moment, which denoted that this simple exterior bore no comparison to the mind within, that encouraged the troops to place reliance on him by whom they were enchanted to be commanded. His own horse had suffered so much from fatigue, that he had borrowed one from the *chef de brigade*, Bessière, on which he met his death wound; and though but a few moments elapsed after the departure of Lebrun and myself, before Savary, his aide-de-camp, came up, the body had been stripped and thrown among a heap of dead. I had seen him but an hour before he fell, commanding the incomparable 19th light demi brigade, making the most difficult movements under a devastating fire, and in situations the most critical, and now my eyes rested upon his bloody and inanimate corpse.

Peace to his name! I had known something of him in Egypt, where his simplicity of dress and address, with his indomitable courage and coolness in the field, had fixed the attention of the whole army, and not a man that had served under him but now felt that he had lost a brother and a friend; while the clemency that had always accompanied his conquests, especially after the departure of Napoleon from the soil of the Pyramids, and the punctuality he manifested in all his engagements, had induced the Egyptians to confer upon him the ennobling title of the Just Sultan.

The treatment of the prisoners by the priests was wretched, denoting a baseness and cruelty of which the ministers of any religion ought to have been ashamed. At the commencement of the action some hundreds of French fell into the hands of the Austrians, by whom they were conveyed to Alessandria. Their entry was announced by the ringing of bells, cries of victory, and rejoicings. Had they stopped here no harm had, been done, because they were no doubt at liberty to prefer the Austrians to the French; but when they proceeded to strike these unhappy creatures, who had been deprived of their weapons, and even to threaten them with daggers, human nature revolts at the idea that educated, civilised persons—men imbued with religion, should have been carried to such excesses, and revolts still more at the recollection that, in a few hours, these very men loaded with caresses those whom they had thus insulted.

Of all the plunderers I have fallen in with, commend me to the Austrian camp followers for rapidity of execution, for surely nothing could be so hateful as the avidity with which they stripped the prisoners. Not one of our men was able to preserve his knapsack, cravat, cap, or shoes; even their ear-rings were in some, instances torn from their ears, without their giving them time to take them out. Many of the men were cut down three or four hours after they had surrendered as prisoners of war.

Chapter 22

Turin

When studying the history of the past, in those imperishable records which nave been handed down to us, how often do we stumble on the melancholy truth that the lessons of experience appear to have been of no more service to nations during their political existence, than they are to individuals in the short career of life. On all animals endowed with intelligence, an all-wise Creator seems to have impressed a sort of mechanical instinct, which induces them to study self-preservation. This, the first law of nature, leads them to avoid that by which they may be, injured; to fly from danger, or to brave it, according to the consciousness of their strength; but it is necessary that danger should be present. Foresight would seem a quality almost divine—an effort of the most perfect reason, more rarely to be met with than genius—for man is naturally presumptuous, inconstant, and wavering, and that in an order of things which is immutable. Man often takes everything to himself, and appears determined not to trace first causes to their constant effects. A creature himself, he would be a creator; and establish new principles, and ever in the advance of the old world physically—by the laws of which he is hampered and restrained, be endeavours to make a moral world always new like himself—a world of which he can modify the rules according to his feelings and his passions. Such is human nature; and why should governments instituted by men be exempt from their faults?

The policy of the court of Vienna may be cited as a proof of these remarks. Untaught by the events of the first Italian campaign, when Napoleon beat in detail all their greatest generals in an incredibly short space of time, they left no more to the discretion of their commanders than the passing events of the hour rendered absolutely necessary. Had a vigorous resistance been made to our descent from the Alps, without resources, and overcome with the fatigues of a passage unparalleled in the history of the world, we should have fallen an easy prey, and the victory of Marengo would never have been inscribed on our banners. Had Melas concentrated his forces on the Po after the capitulation of Genoa, the star of Napoleon would have set to rise no more. Even in the battle he is accused of having committed a great fault, for when he found such a determined resistance in the centre, he thought that by extending his wings, he should cut us off entirely. In carrying this movement into effect he hoped to deceive us, while, in fact, the deception was on his side, for the extraordinary man by whom he was opposed, missed nothing, nothing escaped him, and, although in the centre of a devastating fire, he seized the occasion of victory, and gave on all sides those orders, which the bravery of his troops enabled them to execute.

The name of Napoleon seems, indeed, one to which any other cannot with justice be compared, his who was styled in derision the Bankrupt Brewer of Huntingdon, appears at a distance far remote, and yet is the only one that ought to be classed with it. It was, perhaps, the ready decision of Kellerman, aided by the intrepidity of Dessaix, which led to the result; still there can be no doubt that the trammels which his government had thrown around Melas, were the main cause of his losing the campaign. All things combined to favour the First Consul, who truly seemed a being of another world, determined to achieve one for himself; for he who was indebted for everything to himself—who subjugated so many states—obtained absolute power over a great and enlightened people—scattered crowns among his family—made and unmade kings—who lived to be almost the oldest sovereign in Europe—and who was, without dispute, the most distinguished man of his age—certainly was endowed with no ordinary faculties—possessed a mind of no ordinary calibre—and seems like one of those bright, but evanescent meteors, which dazzle the sight for a short period, and vanish at once from the horizon.

On the 17th of June the exchange of prisoners took place, and the First Consul started for Milan, escorted by the Chasseurs of the Guard. The news of our defeat, which had reached this city, had struck terror and dismay to the hearts of the friends of liberty; but the contradiction and narration of the great event which had taken place, and especially the presence of Buonaparte, changed their depression to a state of enthusiasm. A National Guard and Provisional Government were organised. The Consul, General Berthier, and the whole of the staff, together with an immense concourse of people, attended at the Cathedral, where a *Te Deum* was chaunted in thanks for our triumphs.

As yet the citadel had not surrendered, but by the terms of the truce the officers of that garrison had permission to walk about the city till 10 o'clock p.m. There were two battalions of French emigrants in the service of the Emperor, the one under the command of the Prince de Rohan, the other that of the Chevalier Bussy; and these lost no opportunity of seeing the First Consul, many of them cheering him as he passed. It was said that, some hours before the gates were closed, the Austrian commandant, Nicolet, had held a consultation with the Prince de Rohan, advising him to retire with his corps on Mantua, and magnifying the dangers to which he would be exposed by falling into the hands of the French; to which he replied, that, assured of the faith of Napoleon and his army, he should not quit the city, but trust to fortune, which in this instance did not deceive him.

On the 20th the citadel surrendered, the garrison marching out with the honours of war to the number of 4,000, of whom at least one half deserted on the spot. A battalion of my countrymen passed first, with arms and baggage, and colours flying; and these were followed by the legions of Bussy and Rohan, most of whose men passed over to our ranks, leaving their officers behind.

I was an eye-witness to a singular rencontre between M. Nicolet, the Commandant, and General Zach, whom we had taken prisoner at Marengo. The former, on coming out of the citadel the first time after its investment, proceeded to call on the First Consul, but in utter ignorance of the events which had occurred, was only aware of the order which confined him to the place of his command. You may judge, then, of his surprise, when he beheld the General. "Eh! by what hazard, my dear General, do I find you here?" Zach, surrounded by many curious listeners, replied in German, and I saw at each break in his reply that the Commandant could hardly believe the evidence of his senses.

I was credibly informed that in eight days fifteen thousand men, chiefly French, taken in Schérer's retreat, deserted from the Austrians; in the hospital were a like number of sick and wounded; the number of killed was certainly as great, while that of the prisoners reached twenty thousand. Since our descent of the St. Bernard, the total loss of the enemy in the course of this short but rapid campaign, could not be less than 65,000 men, a loss which, however enormous and incredible it may appear, is nevertheless correct.

In the few fleeting days that had elapsed since we quitted Milan, until our return, how great had been the change in the affairs of Italy. Our second occupation of the city was marked by more decided tokens of approbation than the first; and wherever the First Consul showed himself, he was received with acclamation. The favourite child of victory, Massena, whom he had not seen since his return from Egypt, joined him here. His defence of Genoa had raised him in the estimation of all the generals, and he was appointed to succeed Napoleon in command of the army.

In the meanwhile preparations for the departure of our commander went on, and I had made up my mind to accompany him to Paris, when I was attacked by a low fever, the effects of the incessant exertions to which I had been recently subject. For some days I was delirious, and my life was despaired of, the danger being augmented by the wound I had received at Marengo, which at the time appeared so slight as not to merit attention, but which had now put on an unhealthy appearance, and aggravated my pain.

In a few days a good constitution carried me through, and I was pronounced out of danger; at the same time I was advised to quit the army, at least for some months, and at the earliest possible period seek to re-establish my health by inhaling the invigorating breezes of my native land. "Poor Jean," said Barbanegre to my doctor, "you do but send him home to die." "I much fear it," was the brief reply, which sunk deep into my heart.

At length, when fit to travel, I set forth, loaded with presents from my brother officers, and quitted Milan (no longer endeared to me by the presence of the Marchese) with a heavy heart, and having already disposed of such of my effects as were troublesome to move about, I took the road to Novara.

Oh! who can describe that absolute sickness of heart which comes across the wretch enfeebled by disease, who possesses no hope for the future, as he looks forth upon a world in which he has no tie. How changed was the face of the country since, with knapsack on my back, I tramped along this road a fugitive from justice; and yet it was scarce more changed than the truant boy from him who, though young in years, had already become a veteran by service.

Sad and melancholy thoughts, aggravated by my complaint and the anguish of my wound, came over me, and all the garrulousness of my Savoyard servant, who was overjoyed at the prospect of his return home, could not raise a smile upon my face. Poor Domenico flattered himself he was going back to be a comfort to two aged parents and a happy bride, while I was returning to a home which my conduct had rendered desolate; to find a void by the maternal hearth my imprudence had caused; to friends who, perhaps, had become estranged; to kindred who had no desire to see my face again. There was no comparison in our situations, health and wealth apart, and I was almost angry that he continued chaunting the songs of his country, although he never failed in those little attentions which prove so grateful to the invalid; but as we approached Novara a better frame of mind stole over me, and the syren Hope began to show her face again.

How I pitied the poor peasantry the destruction of their homes; the devastation of their corn-fields and vineyards. Truly the march of an invading army is one of the greatest curses

Providence can inflict on a country. And here, where every yard of ground almost had been contested, the misery was appalling.

Slow marches brought me, at last, to Turin, from which I had been absent nearly five years, four of which had been passed in the busy turmoil of a camp. I had seen as much service as often falls to the lot of those who have grown grey in their harness, and when I entered the city, I went straight to the residence of my late mother, not an inmate of which recognised me until I made myself known. I was well received by my brother, who was two years my junior, and by a sister, who could hardly believe the pallid and broken-down soldier, the gay youth she had parted with.

I had no reason to be dissatisfied at their want of kindness or of care in the management of my property in my absence, to which every attention had been paid since the decease of my mother, and so well had they husbanded my resources, that I found myself master of a considerable sum. Luckily, my uncle did not intrude himself upon me, and in a few days I once more felt the comforts that cling around the magic circle at home.

Chapter 23

Liege

The effects of time and good nursing soon be came apparent, and I slowly recovered my health, although the severity of the attack might still be seen in the waste of flesh I had sustained, and in the pallid and unearthly hue of my countenance; nature had experienced a shock and a severe one; nevertheless, I had cheated the doctor, and was yet spared, again to play a part on that ever-shifting stage—the world; again to become an actor on life's ever-varying scene.

Determined to make my period of leisure of service to my mind as well as to my body, I had, during the latter portion of it, occupied myself in study, and I remained some time in Turin, as much for the purpose of perfecting my education, as to recover thoroughly from hard usage and wounds. Nearly the last four years of my life had been passed in the camp, and if my spirit needed not repose, my body required rest, to repair the ravages wounds and disease had made; I therefore devoted myself to study the theory of my profession, for though, during the time I was not actively employed in the field, I had neglected no opportunity of improving myself, still it had occurred so seldom that I had added little to the meagre stock of information with which I had left school, save such as I had acquired in the practical duties of the service; and I had long since discovered that I had little chance of promotion unless my information kept in advance of my fortunes. Now that I was at leisure, I set about in right earnest to improve my advantages, and render myself master of such things as were necessary to success in the line I had chalked out for myself; history, geography, languages, and drawing, were each followed with an avidity quickened by the knowledge of how much time I had lost; and though this course of study rendered my life dull enough in all conscience, I did not seek to make it more amusing.

Even the most irksome task must be some time finished if we persevere, as the most wearisome day will come to an end, and as avoided all kinds of society and amusement with the tenacity of a hermit, my progress was rapid as my attention was close.

It was well that I made such good use of my time, for scarcely had the hue of health revisited my cheek, and returning stoutness established the soundness of my cure, than I was appointed to a lieutenancy in a regiment of hussars, then forming by General Serres, to whom the organisation of the Piedmontese troops had been entrusted, and under whom I had for a short time served; and between the duties of my appointment, and the course of study in which I still persevered, the months flew rapidly by, until being declared fit for service, we were ordered to Bologna, to join the army under General Bruno, who had just made the passage of the Mincio. I was sorry that I was too late to share in that brilliant affair, as I should have reaped fresh laurels near the spot where my military career commenced, and added to that fame which former success had bestowed on me.

However, on marching into quarters at Bologna, we had no reason to be displeased with our reception, the inhabitants received us with open arms, and the National Guard with an enthusiasm I have seldom seen exceeded. Balls, fêtes, and spectacles, were got up for our especial amusement, and we might have exclaimed with the poet, "How merrily we live that soldiers be."

With returning spring we re-entered Piedmont, when I quitted the Hussars for a regiment which had formerly been Chasseurs, and in May, 1802, we marched into France.

I had now for some escaped the thraldom of the *beau sexe*, never having recovered from the stunning effects produced by the abrupt termination of my first attachment. The remembrance of the Ballerina, like the undying worm, remained to harrow up my existence, and making my heart a void; and so potent had been the charm, that it had carried me unscathed through the fiery ordeal of Italian eyes and Italian temptations, making me almost a convert to the doctrine that man never loves but one, and loves that one for ever.

It is true, that amid the eventful scenes through which the restless activity of our leader or the unerring decrees of fate had led me, I had never met with one whose charms had sufficed to obliterate from my heart the impression it had received, or to heal the wound which the duplicity of woman had inflicted; nor had time, that soother of all ills, and destroyer of all passions, exerted his influence on me. I had not forgotten; for though after years and other scenes may, like the undisturbed moss on the tombstone, fill up and conceal the inscription which is beneath, some strange accident may remove the incrustation—some trifling circumstance rudely tear away the veil, and expose in all its pristine nakedness the bitter reality we would fain believe was eradicated and forgotten.

I had changed name, station, country, even language; and taking new impressions from the scenes around me, endeavoured, and with some success, to be more in keeping with the set with whom my lot was cast, and by the time we arrived at Liege, to which place we were ordered, I had got rid of much of the gravity of my countrymen, and acquired some of the vivacity of my companions in arms. And they were in truth a merry crew, in whose society some of the happiest hours of my life were spent—hours long since passed away, but never to be forgotten.

Well do I remember our arrival at Liege, and good cause have I for doing so, for here, notwithstanding all my assurances to the contrary, my heart was again attacked by the boy-god; in spite of all resistance I was again to become his victim.

The evening after our entry into the town I strolled down to the public promenade, where, strutting in all the glory and grandeur of a gay cavalry officer, I thought myself the most captivating of men; and, forgetting that although I had seen more service than had fallen to the lot of many of my seniors I was yet but a boy in years, I fancied that veteran was stamped upon my face, which certainly of itself was not calculated to scare away the fair sex.

Like the young Cantab of whom I have read, who fancied that all the people be met in London were aware of the honours he had obtained at college, I thought Mantua, Egypt, Marengo, were to be seen in my countenance, and that every one recognised in the dashing soldier before them a survivor of the forlorn hope at Mantua.

It was evening, and the last bright beams of the declining sun, as he lingered yet in the heavens as if unwilling to part even for a night from the beautiful land he was quitting, cast an air of warmth and loveliness around that well accorded with the scene before me. Far away were the fruitful fields of Flanders, thickly studded with the cottages of the peasantry every here and there congregated into villages, and at greater intervals into cities and towns. Groups of well-dressed and beautiful women occupied the public path, some reposing on chairs reading the last new novel, while others were chatting socially together—here a knot of lovely girls, arrived at that delightful age when girlhood has hardly merged into womanhood, though it has already lost the trace of childhood, skipping gracefully about, or thrown together in groups, and conversing with all the gaiety and vivacity of *la belle* France—there a gay and moustached dragoon whispering soft nothings into the willing ears of some city damsel, or a simpering ensign, with his maiden sword still hanging upon his thigh, receiving lessons and advice from a grey-headed veteran of a hundred fights. Farther on a young and lovely mother might be seen watching her earliest pledge of love, essaying his *premier pas,* and nearer two staid and sober citizens of Liege, each armed with the *Moniteur* or the *Gazette,* fighting over again the battles there described, or arguing over the effects which this or that measure were likely to produce.

The after-dinner life of the French, and in this the *Liegeois,* though not strictly French, resembled them, especially during the summer months, and the exhilarating if cooler periods of autumn and spring, has so much of an out-door character, that I can only compare it to those delightful social re-unions I hear the English talk so much of under the name of *pic-nic.* Yet while it partakes of all the mirth and hilarity of those occasions, it has none of that chilling restraint too often witnessed—a restraint which the unfrequency of the occurrence tends rather to maintain. Here all classes meet upon an equal footing, each following its own impulse, and preserving that distinctive trait noticed in their in-door society, the line of demarcation being strictly intact—neither interferes with its neighbour, though to the unpractised eye of a stranger it would seem as if all classes were blended together in one harmonious whole.

And here upon the public promenade of a provincial city was I doomed again to surrender that heart which had been so severely scathed as scarcely to have recovered, though years of unrestrained intercourse with the most beautiful and fascinating of the sex had exerted their influence upon it; thus was the impression rather glazed over than obliterated, and as there is no period so dangerous to the sick man as when he is just attaining convalescence, so I suppose was my heart the more readily susceptible. My time was come, and I was again doomed to bear the fetters of the sex, whose blandishments I had so long defied.

I had taken two or three turns through the promenade, and was standing against a tree, contemplating the scene before me, and feeling the influence of the hour stealing over me, I fell into a fit of musing. What thought I must be his feelings who could behold a scene like this—so rife with beauties, and his heart be yet a heart of ice, unyielding, hard, and selfish! Could not the hour, the scene, attract him from himself, and leave some portion of its loveliness impressed upon his memory in characters slight but unextinguishable? Such were my thoughts, when my vision became obstructed, and there stood before me, in form as palpable as beauty could fashion her, the angel of my future destiny.

In truth, she was beautiful! Nor can I now remember what it was that first so pointedly attracted my attention, but I was again enchained, whether by the influence of the face, the figure, or the moment, or that of the three combined, Heaven only knows. Sufficient that from that hour I became her slave.

CHAPTER 24

Liege

"Gazzola, my man," said a brother officer, the companion of my walk, "what ails you? Here, have I been talking to you for the last five minutes without your deigning to vouchsafe a reply, your eyes as firmly riveted on that fair face, as those of a devout Catholic on the image from which he expects a miracle. Rouse thee, man, and if thy reflections be not of a nature too tender to be communicated to a rough captain of Hussars, at least condescend to bestow on me thy lucubrations, for of all dull occupations commend me to that of an unwilling listener or of a companion to a gay fellow just tumbled into love. Hast thou, the invulnerable, been wounded by Cupid's shaft, or has the impediment which seems to interrupt thy motions, been communicated to thy tongue, and rendered thee speechless?"

Did the galled jade wince? Undoubtedly; for the "rough captain" had unwittingly struck the the right chord, and its vibrations were felt through my whole frame. I gazed till she vanished from my sight, and then taking the arm of my companion, we slowly returned to our barracks, where I shut myself up in my room, determined to concoct some scheme which might lead to the discovery of who she was, and gain an introduction to her.

Calm reflection seemed rather to rivet my bonds than free me from them, while her voice, soft and musical as falling waters, still seemed to strike upon my ear, mingled with the happy ringing laugh of childhood and the more sober prattlings of advanced age.

In truth she was beautiful, rather above the middle height, with a figure that might have served as a model for a sculptor desirous of rivalling the Medicean Venus; eyes bright as the starry firmament, soft, liquid, and blue as the vault of heaven; hair that would have put to shame the plumage of the raven; feet (unlike those of the majority of her country-women) small and well-formed, and covered with a chaussure that might have made a Parisian belle, die with envy: and to this charmer, my heart, long without a tenant, bowed down in utter helplessness, establishing her its sole empress, and discarding at the same moment, and for ever, all traces of its former enthralment.

The stoic philosopher may laugh at my enthusiasm, the sceptic may smile at my credulity, the man of the world turn away with contempt at my folly—a too willing victim to the treacheries of the sex—how could it be otherwise? Yet when the earliest bursts of passion die away, and the heart turns in despair from the false one by whom it has been betrayed, its sympathies are awakened unnaturally, and it clings with more than its wonted tenacity to the first kindred mind it falls in with.

How the wished-for introduction to her, of whose name even I was ignorant, was to be obtained, was a problem I set myself to solve, yet did I not despair, for to the lover all things seem probable. I had declined an invitation to accompany the officers of the garrison to a ball, which was to be given by the municipal authorities, at the Hotel de Ville, in honour of our arrival. The recollection of the one I had attended at Milan was still impressed upon my heart; and I asked myself, "What gratification can you, a stranger, find in an amusement Calculated to awaken any thing but pleasurable reflections? But now the case was altered, for I hoped, among the fair votaries of Terpsichore, to find my charmer of the promenade. The influence of the boy-god prevailed, and, revoking my decision, I dressed myself with the greatest care, and followed our major into the *caleche* which conveyed us to the ballroom.

She was already there—"Yes, most adorable Caroline, in that crowded scene I first made your acquaintance, there my heart drew in long draughts of love, there those hands, which the bonds of the church afterwards united together, first met."

From a garrulous citizen, whose acquaintance I made, I learnt that she was the only child of a rich burgomaster, who dying while she was yet an infant, left her to the guardianship of a mother, more attached to her for the wealthy portion she was destined to inherit, over which, till she came of age, the mother exercised unrestrained controul, than for the beauties of her person or the spotless loveliness of her mind.

I had little difficulty in getting introduced to her, and, before the end of the first waltz, had made up my mind that the fault should not be my own, if I did not inspire her with a like passion to that which raged in my bosom. Again and again I sought her hand; again we joined the mazy throng, roaming, between the dances, from the hall to the refreshment room.

Of all opportunities for a woman to rivet her chains, commend me to the waltz, in which my charmer excelled; and when the hour for separation arrived, I obtained her permission to enquire after her health on the morrow.

The morrow came, and came, and swiftly flew, finding me ever by her side; and the few days intercourse which served to bind me to her for ever, also informed me, that in her mother I should meet a most determined opponent to my suit, and when, after three months of daily intimacy, I received an order to proceed to Maestricht, I hastened to her home, and asked her to be mine, she with much hesitation declared to me, that without the consent of her mother she could not marry for a year, and that consent she had little chance of obtaining, as it would deprive her of more than half her income, an income which even now was inadequate to her extravagances. An appeal to her mother she would not hear of, as it would in all probability lead to my dismissal at once; and so, with protestations of fidelity and devotion we separated, having first arranged a plan of correspondence.

With a heavy heart I departed, and not all the roasting of the mess-room, or my companions on duty could win me from my thoughts. Three dreary months were passed at Maestricht, enlivened only by the letters of my adored, and when at last the route came, and my regiment was ordered to return to Liege, I was more like a culprit for whom a reprieve has been just received, than a man in the possession of his sober senses.

Again the enchanting intercourse was renewed; again I pressed her to be mine, and at length won her consent to make an appeal to her mother.

I have faced death in the breach and on the battle-field, yet never felt the fear that came over me as I entered the room where Madame Fitz was sitting, to ask her permission to wed her daughter. Why repeat the scene? She called me an insolent beggar, and bade me quit her presence, nor dare again intrude myself in the house of one, who feared she had harboured a serpent to rob her of her child. Tears, entreaties, threats, all were of no avail; she was deaf to every appeal, and I left her like a maniac. Love, however, laughs at locksmiths, and if our interviews were less frequent, they were not the less enjoyed; the end was that one bright morning found us together in the church, and a few moments sufficed to make her mine.

We were married, and never, while life exists, shall I forget the thrill of exstatic delight which vibrated through my frame, as twining my arm around the slender waist of what was now my own, I imprinted upon her blushing lips the first marital kiss.

If ever man on earth enjoyed perfect happiness, I did during the succeeding months, the garrison duty extending even longer than was anticipated. What to me were the frowns of the mother, when we met (as yet in ignorance of what had taken place), they were amply repaid by the daughter's smiles? What to me the threatened loss of fortune, unless she gave me up, in a few months all might be acknowledged without fear? We were intoxicated with hope and joy, and I know not how long I might have gone on in the same blissful delirium, if my wife's interesting condition had not awakened us, by warning us that our marriage must be published to preserve her honour.

To me the discovery was the cause of unmixed pleasure, and on the morning when we parted with a pledge to meet again ere night, when she was to communicate to me the result of her confession to her mother, she was as cheerful as I ever beheld her, while I, caring little for her fortune in comparison with herself, had desired her to resign all, rather than forsake me, and bade her adieu with a heaviness of heart I could not shake off—true presage of the events that followed. Truly "coming events cast their shadows before"—for the gloom that overpowered my spirits was at last communicated to her, and I left her in tears. It was our last parting. We never met again! What became of her I never could discover.

I left no stone unturned to discover her retreat, plied her mother with threats, tears, entreaties, menaces—all without avail. She denied all knowledge of her condition—ridiculed my assertion that we were married—laughed at my tears—spurned my reproaches, and slamming the door in my face, bade me quit her presence for ever.

Yes, soul-harrowing fiend, while she denied all participation in the abduction she had planned, and paid for the stratagem by which she was entrapped, at her instrumentality she was removed to a farm in the country, where she was kept close prisoner, and whence she was removed to a convent in the neighbourhood of Rocourt.

Days and weeks elapsed; still I continued the search, still were my endeavours fruitless, till the Colonel, being annoyed at my neglect of duty, warned me of the consequences. What were the consequences to me? I replied hastily, and was put under arrest, and there my spirit chafed, until I wrote a most intemperate letter, throwing up my commission.

He had been my friend, and now came to me, reasoning with me on the folly and madness of my conduct, and having talked me into a better mood, released me on my promising to return to my duty.

One morning on returning from parade, I was behind with the rear-guard, when a boy approached, holding in his hand a basket of fruit; I accepted the present, and emptying the basket, which also contained a note, I returned it to the boy, having first deposited therein a piece of three francs, and pursued my route.

But what was my surprise, when on opening the note, I perceived the hand-writing of my wife! In it I read all the despair of an attached woman, who thought herself abandoned; she detailed to me her situation, and begged of me, if I had not forgotten her, to hasten to the convent in which she was confined and release her.

To disguise myself according to her directions, mount a fresh horse, and gallop off to the spot, was the work of a few hours; but instead of my Caroline I only saw the portress, who informed me that Madame Fitz was then with her, and requested me to return on the morrow, and this I faithfully promised, remounting my horse, and returning to Liege just as the gates of the town were opened.

CHAPTER 25

Mayence

The 23rd Chasseurs will leave Liege at six o'clock to morrow morning. Captain Gazzola with his troop will precede the main body of the regiment, by one hour's march, so as to arrive at Spa before noon.

Such was the order of the day that met my view on dismounting at my quarters, after my return from the fruitless expedition to the Convent at Rocourt, my servant having in vain sought me every where, and only one hour being left to make preparations for my departure. I determined at once not to obey, and immediately repaired to the house of the commandant, Le Vicomte Digeon, requesting permission to delay my journey for three days, promising at the end of that time to return to my duty.

"It cannot be, my dear Gazzola," said the kind hearted man; "your neglect of duty has already caused remark, and had you not been so occupied with your own affairs, you would, ere this have discovered what has been apparent some time to the majority of the garrison. The peace of Amiens is about to be broken, and we have received orders to join the army of the Rhine, there being every prospect of our being engaged against your old enemies, the Austrians. I would willingly oblige you, but my orders are imperative, directing me to recall every man to his regiment, and to lose no time in getting to Mayence. Much as I pity your situation (for I had entered into a full detail) I cannot allow your absence; but if you will march out of town with your troop, you may leave them, if you will pledge me your word of honour to join them again before they quit Malmedy. If you fail, and are found in this neighbourhood twenty-four hours after our departure, I cannot be answerable for the consequences; but to show you how deeply I feel for you, take two of my horses, place them as relays on the road, and God speed you. Remember, we must meet to-morrow."

I had had a fair specimen of the results of resistance, and hard as the terms were, was fain to accept them, determining about my after-movements on a future occasion; so thanking the colonel for his kindness, but declining the loan of his horses, I bade him good day, and joined the troop on parade. Having made the necessary arrangements, I accompanied my men a few miles out of town, and then, resigning the command to my lieutenant, I retraced my steps to a small cabaret situated about half a mile from the gate. Here I waited for the appointed hour, previous to which the head-quarters of the regiment marched by, few of the officers thinking of the unhappy plight in which their comrade was placed; but as the day drew towards a close, my impatience increased, and I found my way to the Convent, at least an hour before the appointed time.

To my incoherent and almost unintelligible enquiries, the old portress replied, that I was too late, for that Madame Fitz, having been apprized of my visit yesterday, had caused her daughter to be removed, but whither she was gone, or by whom accompanied, she knew not. I believe she told the truth, for though I endeavoured to bribe her with all the money I had in my purse, she persisted in her story, and declined my offer. Here then was I again at fault, and as I had no intelligence to gain here, I slowly retraced my steps, and once more sought the habitation of the mother, determined to carry her off by force, or die in the attempt. This heroic resolution was, however, spared being put in practice, for the porter, who was formerly in my pay, declared that Madame had been absent some days, and was he believed gone to Spa, though Louis, the coachman, had told him they were to go Namur.

As this was my destination, I put my willing steed on his mettle, and rejoined my regiment at day-break, but no Madame Fitz had arrived, and on presenting myself to the Colonel, he told me that he had just received a letter from the old lady, stating that having entrapped her daughter into a pretended marriage for the sake of her fortune, she had determined to remove her out of my grasp, for which purpose she had left home, taking care to destroy all trace of her route. She announced her intention of appealing to the Emperor, for to such rank had Napoleon now attained, and concluded by declaring her determination to apply to the ordinary tribunals of the country, to declare our marriage invalid.

Under these circumstances further pursuit was useless, and although unwilling to abandon it, I saw no good in its continuance for the present, especially as I had no means of contending against her wealth; and it was well known that Napoleon, since his assumption of the ermine, was desirous of securing the good will of the citizens, I therefore determined to bide my time, and as there was every prospect of the Emperor himself assuming the command, to wait his appearance and appeal to him myself.

Heavy at heart, I returned to my duty, and at Manheim was joined by my brother, who, tired of a life of inactivity at home, had followed my example, and presented himself as a volunteer. He was admitted into my troop, and between the duties of my appointment, and instructing him, I managed to pursue a sort of mechanical existence, till one of Napoleon's spirit-stirring proclamations roused me from my apathy, and with the rest of the army I passed the Rhine.

On the 6th of October, 1805, we arrived at Donawerth, the division of the army to which I was attached being under the command of Marshal Soult; while the enemy, under General Mach, had advanced to the borders of the Black Forest, where they appeared to have taken their position. The bridge over the Iller was fortified, while ramparts were being raised round Memingen and Ulm.

Napoleon had now joined the army, and directed its movements; and so well had these been planned and executed, that we had avoided the Austrians and the Black Forest altogether, and, passing through the valley of the Danube, found ourselves several days march in their rear.

I had generally the command of the advanced guard of my regiment, and on the 8th we march on Augsburg, crossing the Danube at Lustnau, while another division took the route to Feldheim, and the left bank of the Lech, Murat, at the head of his division of cavalry, advancing on Ulm. At Augsburg I purchased a map of the country; and trifling as this event may appear, it was to me a matter of importance; the information I was able to obtain from it causing me to be employed in many services I should not otherwise have fallen into.

From Augsburg we took the route to Lansberg, and one day I was sent for by our Colonel, and informed that the command of a reconnoitering party was to be intrusted to me, and after giving me my instructions, he commenced enumerating the villages I should pass through. I interrupted him, mentioning my purchase, and was dismissed.

I set off, taking with me 30 men; and ordering my brother and four men to form an advanced guard, I followed with the main body. Arriving at a little village, I made several inquiries of the inhabitants as to the position of the enemy, and while refreshing my men and horses, I espied a fine young man, who appeared to be skulking about desirous of avoiding attention. I arrested him, and finding he was a deserter from the Austrian army, I learnt that their advanced post was distant only two miles. I took him with us, and continued our route towards Lansberg, a little before arriving at which town I was aroused by the report of a carbine fired by my brother, and immediately riding up, found that he had killed the vidette and got possession of the post, the guard, six in number, being taken by surprise, and made prisoners before they had time to mount their horses.

Advancing cautiously to reconnoitre, I found the Austrian camp totally evacuated; for the men, little dreaming of our proximity, had gone to Lansberg to receive the distribution of forage, and a few sentinels were all we discovered, these keeping so lax a look out as not to have noticed the discharge of my brother's carbine. However, before we got near enough to be discovered, I could see the men arrive by twos and threes at a time, and as my force was too small to attempt anything myself, I sent back a sergeant to inform my colonel, who I knew could not be far behind, and in a short time followed him, and soon met the regiment.

Marshal Soult was not far in the rear, so having related what I had seen to my colonel, I was despatched to our commander with the information, and having given my opinion that the enemy were profoundly ignorant of our proximity, and that the camp certainly did not contain more than one regiment, I returned with orders for the engagement.

I had the honour to lead the attack. The road from Augsburg to Lansberg lies partly through a wood, on the outskirts of which we had fallen in with the advanced post that we had surprised. The rain and sleet now began to fall around us, added to which the road was execrable, and bounded on either side by a deep ditch filled with snow and mud. Having advanced a short distance, I perceived, what had before escaped my observation, that it was commanded by two pieces of cannon; but my brother and some men filing off to the right and left, took the cannoniers in the rear before they had time to put their matches to their guns, else we should have fallen a sacrifice, for the road was narrow and entirely commanded by them.

Hardly had we gained possession of this little battery, than we were attacked by a party of Brankenstein's dragoons. We charged, and finding our swords made no impression upon them, suspected they had cuirasses under their cloaks, and counselled our men to aim only at their throats.

This had the desired effect, and they turned, but being supported, again rallied. However, we also were supported in our turn, and remained masters of the field, having succeeded in taking many prisoners.

As this was the first engagement we had been in, we received the approbation of Marshal Soult for our conduct; nor was it without avail, for it cut off the communication between Prince Ferdinand and a portion of his army, besides putting us in possession of two guns and many of his men and horses.

Chapter 26

The Eve of Austerlitz

After the little affair described in the last chapter, we marched on Memmingen, which we carried, taking nine battalions prisoners, with several guns and magazines, and continued our way to Biberach, with a view of cutting off the retreat of Prince Ferdinand. On the 13th of October Napoleon arrived at the camp before Ulm, and immediately made dispositions for the reduction of that place. The attack commenced by our carrying the bridge of Elebingen; and on the 14th, Ney, at the head of Loison's division, passed the bridge and attacked the advanced guard of the Austrians, consisting of 16,000 men. They were beaten at all points, leaving 3,000 upon the field or made prisoners, and retiring in disorder within their intrenchments. In the meanwhile Lannes took the heights which commanded the village of Epfoël, his tirailleurs carrying the head of the bridge of Ulm, creating great disorder and dismay in the town; and Murat, at the head of his cavalry, attacked and put to route that of the enemy. Several divisions of infantry occupied the bridges of Unterkirch and Oberkirch, intercepting all the communications of the enemy upon the Iller.

On the morning of the 15th, Napoleon, who since his arrival had no idea of rest, in spite of the inclemency of the weather, made dispositions for the attack. The corps of Lannes and Ney, supported by that of Murat, were under arms, while the other corps blockaded the town on the left bank of the Danube, encompassing it on every side, and cutting off all communication with the surrounding districts.

Another proclamation roused us for the attack, which began with all the fury of former times. The advanced posts of the enemy were carried at the point of the bayonet, when Napoleon, desirous of avoiding the effusion of blood which must necessarily follow a general assault, addressed himself to Prince Lichtenstein, whom he knew and esteemed—"You see," said he, "your position; if you do not lay down your arms at once, I will carry the town by storm, and shall be forced to do as I did at Jaffa, where the garrison were put to the sword. However deplorable the necessity, it is the fate of war. Spare me then, Prince, and the brave Austrians, so fatal a resolve, since the town is not tenable."

This had the desired effect, and General Mach capitulated, with 19 generals, 33,000 troops, 3,000 horses, 40 standards, 80 pieces of artillery and caissons and baggage in proportion; and thus in fifteen days had Napoleon achieved these brilliant results—results without a parallel in the history of nations.

The head-quarters of the army now moved to Elchingen, the place from which the ill-fated Ney, "the bravest of the brave," afterwards took his title, while Napoleon, though weighed down by fatigue, having been exposed for the last eight days to the pelting of the rain, needed repose. His staff implored him to yield to the imperious dictates of nature, but he refused; he had no idea of rest, and continued night and day to reply to the officers who flocked to head-quarters, and to give new orders.

As generous after victory, as terrible in the battle, he sent for the Austrian officers who had surrendered at Ulm, and keeping them near him while the army passed, he endeavoured, as much as lay in his power, to diminish the sadness of their situation.

"It is not in this army alone that my resources consist," said he, "although it is true that we have obtained great successes. Appeal to the report of those prisoners who have lately traversed France, and you will learn the spirit that animates my people, and with what anxiety they hasten to range themselves under my banners. Behold the advantages of my country and position. With a single word, 200,000 men would rally round me, and six weeks would suffice to make them good soldiers, while your recruits march only by force, and require years to make them effective troops. I have counselled your Emperor, who wages an unjust war against me, to desist, but he hates peace; I want nothing on the continent; ships, colonies, commerce, are what I desire; and these would advantage you as well as myself."

But said the proclamation, "we will not stop here; the Russian array, which the gold of England has transported from the extremity of the universe, is before you, we will hasten to treat them in the same way." Onward was the cry; and although the troops constantly marched through the mud, the rain descending in torrents, nothing could daunt their enthusiasm.

Loud cries of "*Vive l'Empereur,*" issued from the ranks as they passed. "'Tis not with our bayonets, but our legs he makes war," said an old grey-headed grenadier, in the hearing of Napoleon. "True, my friend," was the ready reply, "but it is to save the effusion of your blood that I make you endure such fatigue." On the 15th of November Murat and Lannes entered Vienna. The capital of Vienna was in the hands of the Child of Fortune—garrisoned by the conquering legions of France. They crossed the Danube; and then, for the first time, beheld another enemy, in the advanced corps of the Russian army. On the 15th Napoleon dictated his orders from the Palace of the last descendant of the house of Hapsburg, and never did any member of that ancient family receive more intense homage. Scarcely had he arrived before the benefit of his appearance was recognised by all. All eyes were fixed upon him—all hearts were turned towards him. But with the same delicacy which he had shown at Munich, when occupying the Palace of the Elector of Bavaria, he discountenanced the homage which was offered to him by the people—a people who, in the present occupant of the palace of the Cæsars, beheld one who had risen from the army, to the giddy height of an imperial throne.

We found in Vienna, through which we passed, observing the most rigid discipline, more than 2,000 pieces of cannon, 100,000 stand of arms, munitions of war of every sort and kind, enough to form the equipage of four armies; and advancing into Moravia, the advanced guard, under Marshal Davoust overcame everything that opposed its progress between Brau and Wakesdorf, while Marshal

Lannes took Stokerau,—Bernadotte invested Krems,— Mortier was at Weekesdorf, and another division marched on Gratz.

On the morning of the 1st of December, Napoleon, with inexpressible joy, perceived from the height on which he had bivouacked, the approach of the Russian army. He had met the Emperor Alexander, who with the view of gaining time had inveigled him into granting an interview; but our leader was too clear sighted to be deceived by the ill-concealed policy of the Muscovite, and nothing now remained but an appeal to force. Two discharges of cannon from their advanced posts, preceded a movement which was intended to take us in flank, and turn our right. In an instant the presumption and ignorance of the art of war, which directed the Russian commander, became evident to Buonaparte, who, rubbing his hands with glee, exclaimed, "Before to-morrow night that army will be mine!" The opinion of the enemy must have been directly the opposite of this, for they approached within pistol shot of our advanced posts, and defiled by a march on our flank, along a line four leagues in length, while our army appeared afraid to move from its position. The Russians had but one fear—it was that we might escape.

Every means were employed to confirm them in this imprudent confidence. Murat, at the head of a few regiments of cavalry, advanced into the plain, but suddenly appearing astonished at the immense force before him, he withdrew in haste. This very thing tended to make General Kutusow persist in the ill-calculated operation he had commenced.

Strict orders were given, that as we were in sight of the enemy, who was much superior to us in strength, every means should be used to prevent his gaining a knowledge of our position, and that no fires should be made. It was bitterly cold, and I had made a fire under a bridge, where it was impossible for the Russians to perceive it, and had enveloped myself in cloaks and forage, when I was called by my brother to partake of a supper he had procured. The prospect of a good meal thus suddenly presented to one who but a few minutes before had resolved to retire to a supper-less couch with all the philosophy he could muster, was any thing but uninviting, so I quickly set about demolishing the good things provided, without making very strict inquiries as to how or where they were procured. But hardly had we concluded the meal, than General Margaron, who had the command of the light cavalry of the division, an officer who had always served with heavy troops, and mortally hated us Piedmontese, appeared on the scene. While prowling about for something to satisfy the gnawing pangs of hunger, my brother and my cornet espied the General's supper ready laid out on the table, and finding no one near they determined on appropriating it to themselves. To take the cloth by the corners, bundle up the viands as they were, and decamp with them across their shoulders was but the work of a few moments; and hardly had we devoured these unlooked for delicacies, and thrown the plate, &c, in the brook, than the loss was discovered. Foaming with rage, the General rode up to our Colonel's quarters, and demanded his supper. "It was those rascals of the 26th Chasseurs who have robbed me," said he. "Well," said Le Vicomte Digeon, "what would you have me do, the supper is eaten and half digested ere this? I cannot, my dear General, assist you." "But surely you can find my plate?" said the General; there were lots of silver on the table." Impossible. Neither supper nor plates were ever discovered; the former found its way into the stomachs of famishing soldiers; what became of the latter I never inquired, I guess, however, they were not left in the brook.

It was the eve of the anniversary of Napoleon's coronation, and, as if the pressure of the hour were too great, at the close of day he determined to visit on foot, and unknown, the different quarters, and endeavour to discover what chances he had of success on the morrow. He had not proceeded many paces before he was recognised, and it is impossible to describe the rapturous enthusiasm of the troops at thus beholding the hero they revered. Torches of straw were prepared on the instant, lighted and elevated on thousands of poles, and the whole camp presented themselves before their chief, some saluting him with acclamations to give honour to the anniversary of his coronation; the others exclaiming that on the morrow the army would present a bouquet to their emperor. One of the oldest grenadiers approached him and said, "Sire, you will have no occasion to expose yourself, as you have too often done, I promise you in the name of the grenadiers of the army, that you need only fight with your eyes, and that to-morrow we will bring you the standards and artillery of the Russian army to celebrate the anniversary of your coronation."

Napoleon, quite overcome with emotion as he entered his bivouac, which was a miserable mud hut, without a roof, exclaimed in answer to the remark of the grenadier: "I have, witnessed the most pleasurable evening of my life, but I regret to think that I must lose so many of these brave fellows. I feel—unhappy does the feeling make me—that they are truly my children, and in truth I sometimes reproach myself in consequence, because I fear that it will render me unable to prosecute the war as I should do." The lights soon burned out, order was restored in the camp, and we each retired to rest, to dream of that victory which none doubted would crown our arms.

Chapter 27

The Sun of Austerlitz

I know not if Napoleon had conceived the plan of the campaign, which should terminate in a great battle, as he did that of Italy, which ended at Marengo; at all events, he had so well concealed his plans from the Russians, that they were little aware of the science which laid them, or that they were intended for the purpose of drawing them upon the ground he had previously marked out.

To render this glorious affair more easily understood, I must describe the position of our army, which formed three grand divisions, under the command of Lannes, Bernadotte, and Soult

The left, under Marshal Lannes, was at Santon, a superb position, which had been fortified on the previous day, and where 18 pieces of artillery had been placed. Suchet's division joined the left of Lannes; that of Cafarelli his right, which was also supported by the cavalry under Murat. In front of the latter were the Hussars and Chasseurs, under Kellerman, with the divisions of Watrin and Beaumont, having in reserve the Cuirassier divisions of Generals Nansouty and d'Hautpoult with 24 pieces of artillery.

Bernadotte took the command of the centre, having on his right Drouet's division, and on his left that of Rivaud, the latter extending to the right of Murat.

Soult, who commanded the right, had on his left Vandamme's division, that of St. Hilaire in the centre, with Legrand on his right.

Marshal Davoust, was detached on the right of General Legrand, to guard the villages of Sokolnitz and Celintz; with him were the divisions of Friant, and the dragoons of Bourcier's division. Gudin's division was ordered to march early in the morning to Nicolsbourg, to keep in check a corps of the enemy which might annoy our right.

Napoleon, General Berthier, and his staff were in reserve with the Guard and ten battalions of grenadiers. The reserve was ranged on two lines in column by battalions, at sufficient distance to allow them room to deploy, having in the intervals 40 pieces of cannon, served by the artillery of the Guard. It was with these last troops that the Emperor determined to throw himself on any spot where he found their presence most necessary.

As early as one in the morning he mounted his horse to visit the posts, reconnoitre the fires and bivouacs of the enemy, and to learn as far as possible from the videttes, of the movements of the Russians. He discovered that they had passed the night in debauchery, uttering the most tumultuous cries, and that a corps of Russian infantry had presented itself at the village of Sokolnitz, occupied by a regiment of Legrand's division, to which he despatched fresh troops.

The second of December the sun, or to use the expression of Napoleon himself, "the sun of Austerlitz" rose brilliantly, and this day, the anniversary of the coronation of the Emperor of the French, which was destined to bear witness to one of his most brilliant and memorable engagements, was one of the most delightful of the autumn.

Surrounded by his Marshals, Napoleon waited to give his final orders until the horizon was well lighted up. As the first rays of the sun beamed upon us they were communicated, and each Marshal promptly rejoined his corps.

In passing along the lines Napoleon said, "Soldiers, it is necessary to finish this campaign by a thunder-clap which shall confound the pride of our enemies;" but scarcely had the words passed his lips than caps and helmets were raised upon the points of bayonets and sabre; loud cries of "*Vive! Empereur*" burst from the soldiery, giving the signal for the commencement of the fray. An instant after a cannonade was heard on the extreme right, which the advanced guard of the enemy had already attacked; but being there met by Marshal Davoust, their impetuosity was checked.

The soldier on the field of battle is merely a component part of that great whole by which certain effects are to be produced, and knows little of what is going forward save as far as his own individual self or those more immediately surrounding him may be concerned. A regiment is but a portion of the machine set in motion by the will of the General who directs the various forces under his command as the player does the pieces on the chessboard. Marshal Soult had appointed me an extra officer of ordonnance, thus giving me an opportunity of witnessing the movements of the various divisions of the army, and seeing more of the details of a general engagement than had hitherto fallen to my lot.

The division of Soult went into action at the same time as Davoust's, Vandamme's brigade with that of St. Hilaire attacking the heights of Pratzen, and cutting off entirely the left of the Russians, whose movements henceforth became uncertain. Surprised by this manœuvre, and finding themselves attacked where they fancied they were acting on the offensive, they wavered, and already considered themselves half beaten.

Murat, with his division of cavalry, advanced, while the left, under Lannes, marched in echelon, like a regiment on parade; a thundering crash of artillery was heard along the whole line, more than 300 pieces of cannon and 200,000 men made an awful noise. Hardly had the fight lasted an hour than the whole left of the enemy was broken; his right was already at Austerlitz, which was the head quarters of the Emperors of Russia and Austria, who immediately moved up the Russian imperial guard to re-establish the communication of the centre with the left. Napoleon, perceiving this, despatched Marshal Bessieres with assistance to our right, and, in a short time, the two imperial guards found themselves opposed to each other.

From the heights of Austerlitz, the two emperors witnessed the total defeat of the Russian guard. How I longed to be with my old comrades, as I saw them prepare for their last charge; down they came powdering their enemies to the dust, riding down and sabreing all who came in their way, and so engrossed was my attention that I was near forgetting that my instructions were to aid in the route, rather than sit calmly by as a spectator.

Bernadotte now moved up the centre, and received three charges of cavalry—charges well made and nobly sustained—without giving way; while the left, under Lannes, bravely maintained their ground. All these movements seemed so well combined that the victory, though not yet achieved, was no longer doubtful.

I had ridden up to Murat with an order from Soult to advance the Light Dragoons, just before the last charge of the Imperial Guard was made, and, as I have before said, was paying more attention to them than my duty allowed, when a rough voice exclaimed, "What are you doing there ?—join your regiment." A loud burst from my old comrades welcomed the Emperor, and, forgetful of all but the excitement of the moment, I rose in my stirrups, and joining wildly in the cry, joined my former companions, and assisted them to ride down their formidable opponents. On we went, powdering on, upsetting or cutting down the formidable body guard of the Russian Emperor; and it was not till the bugle sounded "halt, retire by squadrons on the right," that I recovered my senses, and galloped back again to my commander.

Success was no longer doubtful—the Russians were soon *hors-de-combat,* the veterans of Napoleon's guard totally routed their opposers—colonels, officers, artillery—standards all shared the same fate. The regiment of the Grand Duke Constantine was cut in pieces, the prince himself only owing his safety to the speed of his charger.

The field was now won. The cannonade ceased except on the right. The Russian corps under Buxhoëwden, which had been driven from the heights, found themselves in an awkward position, near one of the lakes or pools of water with which that part of the battle-field was studded. There went Napoleon with a strong battery, which, opening on these unfortunate troops, drove them from position to position, until at last was witnessed one of those appalling sights which seldom happen more than once in a man's lifetime, but so happening, can never be forgotten. Twenty thousand men, and a park of artillery consisting of fifty pieces of cannon, in order to escape the conquerors attempted to pass over the frozen surface of the lake, which, unable to bear this enormous weight, broke, consigning to the grave the whole of this unfortunate corps. In this affair the Russians lost 45,000 men, 20 generals, many *aides-de-camp* of the Emperor Alexander, besides a great number of officers of distinction, 550 pieces of cannon, 45 standards, among which were those of the Imperial Guard, many of their men laying down their arms after the last charge.

When the firing ceased, the old grenadier who had addressed the Emperor the night before, and who had escaped the dangers of the battle-field, stepped forth from the ranks, and, pointing to the plain before him, thus covered with the dead and the dying, exclaimed, "Behold the beautiful bouquets which we promised to our brave Emperor!" Loud cries of "*Vive l'Empereur,*" burst again from their lips, amidst the clanking of arms and the waving of caps and shakos.

CHAPTER 28

The Night After the Battle

The whole day had been devoted to a series of manœuvres, which had been so ably planned and supported as to have been attended with the most complete success, for the Russian army, surprised in a flank movement, was cut into as many pieces as there were columns brought up to attack. They fled towards the frontier, abandoning guns, caissons, baggage, wagons, and other equipages, which literally blocked up the route.

Among those stricken down on this "glorious and decisive day," was my brother, who had lately been made a corporal-major in my troop, and when on my return to quarters I discovered my loss, I immediately retraced my steps to the field of battle, and while occupied in turning over the dead and the dying, in search of him who had been nourished at the same breast as myself, a rough voice exclaimed, "What seekest thou?" It was the Emperor, who was employed looking after and succouring the wounded, in which occupation he passed along the whole line, where the different regiments had been engaged. Evening drew on apace, and his steps were ever and anon arrested and silence proclaimed, in order to allow those who accompanied him to hear the cries of the wounded, and to render such immediate assistance as the case required. "What seekest thou?" was again the demand, when turning round, not immediately recognising the voice, I replied, "My brother, a corporal-major in the 23rd Chasseurs a Cheval." "Ah!" was the quick reply, "who art thou? Surely we have met before." "Yes, Sire, in the grand place at Mantua, and at Marengo." "'Tis well, my friend, we will assist thee," and dismounting from his horse, he superintended the search; and when it proved successful, none rejoiced more than he. In the midst of a heap of wounded and dead, so thick and numerous that a hand-to-hand encounter must have taken place at the spot, we found poor Jaques: his horse had been killed under him—probably killed by the same shot that had shattered his left leg—and having fallen upon it, there they lay together, Jaques unable to free himself from the animal, which pinned him to the ground, and faint from loss of blood from a large sabre cut that had laid open his cheek; and here in all probability his mortal career had ended but for the humanity of the Emperor, who poured a glass of brandy down his throat, and assisted with his own hands in placing him on the litter which was to convey him to the hospital. "Brave boy," said he to me, "see him well taken care of, and return."

I accompanied the litter to the rude hut which was used as a hospital, and having ascertained that there was every prospect of his doing well, I returned to the field. It was now quite dark, and I remained with the Emperor, who was attended by Savary, his *aide-de-camp*, and a squadron of the guard. We passed the whole night taking off the cloaks of the Russian dead, for the purpose of covering the wounded with them. The Emperor ordered a large fire to be kindled near each heap of the wounded, which the troopers had drawn together to await the ambulance, and sent for a muster-master, till whose arrival he did not stir away; and having left them a picket of his escort, he enjoined the master not to quit the wounded until they were all safe in the hospital. These brave men loaded him with blessings—blessings more grateful to his heart than the honied words of flatterers, or the fawning blandishments of court parasites. The devotion of his troops, and his conduct to them, has oft-times been the theme of scorn; those who have witnessed both are aware of how be won the affections of his soldiers, who well knew that when their usage was hard the fault was none of his, and for this reason they never spared themselves when he called upon them.

"And you were at Mantua, and the Pyramids, and Marengo?" said the Emperor, again addressing me; "are you decorated?"

"No, general; for my share in the forlorn hope at Mantua I received a sabre of honour; my reward at Marengo was a wound, which spared my life again to be devoted to your service."

"Ah! my hero of the breach, how is it that you left the guard?" I narrated the circumstances, and was desired to appear at headquarters early in the morning.

Thus passed the night; the most ready assistance was rendered to the wounded, no matter to what nation they belonged, and many an Austrian and Russian received succour from the hands of Napoleon himself. The custom of carrying off their own wounded before those of the enemy has never prevailed with the French; they are too humane to turn a deaf ear to the voice of the unhappy stranger who implores their assistance. It has been said that we left the wounded Russians and Austrians to perish on the field; never was truth more grossly outraged than in this report. That such was not the belief of the Russians themselves is evidenced by the fact that, in the greater part of the towns and villages where detachments of our army entered in pursuit of the enemy, we found the farms and churches occupied by their wounded, who were abandoned without assistance. General Kutusow was contented with placing a placard over the door, on which was written in French, *I recommend these unfortunates to the generosity of the Emperor Napoleon, and the humanity of his brave troops.*

If our success was pleasing, no less were we gratified at the proclamation which Napoleon addressed to us on the following day; not the least gratifying portion of which was that which even in the hour of victory admitted that he owed his power to the will of the people. "Soldiers," it concluded, "when all that is necessary to assure the happiness and prosperity of our country has been accomplished, we will return to France, where you will be the objects of my tenderest solicitude. My people will behold you with rapture, and it will be sufficient for you to say, 'I was at the battle of Austerlitz,' to elicit the ready answer, behold a brave man.'"

My brother's hurt not being so serious as I anticipated, I slowly wound my way to the quarters of the Emperor. There I was met by my Colonel, who said he was ordered to offer me my old grade in the Imperial Guard, and to congratulate me on the determination of Napoleon to bestow on me the cross of the Legion of Honour. I did not hesitate to accept the preferred appointment, which was rendered still more pleasant by an assurance that on my brother's recovery he should be transferred to the same corps. Again was my tide of fortune on the point of flowing, and this time I hoped no adverse circumstance would occur to prevent its continuance.

While I made preparations for my change of service, the Emperor of Austria had had an interview with Napoleon, an armistice was concluded, and the principal conditions of the peace which was afterwards negotiated, were discussed; in which also the Emperor Alexander's consent was desired.

The aide-de-camp of Napoleon, General Savary, accompanied the Emperor of Austria after the interview, to the Russian camp, to ascertain if Alexander embraced the capitulation; I chanced to make one of his suite. We found the Russians without artillery or baggage, in irremediable disorder. It was midnight when we arrived, General Meerfield had been repulsed at Godding, by Marshal Davoust, and thus the Russian army, surrounded on all sides, was, in some measure, prisoner.

Prince Czartorinski introduced General Savary to the Emperor Alexander. "Say to your master," said the latter, "that I am about to depart, yesterday he accomplished miracles, that to day has increased my admiration for him, that he is one predestined by Heaven, and that my array in a hundred years could hardly equal his. But, may I retire with certainty." "Yes, sire," said the General, "if your Majesty ratifies that which the Emperors of France and Austria have agreed upon at their interview." "And what may that be?"

"That your Majesty's army shall retire by such marches as the Emperor Napoleon shall direct, and that you shall evacuate Austria and Prussian and Austrian Poland; on this condition being accepted, I am ordered to send to our advanced posts, which have already turned your leading columns, and to protect your retreat. The Emperor would respect the friend of the first consul." "What guarantee does he require?" "Sire, your word," said the aide-de-camp. "It is given," replied the Emperor, and on our quitting his presence, I was immediately despatched to Marshal Davoust with orders to cease all movement and remain tranquil.

The Russian army marched off six days after the battle, in three columns, the Emperor Alexander and his brother Constantine going at the head of the first.

Our army was now scattered about in divers places, and I quitted my comrades of the 23rd with regret, and accompanied my old corps to Schoenbrünn, where the Emperor took up his residence. On the 29th of December he addressed a proclamation to the Viennese, which flattered them considerably; and having dined with the Arch-Duke Charles, and presented him with a magnificent sword, with which he seemed well pleased, we started for Munich. At Munich we remained some days, and as the cause of our detention is stated in a letter to the Senate, I cannot do better than give it here.

Senators,—Peace has been concluded at Presbourg, and ratified at Vienna, between the Emperor of Austria and myself. I will, in a special sitting, convey to you its conditions, but having some time since arranged with the King of Bavaria for the marriage of my son, the Prince Eugene, with the Princess Augusta, and finding myself at Munich at the time when the celebration is to take place, I cannot resist the temptation to behold the union of two persons who are models of their sex: I am, besides, desirous of giving to the Royal House of Bavaria, and the brave people who in this circumstances have rendered me such services, and shown me so much friendship, and whose ancestors were constantly united in politics and in soul with France, this proof of my consideration and particular esteem.

The marriage will take place on the 15th of January, and my arrival among my people will thus be retarded some days. After having been without ceasing devoted to the business of the camp, I find a soft enjoyment in occupying myself with the details and duties of a parent, but unwilling to retard the publication of a treaty of peace I have ordered that it should be communicated, without delay, that it may be published as a law of the empire.

CHAPTER 29

La Belle France

It has been said that if at the termination of a campaign the number of casualties which each party reports to have occurred to the enemy were added together, the gross amount would be more than the effective force employed; however true this appear, some excuse may be made from the fact that the number of wounded left upon the field of battle is generally included in that of prisoners, and it is very difficult, even for persons on the spot, to calculate exactly the loss of each party.

French, Germans, Russians, Italians, Poles—the swarthy Croat and dashing Hungarian, had all inundated with their blood the plains so often watered by that of their barbarous ancestors, and the frequent skirmishes which took place, preludes to more important engagements—were often equal to those immense carnages which have sometimes destroyed a great people.

War, however, was over for a time. The Emperor was employed at Munich in soft dalliance with the Royal Family of Bavaria, and the different divisions of the army had moved off from the scene of our triumph. I had obtained leave to join the detachment by which the standards taken from the enemy during this short but brilliant campaign were conveyed to Paris.

On our arrival at Frankfort, the captain of the troop persuaded me to accompany him to the theatre, where a company of Italian artists, driven out of Austria by the approach of the contending armies, had pitched their tent. The opera was Mozart's masterpiece, *Il flauto Magico*, pretty well performed by a second-rate company. The name of the ballet I forget, but the principal *danseuse* was the Ballerina in consequence of whose acquaintance I was obliged to quit my home.

Time, and the life she had necessarily led in the pursuit of a profession, which is, perhaps, of all others the most exhausting to the energies of the frame, had laid a heavy hand upon her, and I thought how mad I must have been to have abandoned home, friends, and country, for such an ordinary person.

But great as had been the change in her, it was nothing when compared to what had taken place in myself, for had she remained exactly as she was when we first met, my surprise would have been the same. My acquaintance with, and subsequent marriage to, my wife, had dispelled the misty haze that had enveloped my first attachment, and now robbed of its deceptive colouring, it stood forth as it was in reality; rather the impulse of passion than the fruit of affection. It gave room, however, for moralising, and I have come to the conclusion that at fifteen and forty we look upon the world through different ends of the telescope.

In every town through which we passed, after entering France, we were received with acclamation, for the genius of the country was essentially military, and our march was one of triumph.

I obtained leave of absence for a week to visit Liege, promising to meet the detachment at St. Denis, previous to its arrival at Paris.

With a heavy heart I pursued my way, and on my arrival went to the hotel of Madame Fitz. All was there a blank;—she had never returned to it since my departure, nor could all my inquiries obtain a clue to her residence. One person only was supposed to possess the information, and nothing could wring the secret from him.

I determined to try the convent at Rocourt, and for that purpose proceeded there. I met with as little success; and now, despairing of ever meeting with my wife again in this world, I turned my horse's head towards France, and proceeded on my journey.

I pushed on, my anxiety and impatience often putting my horse to the top of his speed, which I would at times check, and pursue my way more slowly, and, sunk in gloomy abstraction, seem to take little notice of external objects. The excitement of duty had ceased; and now, left with nothing but my own sad thoughts to rest my mind upon, I bid fair to become one of those all-but automatons who we occasionally meet with in this world, though they seem not to belong to it.

Wrapt in one of these gloomy fits, I had not noticed that the shades of evening began to steal on, and that I was still far distant from my resting-place, when I was accosted by a demand of how far it was to the next village? Roused from my reverie by the voice of the questioner, I prepared to reply to the best of my ability, when on raising my eyes I beheld a man in the garb of an ecclesiastic slowly pursuing the same road as myself, the mule on which he rode, evidently well fed and cared for, seeming determined not to part company with my quicker moving charger. As our road lay together for the next stage, we soon got into conversation, and on arriving at the cabaret where we were to to pass the night, the warm smell of the viands, and the comfortable appearance of a wood fire, soon chilled the restraint that might be expected to exist between two strangers, and the old man having refreshed himself, proceeded to inform me of the history of his journey.

"I have been," said he, "for many years an inhabitant of Liege, in which place I hoped to end my days in peace, when I suddenly received a summons to attend the only child of my former patron, then at the point of death, and my old heart has been wrung by a scene such as I never hoped to have witnessed. Spare me the recital, however, my son, for I find my feelings too much harrowed up to enable me to speak of it with calmness, and I will, if you please, retire without the preferred report."

"Not so, father; for the scene of your labours has, alas! peculiar interest for me;—there some of the happiest, as well as the most miserable hours of my existence, have been passed; and if, as you say, you are an old inhabitant of Liege, perhaps you can aid me in a search which has induced me to quit the army to undertake."

"I have heard you say you had dwelt at Liege, and yet I know you not. Your name and occupation?"

"Captain Gazzola, of the 23rd Chasseurs à Cheval."

"Great God," he exclaimed, as he raised his hands in the attitude of prayer, "I thank thee for this opportunity of meeting with one for whom I was in search. Yes, young man, I was about to seek thee, for now that peace has been proclaimed, I doubted not that thou would'st be found amongst those whom the fortune of war had allowed to return to France. I was long the confessor of Madame Fitz. Nay start not; I knew thy wife, for such alas I discovered was the fact, when the discovery came too late."

To start from my chair, clutch the old man wildly by the arm, and demand the present abode of her my soul held most dear, was but the work of an instant, while he with feeble efforts attempted to shake me off, and finding this ineffectual, entreated me to be calm, and resumed his seat.

"I said that I was the confessor of Madame Fitz. Some six weeks since I was sent for to witness the closing in death of those eyes, which in youth I had often contemplated with delight; but let me not digress. When you went first to the convent at Rocourt, Madame determined to remove her daughter farther from the sphere of your duty, and took her to a convent of Ursulines at Namur; and here every stratagem that could be devised was made use of to induce her to believe that you had abandoned her. Her marriage was ridiculed as a farce, and her seclusion pointed out as the only means to preserve her character. With a woman's reliance on him to whom her virgin heart had been given, she received all their tales with distrust, and not doubting that you would sooner or later discover her retreat, she passed her time in tears for her bereavement and prayers for your return. It was the old lady who procured the order for your sudden departure, and by some means or other she obtained a correct account of your movements; for after the battle of Lansberg, in which your regiment was engaged, the particulars of which she had received, she entered her daughter's apartment one morning, and throwing an open letter on the table, exclaimed, 'At length, thank God, the viper has received the reward of his crimes; yes, Adela, the wretch who would have seduced you from your home, now lies a stiffened corpse under the walls of Lansberg. Ill-judging woman, so sudden was the announcement, so apparently true the news, that uttering a loud scream, your wife fell to the ground, from which she was carried to her bed, never to rise from it again."

"Premature labour came on—a dead child was the result; and while the mother occasionally seemed to have moments of recollection, the greater part of her time was spent in perfect unconsciousness of all that was passing around her, the only change being from low muttering delirium to raving insanity."

" I had been the intimate friend and spiritual adviser of her father, and loved her as my own child; and in this dilemma her mother, whose presence always made her much worse, wrote to me, and I went to her. In one of her lucid intervals she recognised me, and ere the immediate approach of death a merciful Providence vouchsafed a return to reason, and she gave me the particulars of your acquaintance and marriage. Thank God! what appeared to me a heavy sin was thus lightened, and in these old arms, on this bosom, she breathed her last, enjoining me, as I hoped for peace here and forgiveness hereafter, to seek thee in the armies of the Emperor, and, if living, convey to thee this thy first gift, and to her, next to thy affection, her dearest treasure. In this packet thou wilt find much that will inform thee of the past, may it afford thee guidance for the future; and should it make thee a wiser and a better man, I will not regret that my mission has drawn me far from my home and the more immediate sphere of my duties. Young man, I bid thee farewell; in this world we may not meet again."

Rising from his chair he took the light from the table and left the room, while I, stunned by the recital of what I had heard, remained fixed to my seat. When I in some measure recovered myself, his chair was vacant, and all seemed a dream, a cheat of an over-wrought fancy; but the packet was upon the table—it was in truth no cheating vision of the mind—and snatching up the remaining candle, I hurried up stairs and besought the old man to return to me again.

Tears, entreaties, threats, were of no avail. "In this world we may not meet again," was his reply, and I slowly descended to peruse the last traces of my adored but lost Adela.

Thus passed the night. From the prying eye of the world these last memorials of my fond one are sacred. There were many letters, some in accents of despair, bewailing my absence, others in terms of passion denouncing my desertion; still through all there beamed the most devoted affection—all were blotted and marked by tears. As the morning came on exhausted nature claimed repose, and on awaking from a sound slumber and seeking the stable of the inn, I found the old priest had departed while I slept, determined to prevent a recurrence of our meeting. Farther pursuit was useless, so having paid my bill I mounted my horse, and, with feelings hovering between madness and despair, pursued my way to St. Denis.

Chapter 30

Paris

Paris! dear, enchanting Paris! what a host of recollections come thronging o'er my brain, as I recall my first entry into thy crowded streets with the hundred veterans, chosen from the ranks of a gallant army, to bear the trophies of our prowess to the capital of the world!

The *cortége* traversed the principal streets, having entered the city by the Porte St. Denis, each street lined by a triple row of spectators, all with eyes filled with pride, mingled with respect, eagerly gazing on the standards, which borne aloft fluttered in the breeze, emblems at once of our devotion and our courage. Each of the veterans who accompanied them was decorated with the cross of the Legion of Honour—a cross only gained on the field of victory by the most determined heroism, and proving of itself, an insignia of glory, and a sufficient guarantee that those who bore it had a right to the honourable mission with which they were charged.

As these glorious spoils—these astounding witnesses of the heroism of the French army advanced, the population became more dense; and the windows of the different houses crowded with well-dressed women. Loud cries of "*Vive l'Empereur!*" "*Vive la Grande Armée!*" burst from all sides; their hearts seemed swelling with a mixture of admiration and joy, which only relieved itself by cheering; and although their cries rent the air, it seemed as if the utterers were unable to give sufficient vent to their feelings, but wanted the lungs of stentors to increase their expression.

In this way we advanced, till passing by the Boulevards to the

Place Louis XVI. we drew up a few minutes, as much to allow us to re-form our procession, broken by the pressure of the crowd, as to afford the municipal authorities an opportunity to join us ere we proceeded to the *Invalides*.

I had seen the entry of a conqueror into Milan—the progress of a successful general into Munich—the passage of an Emperor to Vienna—but these scenes were tame compared with the enthusiasm of the Parisians as the procession crossed the bridge, and took the route to the *Hotel des Invalides*. On arriving at the Esplanade, the municipal guards of Paris, and such regiments as were in garrison were drawn up; and the oldest grenadier passing into the church first, deposited his standard on the altar; one by one we followed, till all were laid in their last resting-place, though we little thought that their slumber was to be so soon disturbed.

On the night of the 30th of March, 1814, the eve of the entry of the allied armies into Paris, Joseph Buonaparte ordered the sword of Frederick the Great, which was deposited in the *Invalides*, to be broken, and upwards of 3000 stand of colours, among which were those I assisted to bring in, the memorials of innumerable triumphs of the French armies, to be burnt. This wanton devastation was carried into effect, and while the hospital was robbed of one of its greatest ornaments, posterity was deprived of the contemplation of those marks of valour which prove incentives to the rising generation.

Having entered the barracks of the Imperial Guard, my first enquiry was after my brother, and learning that he was so far recovered as to be able to bear the journey, and was soon expected in Paris, I gave myself no farther uneasiness on that score, but set about my duties with an alacrity, sharpened by the necessity of overcoming the demon thought which weighed upon my spirit, and bowed my energies to the ground.

Of all the madnesses to which an excited mind can give way, may Heaven preserve me from the *salon de jeu;* I have drank, and deeply, of the stream of dissipation, and wasted the savings of months—the prize money of many a battle field—in less time than it would take me now to count it. What matter; I sought excitement, and as the wine cup is seldom resorted to with us,

I found a sure and more desperate method of stimulating my brain to frenzy. Over the mad folly of those days let me draw a veil, and narrate a circumstance that first disgusted me, and then drove me from this temple of sin.

Among the players who frequented the house in which I passed most of my evenings, was a Frenchman, who had originally been master of arms in one of the cavalry regiments, but for some act of bravery in the field, had been promoted, and then held a sous-lieutenant's commission in the artillery of the Guard. From so frequently meeting at the same table, a speaking acquaintance arose between us—an acquaintance which perhaps might have ripened into intimacy, but that I noticed in him a recklessness of language which ill-suited my feelings, and which was calculated to make strife between him and any of his intimates.

One evening fortune had frowned upon him; he had lost several heavy stakes, and having applied to the banker for a loan and been refused, he got up from his seat, and crossing to where I stood, occasionally throwing a small stake on the table, demanded, rather than requested, a thousand francs.

There was a fierceness and abruptness in his manner which I did not like, and I civilly declined, continuing to leave my stake upon the table, until the red having won five or six times successively, it had accumulated to a large sum. "Why do you not pick up your winnings?" said Laroche "see what luck you have had, and yet decline to lend a poor devil, who is cleaned out, a paltry thousand francs." I took no notice of him, and suffered my stake to remain. Again red came up. "Fool," cried he, "remove your money." "Gentleman," said the croupier, "make your game." "The game's made—red wins." Maddened beyond endurance at my success, Laroche seized a rake, and began to pull the money towards me; and this, or perhaps a feeling of dislike induced me to desire him to desist. I coolly replaced the money, again the cards were dealt, again red won, when I took the money from the table, pocketing some ten or twelve thousand francs. The gestures of my companion could no longer be mistaken. Maddened by disappointment and rage, he applied an epithet to me the most unwarrantable; when drawing my sword, I should have inflicted personal chastisement on him on the spot, but that the people round the table interfered and prevented me. A meeting was demanded, and accorded, and at six on the morrow I was to parade in the Bois de Boulogne, to make my first essay in the duel.

So little was thought of an affair of the kind at the time, that I made no preparations, and true to the appointed hour, appeared the next morning in the field. A thick mist hung upon the trees, and a cold frosty air struck a chill through my frame; nor was my equanimity at all increased at finding that my adversary had made choice of pistols instead of swords. I flattered myself that with the latter weapon I was a match for any man in the army, with the former I had little acquaintance; and when on arriving at the spot I found my adversary already there, who, with a meaning look, threw up a half franc, and firing at it in the air, struck it at ten paces distance, I confess I longed to be again on the field of Marengo, or even in the breach at Mantua.

My second noticed my trepidation, and augured ill for the result, but being more *au fait* at such matters than myself he took me aside, and cautioning me to fire quick as my only chance, bid me keep my eye on him, and let go the moment the word was on his lips. This timely hint no doubt saved my life. The ground was measured, and we took our places, one, two, were given, and before the sound of three could reach my ear, my ball had struck my adversary's right arm, shattering the bone to pieces, while his ball, discharged a second after, had just missed my head, carrying away a piece of my left ear. The loss was trifling in comparison with the narrowness of my escape, and as my adversary was *hors de combat,* there was no prolonging the fight, and thus ended my first duel.

I have been in many an encounter of the kind since then, but have always declined the use of pistols; a certain tingling in my left ear warning me that the next time I might not be so fortunate.

A life of dissipation however soon palls, and garrison duty, although in attendance on a court, has little attraction for one whose time has been spent in the bustle of a camp. I sighed for more stirring scenes, for although we had reviews, inspections, sham fights, and what not, and plenty of drilling and such like amusement, to me there was nothing like the bivouac, and the watch-fires; and I longed to be. once more with my dashing companions of the 23rd, who were on duty in the north of Italy.

My duties were, however, confined to an attendance on the court, and though belonging to it, I could never become one of it; dissipation brought each succeeding day to the close, the later hours of the twenty-four being generally spent in the s*alon de jeu.*

Chapter 31

Paris II

How few are there in this life sufficiently mindful of the star that might guide, or the chart that might direct them in their voyage towards eternity, who, while they are conscious that they are floating onwards to that gulf which must eventually receive them, are yet sufficiently careful that their course may be aright. Though they are careless of what ought to be the great object of their existence, and by that very carelessness exposed to all the contingencies which such a changeful state of being as ours exposes them to, yet on they go, alike regardless of the dangers to be dreaded, the shoals by which they are encompassed, or the rocks by which they are threatened, borne forward by an impulse, which, though invisible, is not the less irresistible.

Such, indeed, was my case at the period of which I speak; and though my conduct in the duel had gained me much credit with my comrades, still was that conduct reprehensible. I had been assailed in a gambling-house, and had no right to be satisfied with the circumstance which had placed my own life, as well as that of a fellow-creature, in danger. I recoiled with horror, it is true, at the thought of becoming a duellist, yet such was the character of my adversary, and if the general reports were true, he was too implacable an enemy to let the affair remain as it was.

With all these impressions crowding on my brain, my visits to the saloon were not the less frequent; and as his wound necessarily confined him to his house, the affair had passed from my mind, and I pursued the blind goddess with that variable success which generally attends the *habituées* of such places.

Among the frequenters of the saloon was Lajarre, who, though suffered to go at large, was under the surveillance of the police, Fouché the indefatigable director of that force, having information that he was in correspondence with parties in England. He was a remarkably pleasant person, and played very little, contenting himself with an occasional *coup* or so, his time being spent in conversation. I passed many hours in his society, little dreaming of the net I was weaving around me, or of the events which this casual intercourse was likely to produce. As ill luck would have it, I was engaged in conversation with him the first evening Laroche made his appearance since the duel, about six weeks after our meeting, and having had a greater run of ill-fortune than usual, my mind was soured in proportion. He entered the saloon with his arm in a sling, and throwing himself into the first vacant chair, laid down his stake. He was unsuccessful. Again and again the result was the same; when, turning round with an audible curse, his dark scowl rested upon me; the expression of his wan and pallid features satisfied me that although we had met, and he was the sufferer, he was far from being satisfied with the result.

Had I been mindful of the quicksands that surrounded me I should have left the room, and there the matter might have ended, I, however, returned scowl for scowl, and with dark thoughts mantling in my bosom, remained at the table.

Fortune, however, seemed out of temper, with each of us, for we both backed the same colour, and lost, till having declared slightly in our favour, Laroche seized a rake, and, while my back was turned, in reply to the casual observation of a bystander, removed my money as well as his own. On my demanding my stake he replied, with a low derisive laugh, that I was entitled to none, and bid me seek it of the croupier. Now he well knew how useless would be such an appeal, for when two or three persons win on the same colour, the croupier merely puts down the gross amount, leaving each party to reclaim his own stake.

"You had no stake," was repeated, "and if you had you should have attended to your game and claimed it; I took none of yours, and none will I return."

It was evident, from his manner, that he was desirous of fastening a quarrel on me, which I was equally anxious to avoid, as much from his crippled condition as from any fear for myself. Nothing, however, would do, and I prepared to quit the table, when a friend of his called me aside, and said that as I had accused Laroche of stealing my stake, I must give him a meeting.

I applied to Lajarre, and left the two in conversation, while I awaited the result of the conference.

Now, although duelling may, and ought to be condemned, when had recourse to on trifling occasions, still there are circumstances which render it not only venial but necessary. The equality upon which the pistol puts the strong man and the weak—the chastisement it affords for crimes unnoticed in the statute book, and therefore without the pale of the law—the redress it affords for grievances that must otherwise go unredressed, may in some measure palliate the practice and although the legist and the citizen may censure it altogether, society has become too civilized, and consequently too artificial, to admit of its total abolition. In the French army, too, it had unfortunately become common I was not, therefore, much surprised that on Lajarre's return he informed me that Laroche demanded another meeting on the morrow.

"Let him wait till he is well," was my reply, "and I will then accommodate him."

"Not so, you must meet him at once; and as his arm is disabled, he proposes that you should have two pistols, one loaded, the other empty, and having deposited them in a bag, toss for choice, and draw them forth. Standing at the two corners of a pocket handkerchief, let each man pull, and the one who has the ill luck to get the empty weapon, must then inevitably fall."

I declined a meeting the result of which could be nothing less than murder; and as he, being the aggressor, had no right to the choice of weapons, declared my intention of appealing to the Emperor, unless he were content to meet me in the usual way, for which purpose I would wait till his arm was sufficiently recovered.

Stung by my denial, he denounced me to the police as the friend and accomplice of Lajarre; and on returning to my barracks one day from Versailles, whither I had been in attendance on the Emperor, I found my drawers had been searched, my papers removed, and an order for my immediate arrest.

On appearing before the Prefect of Police, my innocence was soon made manifest, nothing being found amongst my papers that could warrant my detention; and Lajarre, who was also privately examined, denying all knowledge of me, except as a frequenter of the *salon* in fact, so perfect was the system of espionage, that had any connection existed between us, the police would have had cognizance of it, so I was ordered to return to my duty.

All this was bad enough, and my life would have been intolerable, as I had somehow contracted a habit of visiting the saloon each evening that I was not on duty, if my brother had not arrived in Paris, and between anxiety for his health, and constant attendance on the Court between Paris and Versailles, I had enough to do without troubling myself about Laroche. Our major, to whom I had confided the whole affair, decided that I was right, and declared that if notice, were taken of the matter during my absence he would prevent any stigma being cast upon my character, by appearing in my place Gratified by this assurance, and satisfied that I was confiding in one on whom the breath of reproach never rested, I took no further care about it and thus the matter rested, for Laroche being detected soon after in an attempt to cheat the bank, was ignominiously driven from the room, and would in all probability have been taken up by the police had he not thought it prudent to absent himself from Paris.

I was on duty one evening at Versailles, and on strolling through the gardens of the Palace, I came unawares near the little Trianon, then the favourite haunt of the Empress Josephine, as it had previously been of the unfortunate Marie Antoinette. It was about the middle of the month of July, and the atmosphere was warm and sultry, when divesting myself of sabre and sabretache, I stretched myself under one of the trees, whose shade extended almost close to the building. How long I may have slept I know not, but on awaking I was not a little alarmed at finding that my arms were gone, and I was that anomalous animal, a soldier on guard without his sword.

I confess my reflections were anything but pleasant, and I was cogitating over my situation when a merry ringing laugh from within aroused me from my reverie, and stepping up to the door I knocked. It was opened by the Empress, who advancing, requested, with much solemnity, to know my errand. Stammering out my loss, I beseeched her to inform me if she knew by whom I had been robbed, when a laugh from behind the door revealed one of her attendants, with whom I had oftentimes exchanged a joke while on duty.

"Ah! Captain Gazzola," said she, "fairly caught, and, but for the intercession of our good lady, I should certainly have carried your arms and laid them at the feet of his Majesty, who, Heaven knows, would have much reason to be grateful for so good a watch."

"Cease trifler," said the Empress, "and return the arms, which I assure you, captain, would never have been brought here, but that this madcap found them while you slept, and had taken possession of them ere I was aware. May they prove as useful in our defence as I see they have hitherto been; for the cross you wear is a sufficient proof that they have not always been forgotten as they were this evening. Remember that a good soldier is never found sleeping on his post. But hist, begone, for see the Emperor approaches."

Bending on one knee, about to kiss the hand extended me, I was not aware that Napoleon was so near, till his deep voice exclaimed, "*Arrete*," and I recovered my position.

"Whence come you, and what do you here?" was the brief exclamation.

Thoroughly alarmed, the Empress motioned me to be silent, and explained that she supposed some little love affair brought her attendant and myself together, when he roughly exclaimed, "I will have no love affairs with the Officers of the Guard, hence sir, return to your barracks, and remember that your presence here can be dispensed with until I require it."

I made no reply but scampered off to my quarters, and the next morning received orders to accompany the relief that was going into Paris.

CHAPTER 32

Weimar

It has been well said that idleness is the prolific parent of evil, and since my sojourn in Paris, I had added another to the already innumerable illustrations of the truth of the proverb. In addition to the affair with Laroche, from further consequences on which score his own conduct had released me, I had been in two or three minor escapades, which I have not thought it worth while to record, and now my unfortunate slumber in the garden at Versailles seemed a crowning misery, having put me under the ban of him without whose smile the career of the soldier was not likely to be a very fortunate one. I ought perhaps to have felt flattered by the explanation of the Empress, for she whose name was thus sought to be coupled with mine was, in addition to the gifts of nature, in possession of many of those received with favour in the world, yet though wealth, titles, estates were hers, I was anything but satisfied; but as she had volunteered, and might perhaps have felt annoyed at the liberty her attendant had been taking, as in some measure countenancing an acquaintance which had no right to exist. I could not undeceive the Emperor, and submitted to the banishment with the best grace I could, hoping that the proverbial restlessness of the French would soon plunge them into war, and that I should again resume my station in the camp and the battle field, which seemed more congenial to my taste, and conducive to my success in life, than the gilded precincts of the court, or the gay society of the capital seemed destined to be.

However, neither my devotion to the latter, nor my attention on my brother, who now, perfectly recovered, had resumed his duties with the regiment, had prevented me from frequently presenting myself at the *levees* at the Tuileries. A hope of obtaining the first majority that fell vacant animating me. I felt myself misplaced in garrison, and liked not the listlessness that attends a want of employment, more varied duties and stirring scenes falling in with my taste. Now, however, all chance of promotion seemed at an end, and I was beginning to despair, when suddenly Paris became alive with the report that the Emperor of Russia had failed to ratify the treaty submitted to him, and that, in order to be prepared for anything that might occur, the Emperor had determined to concentrate a large force on the Rhine.

All was now bustle and confusion regiment after regiment commenced its march, and in a short time Strasbourg, Mayence, and Franconia were occupied, and the army awaited but his presence, who was again to lead them on to victory. On the 25th of September, 1806, he quitted Paris, sped on without delay to Mayence, and having established his head-quarters at Bamberg, became aware of the treaty between Russia and Prussia, and that it was not with the former alone we were to contend.

On the 6th of October, at Bamberg, he addressed his first proclamation to the troops and then having divided them so as to march on three different points, we were once more in motion.

The right, composed of the corps of Ney and Soult and a division of Bavarians, marched on Bareuth the centre, formed by the reserve, under Murat, Bernadotte's corps, Davoust, and the Imperial Guard, debouched by Bamberg on Cornach, and arriving at Saalbourg on the 8th, marched by Schleitz on Géra while the left, composed of the corps of Lannes and Augereau, advanced by Schweinfurth, on Cobourg Graffenthal, and Saalfield.

Napoleon having made these dispositions, his troops were animated by his presence with the wildest enthusiasm. The battle of Austerlitz had annihilated at once the ancient prejudice of the superiority of the Russians, and now we were about to destroy, without the chance of restoration, the reputation for manœuvre which the Prussians had maintained since the time when the great Frederick directed their movements.

There can be no doubt that the Russian and Prussian alliance was effected in the hope of finding France unprepared instead, however, of attacking her at a moment of weakness, she had never been stronger or more fit to resist the aggression. The event justified the conclusion, for we find this great Captain, marching at the head of large armies, moving with an astonishing facility extraordinary masses of infantry, cavalry, and artillery, and so disposing them as to have always ready to his hand, and without the least confusion or derangement of his plans, such a force that victory was constantly ranged on his side. Generals worthy to execute the designs of the first Captain of Europe had conducted their divisions to the places assigned to them. The memory of former victories, the feeling of injustice on the part of our enemies, the desire for revenge, the determination to succeed, animated each breast, and combined together to promise a favourable issue to the projects of Napoleon.

The Prussian army, under the orders of the Duke of Brunswick, reinforced by the Hessian and Saxon troops, passed the Elbe near to Minden, and while one portion occupied Eisenach, the other advanced on Hall and Leipsic. It was composed of 130,000 men, under the command of the King, whose counsels were supposed to be animated by the spirit of his great predecessor, who had left the Prussian troops second to none.

Napoleon having been informed that the Queen of Prussia, wearing the uniform of the dragoons of the guard, and riding *en cavalier,* was in the camp, from whence she issued letters to excite the inhabitants to rise up against us, said to Berthier, "Marshal, they have made us an appointment for the 8th; an appointment from which a Frenchman would never shrink; but as I am told that there is a lovely Queen who wishes to be a witness of our encounters, let us be courteous, and make a forced march on Saxony."

We first encountered the left of the enemy, who had concentrated his forces between the Saale and the Verra, his right on Eisenach, and his left extended from Weimar to the heights which overlook the country between that town and Jena. He had fortified Schleitz, Saalfield, Saalbourg, and Hoff; numerous advanced posts protected the whole of his line; the Thuringian woods and the mountains which on one side bounded the frontiers of Saxony, covered his front, and rendered his position a formidable one. In one respect, however, it was a bad one, because it prevented him sufficiently extending his forces on the left, and this circumstance was in part the cause of his defeat.

On the 9th of October Soult carried Hoff, as well as the whole of the magazines, taking some prisoners; Murat crossed the Saale at Saalbourg, driving before him a Prussian regiment which opposed his passage; while Napoleon, with the corps of Bernadotte, carried the village of Schleitz, although 4,000 Prussians and 3,000 Saxons endeavoured to defend it. General Watier endeavoured to pursue them, but had calculated badly, and being attacked and repulsed, was driven back on the infantry, who charged the enemy and rescued him, giving time to General Lasalle to come up, who took 300 prisoners and 400 horses. While Bernadotte occupied Auma, Murat advanced on Géra, and Lasalle following up his success, overthrew the baggage guard, taking 500 caissons and baggage wagons.

Lannes was at Cobourg, and Suchet's division at Saalfield attacked the corps under the orders of Prince Louis of Prussia. Our infantry there occupied a bog, or were dispersed through a wood. The Hussars charged with such impetuosity that the enemy's horse were thrown in disorder. In vain the Prince sought to rally them—in vain he cheered them on—all was useless; a ball struck him from his horse, and he expired in the field of honour, as became a warrior. A thousand prisoners, six hundred left dead on the field, and thirty pieces of cannon were the results of this brilliant affair.

These affairs, like the first flourishes of the maestro ere the serious business of the orchestra commences, were but the preludes of more stirring actions to come. I had shared the advance of Lasalle, and partaken of the plunder which the enemy's baggage wagons afforded; added to which I hoped that my bearing in the field had in some measure obliterated the remembrance of the Little Trianon. He had noticed me once and kindly, and as the acts of every soldier were known to him, I did not doubt that an unwearied perseverance in my duty would meet its reward. The enemy, moreover, astonished by our success, seemed a little confounded also; while the Emperor, determined to take advantage of the season, which was beautiful, ordered forced marches in advance, took the magazines of the Prussian army, turning it entirely, and by this daring and well-planned manœuvre disconcerted the whole plans of the Duke of Brunswick and his generals.

The duke thought he should oppose great obstacles to the movements of the French army, by debouching on Frankfort with his right, Wurtzbourg with his centre, and on Bamberg with his left; such was said to have been his intention, but it has been doubted; for if we believe that he really meditated and intended to execute these simple manœuvres, we must give Napoleon credit for first discovering and then preventing them, and by so executing a flank movement as to turn his left, and occupy so favourable a position himself that he had effected the destruction of the hopes of the Prussian general, and destroyed all his plans. Whether this were correct or not remains for ever uncertain; the facts are indisputable; the bravery of our troops, the rapidity of their movements, the forethought of our general, and the execution of his well-laid plans, all combined together, satisfied the most desponding that the long-expected day must soon arrive when the two armies would be opposed to each other in force instead of by detachments; and when on the 13th of October we arrived at Weimar, the moment for the struggle appeared to have arrived.

I was again with the "Old Guard," and having witnessed the Pyramids, Marengo, Austerlitz, did not for one moment doubt another great victory would crown our arms. I had won the cross of the Legion of Honour—fresh laurels were to be reaped, an indiscretion to be wiped off. I therefore determined "to bear me as became a man," let what might be the result, resolving at the same time that my brother, who was now my constant companion, should also share in the harvest.

CHAPTER 33

Jena

At two, p.m., on the 13th of October, Napoleon arrived at Jena, and from the height of a plateau which was occupied by the advanced guard, perceived the dispositions of the enemy, who prepared to manoeuvre for the attack on the morrow, and open the different debouches of the Saale. The Prussians defended the road from Jena to Weimar by an imposing force, and an unassailable position, seeming to think that the French could not descend into the plain without opening this passage. It appeared impossible to get the artillery on the plateau, which was besides very confined, but by working all night a road was made through the rock, and the guns were got up.

The heavy cavalry, which was not yet united to the army, could not arrive before mid-day, and the cavalry of the guard was dispersed in various places, some being at a distance of ten leagues. These considerations, however, did not weigh with Napoleon; he drew out in battalion on the plateau which the advanced guard had occupied, and opposite to where the enemy was in position, the whole corps of Marshal Lannes, and the Foot Guards under the orders of Marshal Lefevre, and bivouacked in the midst of them.

From this position he addressed a letter to the King of Prussia, which might in all probability have terminated the war, but that unfortunately it was not delivered till the moment when the battle of Jena was lost. The General Hohenlohe had suppressed it, without respect for the King his master, or the French Emperor, and by thus failing in his duty, plunged the Prussians in the miseries into which they afterwards fell; an act of infidelity which was productive of the most disastrous consequences.

It may be said that I place too much reliance on the forethought of the Emperor, and often give him credit for that which was the result of chance, or of fortuitous circumstances. My experience of his genius warrants me in according him the highest rank amongst contemporary generals, if not amongst those that have ever lived. He alone had the talent to foresee the results of a great war, complicated as this was; his genius only seemed sufficient to point out the effects which followed, for at an early period of the campaign he wrote to his Minister of War, "that three or four days after the opening of the campaign he should gain a great battle, which would render him master of the Elbe and of Berlin, and carry him to the Vistula." This prediction was accomplished; although with an army composed of old and picked troops he might be assured that he should conquer everywhere, and at all times secure a victory. But let me not anticipate.

The night of the 13th of October presented the spectacle of two great armies, the one of which deployed its front over an extent of six leagues, embracing the horizon with its fires, while the second appeared to concentrate its forces on a small point. On either side all was activity and movement. The watch fires of the two forces were not a cannon shot apart; the sentinels of each could hear the challenge of his enemy, and it was hardly possible that the patrol of one army could go his round without falling in with that of the other.

Day broke, or rather endeavoured to struggle into existence through a thick fog which obscured even the sun's rays, and our army was immediately under arms. Napoleon passed down the lines, recommending every soldier to be prepared against the Prussian cavalry, which they had pictured as unconquerable. He reminded them that only a year ago, at a similar season of the year, they had taken Ulm; that the Prussian army in its turn had been surrounded; that it had lost its line of operations, and its magazines; that at this moment it did not fight for glory, but to secure a retreat; that it sought to find a road at different points.

He added, that the corps of the army that suffered it to escape, would lose its honour and its reputation. To this animated discourse the soldiers replied by loud cries of "*Vive l'Empereur.*"

The action was commenced by the tirailleurs, but in a short time the firing became general, and whatever confidence the enemy might have had in his position, it was quickly disturbed, for the French army advancing on the plain, commenced taking up its position in order of battle.

The Prussian army, which decided to attack us as soon as the fog dispersed, was soon under arms. A corps of 50,000 men on the left marched to cover the defiles of the mouths of the Koësen, but Napoleon had foreseen their design, which he prevented by moving up Davoust's division. The two other Prussian corps, composed of 45,000 men, threw themselves on our army, as it debouched on the plateau of Jena.

For two hours, the thick fog covered both armies, which gradually dispersing under the influence of the rays of an autumnal sun, discovered the French and Prussian forces within gunshot of each other. The enemy deployed, and his cavalry, which was very steady and splendidly mounted, moved with rapidity and precision but if the troops were brave, they were deficient in those essentials which the veteran legions of France, to whom they were opposed, possessed.

It was the wish of Napoleon that the first hours of the morning should pass away, before we became seriously engaged, in order that the troops, which were yet at some distance, should arrive and take part in the battle, his army being deficient in cavalry, but the ardour of the French prevented this, many battalions being engaged at the village of Hollstedt, from which the enemy endeavoured to dislodge them. Lannes was ordered to move his division *in echelon* to its support, while Soult had attacked a wood on the right, and the Prussians, having made a movement with their right against our left, Augereau was ordered to charge them. In less than an hour the action became general, 26,000 men with 700 pieces of artillery sowing death on every side.

On either side, the various manœuvres were executed with the greatest precision, our troops moving without the least confusion; victory was never for one moment doubtful, Napoleon was always surrounded by the Imperial Guard, and such other picked troops as were necessary to execute any unforeseen movement.

Soult, who had been two hours attacking the wood, at last succeeded in carrying the enemy's position, and advanced, and the same moment the Emperor learnt that the division of cavalry forming the reserve had arrived, and that two divisions of Ney's corps were already in the rear of the field of battle. These were immediately moved up to the front; and thus, finding himself beaten on every point, the enemy commenced his retreat. For an hour preparations were made for a retrograde movement, but the rout soon became general, and the moment when our division of dragoons and cuirassiers took part in the action, throwing themselves on the enemy on all sides, the Prussians turned and fled, for the cavalry and infantry, unable to sustain the shock, gave way at all points—in vain the infantry were formed in squares, five battalions were surrounded, artillery, infantry, cavalry—all gave way!

The Prussians fled precipitately from the field, and we as hotly pursued, arriving at Weimar nearly as soon as they did. On our right Davoust performed prodigies, for not only did he hold his own, but he absolutely obliged the main body of the enemy, who had endeavoured to debouch on the side of Koësen to give way, killing 12,000 men; and taking 3,000 prisoners, many standards, and 100 pieces of artillery.

Great as was our success, and immense as was the loss of the enemy, both would have been increased had Bernadotte, in conformity with his instructions, moved up by Overburg and Apolda to support Davoust. Nevertheless, his sudden appearance on the field, about 3 p.m., obliged the old Field Marshal Mollendorf, who attempted to rally his division, and check the impetuous advance of our right and centre, to retreat. This finished the affair, and a brilliant one it was, leaving us nothing to do but to pursue our flying opponents.

Forty standards—three hundred pieces of cannon—forty thousand prisoners, of whom thirty were general officers—twenty-five thousand killed or wounded—immense magazines and munitions of war—were the fruits of this memorable day, and the glorious proofs of the bravery of the French army, and the military genius of the Emperor.

My share of the action was trifling, being confined to one charge, when the Prussian troops began to give way. Till three o'clock I had been a silent spectator of the scene, moving about with my corps of the guard, as the Emperor thought our services were likely to be required. Ever expecting the word to "charge," which though it appeared constantly on his lips, did not salute our impatient ears.

At length, when the serried ranks of the Prussians were broken, and the dense masses became confused, and turned and fled—"Grenadiers of the Guard—forward—charge,"—became the cry, and putting our horses to their speed, we bore down on the flying foe, sabring and riding down all that opposed our progress. "Halt—form," was the word. Again we formed for the charge—again bore down on the fugitives, few asking, still fewer receiving, quarter, till the work of destruction was considered to be complete, and the bugles sounded the recall.

Among the individual acts of bravery of which I was an eyewitness, one particularly deserves to be recorded. Our trumpeter, carried away by the ardour of the pursuit, found himself surrounded by a number of Prussians. Called upon to surrender, he replied by killing the foremost of his adversaries, hut receiving many sabre-cuts, one of which went through his trumpet as it lay upon his thigh, and a ball at the same moment breaking his arm, he gave himself up for lost, and dropped his reins, which were soon seized by a Prussian dragoon, who endeavoured to drag him along. His presence of mind never forsook him, and watching a favourable moment, he wheeled suddenly round, and driving his spurs into the sides of his horse, galloped back to our ranks amidst the cheers of his comrades. His courage was rewarded by a trumpet of honour, which the Emperor ordered him to be decorated with.

CHAPTER 34

Berlin

How often, in after years, when a prisoner in the gloomy island of St. Helena, wistfully gazing on the white sails which sped over the ocean towards that France to which he was never destined to return in life (though I trust his remains may go there), insensible alike to the praise and censure of the world, from which he was excluded, must the mind of Napoleon have dwelt on the passages of former years, and on none with less regret than those of 1806, which witnessed the memorable campaign of Prussia. How often have I recalled them, together with the devotion, amounting almost to idolatry, with which he was regarded by the troops he so frequently led to victory. Himself "every inch a soldier," he knew our wants and our privations; and while the strict arm of discipline kept us in our places, he was the first after a great battle to care for the wounded. But for him my poor brother Jaques had never been carried alive from the field of Austerlitz; but for him many a gallant fellow, Russian as well as French, who now lived to dare the power of death in the battle strife, had never risen again from the cold sod on which he fell; and now the roar of artillery, and the crash of charging squadrons over, his attention was again directed to the wounded; an attention which he took care always to pay, regarding it as the sacred duty of every general.

On the field he released six thousand Saxons, with three hundred officers of all grades, and dismissed them to their homes, first exacting a declaration that they should not again bear arms against France or her allies.

Pursuit of the enemy was carried on hotly, the object of the Emperor being to prevent his rallying; and when the King of Prussia asked for an armistice of six weeks, he replied "that it was not prudent after a victory to allow the enemy to collect his scattered forces." Foiled in this, the King asked for a truce of three days to allow them to bury their dead. "Think of the living," replied Napoleon, "and leave to us the care of interring the dead; there is no occasion for a truce for that." It is certain that the demand was as ridiculous as the reply was suitable; nevertheless the Prussians scattered abroad a report of an armistice, and many of our generals believing it, suffered some columns to pass. However, when the trick was tried upon Marshal Soult by General Kalkreuth, who positively asserted the existence of the armistice, the former replied "that it was impossible the Emperor could have been guilty of such a folly, and that he would believe it when he received official notice of it." Kalkreuth desired to see him, and an interview took place.

"What would you, Marshal?" said General Kalkreuth. "The Duke of Brunswick is dead, all our generals are killed, wounded, or taken, the greater part of our army in retreat; surely your success is great enough. The king has asked for a suspension of arms, and it is impossible but the Emperor must grant it." "Monsieur, the general," replied Marshal Soult, "it is not long since we have acted against you, and now that you are defeated you appeal to our generosity, forgetting an instant after the magnanimity we have shown towards you. After the battle of Austerlitz the Emperor granted the Russians an armistice- That armistice saved their army, and now behold the unworthy manner in which they act, burning, it is said, to meet us again, and wipe out their disgrace. Had they been equally generous as we were, they would have surely appreciated the moderation we displayed in the hour of victory, and left us to ourselves. What have we done to provoke the unjust war you have waged against us; a war which you commenced with all the *gaité de cœur* imaginable, but which has been checked by the battle of Jena, which in all probability will decide the campaign. Our duty is to inflict all the evils upon you which we can possibly effect; to that duty we are devoted; lay down your arms, and in that situation I will await the orders of the Emperor."

What could the Prussian reply; foiled in his argument, beaten by the force of truth in his attempt to deceive, he silently retired, and immediately the French flew to arms, and hostilities were recommenced, the result being his defeat.

While these things took place, Murat on his side advanced with the cavalry on Erfurt, and accorded an honourable capitulation to the troops which had taken refuge there, taking at the same time twenty pieces of cannon. Napoleon now occupied Weimar, living in the same palace which the Queen of Prussia had resided in, while she precipitately fled before those whose defeat she thought to have witnessed, and, with the king, narrowly escaped being taken by Marshal Soult at Greusen. If this princess, by her fatal influence over the counsels of Frederick, did bring misery and disgrace on his kingdom and arms, still she had great claims on them, sharing his reverses with firmness and constancy, and cheering him in his misfortunes, never quitting his side.

Kalkreuth having retired precipitately on Magdebourg, was pursued by Soult, who took eleven thousand men, thirty pieces of artillery, and more then two hundred caissons and baggage wagons. This city had been named as the rallying point of the Prussian army, and a *corps de reserve* under Prince Eugene of Wurtemberg directed its march there, to which other columns from the interior of Prussia were also hurrying; but Soult's division appeared before the town with such rapidity, that these different columns had not even time to throw themselves within the walls. Vigorously attacked by Legrand's division, in a sort of entrenched camp, they threw down their arms; the town was quickly invested, but the weakness of the immense cordon which it was necessary to form, allowed the King again to escape and to retire behind the Oder. Bernadotte in the meanwhile attacked a reserve of twenty-five thousand men at Halle, and after an obstinate engagement, succeeded in capturing five thousand, twenty-five pieces of cannon, and two standards.

Lannes advanced on Dessau, but the Prince of Wurtemberg destroyed the bridge and checked his advance. Nevertheless three days afterwards we entered Potsdam, at the same time that Davoust advanced on Berlin. The other corps of the army followed by different routes, and, by concentrating, destroyed more of the fragments of the Russian army.

Napoleon arrived in Potsdam, and there contemplated the simple tomb which enshrouds the remains of the great Frederick. Seizing, with enthusiasm, the sword-belt and cordon of the Black Eagle, which formerly adorned that illustrious monarch, he exclaimed, "I had rather these than twenty millions, for I will present them to the governor of the *Invalides*, by whom they will be preserved as a memorable witness of the triumphs of the grand army, and of the vengeance which it has inflicted for the disasters of Rosbach."[1]

On the 18th of May, 1807, the sword, &c, were translated to the Hotel *des Invalides*, when Mons. Fontanes, President of the Legislative Council, pronounced a discourse terminating in the following words:

> In former times, when in a city, the mistress of the world, an illustrious Roman had suspended on the walls of the capital the spoils of the kingdom of Macedon, he was affected, even to tears, at the remembrance of the exploits of Alexander the Great, and of the calamities which had befallen his successors. The hero of France was scarcely less affected, when, on entering the sad and desert palace, which was formerly occupied with so much eclat by the hero of Prussia, he seized with a religious enthusiasm this sword, which he has so nobly presented to his veterans, but with a delicacy worthy of himself he desired that the arms and the standards, together with the mass of trophies taken from the descendants of the late king, should not traverse the place where his ashes repose, further to desecrate his manes or insult his memory.

---

1. Frederick the Great having won the battle of Rosbach on the 5th of November, 1757, erected a monument on the field of battle, which was inscribed to the defeat of the French, but Napoleon, after the battle of Jena, a battle equally celebrated as that of its predecessor, removed the column, and had it taken to France.

The entry of Napoleon into Berlin was triumphant, a deputation of the principal inhabitants meeting him and presenting the keys. He, in a short time, restored order and abundance, and then, to bear witness to the bravery of his troops, he addressed them in a proclamation, telling them of what they had done and what remained to be achieved.

I have said that the devotion evinced by the soldiers towards their Emperor amounted almost to idolatry, and he truly loved them, and this mutual attachment formed a community of glory, which, in the hour of peril or the day of battle, did not fail to operate on all generous hearts. It is true that great talents make illustrious captains, but their reputation is deficient, if humanity and clemency do not heighten their other brilliant qualities. None more than Napoleon possessed these two virtues so worthy of a throne, and of numerous examples which fell under my personal knowledge I shall relate one which happened at Berlin.

The Emperor held a levee, which was attended by the whole of the generals and staff officers of the army, the municipal authorities, and some of the principal inhabitants of Berlin. Among the rest was the Prince of Hatzfeld, who, on passing out of the palace, was arrested. I was on duty, and the consternation was extreme; the officer in charge, however, was certain as to his prisoner, and soon satisfied me that he had warrant for what he had done, for letters addressed to General Hohenlohe had been intercepted, letters fully confirming the accusation of having while the pretended friend of France, travelled out of his line as civil governor of Berlin, and instructed the enemy of our movements.

For this offence he was to be tried by a military tribunal, by which he would inevitably have been condemned to death. His wife, who was the daughter of the minister Schulembourg, demanded an audience of the Emperor, and threw herself at his feet, believing that the hatred which her father was known to entertain towards the French was the cause of his arrest. Napoleon raised her from her kneeling position, and informed her that certain papers, in the hand-writing of her husband, had exposed the double part he was playing, and that the laws of war knew no pardon for such crime.

"Impossible, Sire," said the Princess; "some enemy of my unfortunate husband must have forged them to ensure his destruction." "You know the hand-writing of your husband," said the Emperor; "I will make you the judge, at the same time putting a letter into her hands.

The unhappy Princess, who was near her confinement, was in a lamentable state of distress at thus witnessing the incontestible proof of her husband's guilt, and again throwing herself on her knees, in cries of pitiable anguish bespoke the Emperor's clemency.

Touched with her distress, the Emperor said, "The letter you hold in your hand is the sole proof of your husband's guilt which I possess; rise, Madame," and, pointing to the fire, "that destroyed he is free." The Princess obeyed, and a few seconds saw every vestige of the letter destroyed, restoring to the arms of an unhappy lady the husband who three hours later would have been shot.

This affair quickly got wind, for the Princess related it in every house she went into, and surely such magnanimity ought to give the lie to the frequent assertion of contemporary writers that Napoleon was a monster deficient in every virtue; to us who knew him well it did but add another leaf to that crown of immortality which his conduct in the field and the cabinet was fast acquiring him.

Chapter 35

Prussia

After the battle came the rewards to the victors—the naming of officers to fill the vacancies occasioned by the fortune of war. Davoust's division, with the Imperial Guard, were reviewed by the Emperor in person at Berlin, and a splendid field-day we had; but although the guard had partaken but slightly in the affray, I missed many familiar faces that would have been gladly welcomed.

As Napoleon rode on the ground, surrounded by a brilliant staff, every cap was raised—every tongue was loosed; loud cries of "*Vive l'Empereur! Vive la France!*" burst from the ranks, making the welkin ring, and waking up the echoes of the spot. Having filled up the vacancies, and named the soldiers to whom decorations were to be given, the Emperor desired the troops to ground their arms; and, having formed the officers and sub-officers into a circle, he said:

> Officers and sub-officers of the third division of the army, you have covered yourselves with glory by your conduct in the field of Jena—the recollection will quit me only at my latest breath. The brave men who have fallen have fallen with glory, and it should be the prayer of every one of us that his fate may be as glorious.

More stirring scenes demanded us, and although I would willingly have lingered in the gay city of Berlin, the call of duty must be obeyed. How immutable are the decrees of fate! I had been present when the First Consul dictated his mandate from the vice-regal palace of the Archduke at Milan; had helped to give publicity to the proclamation dictated from the palatial mansion at Munich; I had kept guard at Vienna when Napoleon occupied the palace of the successor of the Cæsars; and now the royal residence of Prussia was the abode of the soldier of fortune, who had stepped from the ranks of the artillery to the dazzling height of first magistrate of France—pulling down and setting up kings—overwhelming with his brave troops the ancient monarchies of the world, and instituting new laws, dictating fresh ordinances. We came like the sulphury breath of the *simoom*, leaving death and destruction in our track; but, like the genial shower which succeeds the thunder, restoring order, plenty, and happiness to the land.

But we had only scotched the snake, not killed it; great as had been the loss of the Prussian monarch, he was not yet subdued. Though we occupied his capital, his generals still made head in the provinces; so Bernadotte left Brandenbourg for Orangebourg, whither Murat had already advanced against Blucher and Hohenlohe, who were obliged by this movement to fall back on Mechlenbourg. Lasalle fell in with the Prussians at Zednik, where, after a smart faction, he succeeded in capturing three hundred men of the Queen's regiment, together with the standard, embroidered by her Majesty's own hands; while Murat advanced on Samplin and Prentzlow. General Milhaud, detached towards Boitzenburg, was in danger of being turned at Vigninsdorf by the grenadiers of the king, when Grouchy coming up to his support, fell upon them, taking five hundred prisoners and four standards.

In the meanwhile Hohenlohe, who stood his ground at Prewtzlow, was obliged to capitulate. Six thousand men—almost all infantry of the *Garde Royale d'élite*—six regiments of cavalry, forty-five standards, and sixty pieces of artillery, were the result of this affair; while on the morrow six thousand men of the same corps surrendered to some regiments of dragoons and chasseurs: Lannes, who had advanced on Stettin with the division of light cavalry, summoned the governor, who opened the gates, giving up six thousand men and sixty pieces of cavalry, which defended the fortress.

Great as were our successes—immense as were our trophies—numerous as were our prisoners, Blucher had been suffered to escape by a mistake which happened to General Klein at Weissensée. Under the false pretext of an armistice, he fled with six thousand men towards Rostock, where, reinforced by the column of the Prince of Weimar on the bank of the Wahren, he hoped to embark and gain the Baltic; but finding himself cut off from Stralsund, and hotly pursued by our cavalry and Bernadotte's corps, he threw himself into Schwerin, after having lost four thousand men. Attacked at Schwerin, he resisted long enough to cover his retreat on Lubeck. A sharp engagement between bis cavalry and our own gave time to the Swedes who occupied the place to embark and fly; while the infantry, shut up in Lubeck, showed a determination to make a stand, hut the redoubts which defended the gates were carried at the point of the bayonet, and then, troops entering the town, the streets became the scene of a hand to hand conflict, and the Prussians in vain attempted to fly—the advanced guard under Soult were at their heels. Broken, dispirited, they fled to the bastions, and, laying down their arms, surrendered at discretion. Blucher, who had sought an asylum on the frontiers of Denmark, with his cavalry, was again attacked by Drouet's division, and capitulated at Schewartau.

Our life was, indeed, one of desperate fatigue, although a succession of triumphs. Each day in the saddle, the trumpet sounded the advance, the enemy's corps were charged, prisoners taken, sent to the rear, the men bivouacked on the field to awake and re-enact the same scenes on the morrow. No courier, riding post, spent more hours in the saddle than did the cavalry—no recruit at a punishment drill was under arms more hours than the infantry—forced marches were the order of the day, and if our hands were never idle our feet were never at rest. Twenty thousand prisoners, four thousand horses, an immense number of killed and wounded, one hundred pieces of cannon, and the last Prussian standard that floated in the breeze on the left bank of the Oder, were the results of the reduction of Lubeck and Schewartau.

While these brilliant successes crowned the efforts of that corps of the army to which I was attached, extending our conquest to the very shore of the Baltic, Ney, on his side, was not idle; Mortier and Savory seconded his efforts, till the whole of the Hanseatic towns and the ports at the mouths of the rivers of Germany successively fell into our hands.

The end of the year approached—the army of the King of Prussia was destroyed—his estates were summoned—and, reduced to despair, he implored the generosity of the conqueror, as the Emperors of Austria and Russia had done before him, and Napoleon granted a suspension of arms, which took place on the 16th of November, 1806, in the hope of establishing a treaty of peace. This, so desirable an end, was not accomplished, for the Russians were advancing by forced marches, and we once more assumed a warlike attitude.

Our army was in position as follows—Ney, Soult, and Bernadotte occupied Berlin; Mortier, Lannes, and Augereau Hamburg, Thorn, Bromberg, and Grandentz; Davoust with his corps, and Murat with the cavalry division, Beaumont, Klein, Becher, Nansouty, and Milhaud marched on Posen and Warsaw. The corps under the orders of Jerome Napoleon invested all the places in Silesia, and besieged Glogau, the Imperial Guard and the staff remaining at Berlin, Potsdam, and Charlottenbourg, while the corps of reserve coming from Bas-Rhin marched in divers columns by Munster, Osnabruck, and Minden to follow the movements of the grand army.

Thus may be said to have terminated the campaign of Prussia. I had commenced a simple captain of cavalry, decorated with the cross of the Legion of Honour, but short, sharp and decisive as it had been, my advancement was as rapid. From captain I had advanced to be *chef d'escadron*—the order of the iron crown of Italy hung side by side with the cross of the legion—my brother had gained a sous-lieutenancy in my corps, and everything promised well for our further advancement.

We did not much regret that, though winter with all its horrors was coming on, the treaty of peace had never been concluded, and prepared for the cessation of the suspension of arms, and the order to advance into Prussia. A new enemy awaited us, for the Swedish monarch, blind to the designs of a neighbour, who would have been the first to annihilate him had the French army been routed at Jena, joined the Russians; but the prestige of success hung over us, "we had," said Napoleon, "been successful everywhere; from the banks of the Po to those of the Oder, and what right had the Russians to believe they held the balance of fate? what gave them the right to reverse its just decrees? Were we not the soldiers who conquered at Austerlitz?"

CHAPTER 36

Eylau

As Napoleon had announced in his last proclamation he advanced into Poland, and the army, animated by his presence, pressed forwards to Warsaw, the capital, the head quarters being at Posen.

Murat's cavalry and Davoust's corps having passed the Vistula, took Praga, where the latter established his head quarters, Murat remaining on the banks of the Bug. Ney passed the Vistula at Thorn, pushing his advanced posts as far as Sharburg and the surrounding villages, and falling in with a part of the Russian force, which he soon compelled to retire, on which Davoust passed the Bug with his whole force.

The Emperor arrived, and business began in earnest. The enemy's entrenchments at Czarnowo, on the Warta, were ordered to be carried, but being defended by 15,000 men, the command was not easily obeyed. Obstinate as was the resistance they were at last forced to succumb, seeking safety in flight, and abandoning six pieces of cannon.

Daily skirmishes occurred between the enemy and different corps of the French army until the beginning of February, when on the 7th of that month, on arriving at Eylau, a town of Prussia, eleven leagues south of Konigsburg, we found the Russians in full force, occupying a position which, only a quarter of a league distant from the town, defended the plain. Marshal Soult received orders to carry this plain, which he attempted to do with two regiments of the line, who were received warmly; and a column of cavalry, at the moment of the advance, charging the left flank of one of these regiments, threw them into disorder, and placed one half of the men *hors de combat*. To remedy this, Klein's dragoons, with Hautpoult's cuirassiers, and several other regiments of infantry and cavalry were ordered up, and falling upon the advancing foe, mowed down whole ranks, throwing them into disorder, which quickly arrested their progress, and the position was carried, a great number of men and guns falling into our hands.

Legrand's division bivouacked before the town, that of St. Hilaire on the right; Augereau's corps was placed on the left, while that of Davoust marched to fall on Eylau and the enemy's flank, if he did not change his position. Ney was marching forwards with a view of passing his right flank, and the cavalry under Murat were in the rear of the whole of these corps. In this position the army passed the night, Napoleon in the centre of the guard bivouacking on the plain.

The night was a bitterly cold one, a sharp hoar frost covering the ground with glittering icicles, and chilling our very life's-blood. Seated round a watch-fire with half a dozen companions, endeavouring to while away the time by smoking and drinking, and ever and anon breaking into some wild chorus or bacchanalian song, little heeding its progress, or the events that were passing around us, we had remained for two or three hours, when Le Beaujolais, an officer who had lately joined, was called upon to explain by what accident he had left Paris, where the whole of his military career had hitherto passed. It seemed that love affair with a protege of the Empress had led to his dismissal from the court, for, having had the imprudence to address himself to Josephine, she had requested his removal, and he had been ordered to join the guards at Posen.

To a youth brought up amid the dissipation of the capital, the change was anything but an agreeable one, and he was blaming the Emperor for the lot that had befallen him, when he felt a hand placed on his shoulder, and the very man stood beside him, his small bright eyes beaming full upon him, as if he would read his very soul.

"And how long, sir," said the Emperor, "have you taken upon yourself to canvass the actions of your superiors? In what campaigns have you joined? At what actions have you been present, that your services have been unrequited? You complain of a want of due reward; how have you deserved it?"

Now it was well known to us all that Le Beaujolais owed his present position to family influence, and not to his own deserts. Though a captain in the guard, this was his first campaign; and he had been advanced to his present grade over the heads of men who had witnessed Marengo and Austerlitz.

"Where have you been, *coquin*?" repeated Napoleon, the watch-fire throwing its lurid light upon his face, now pale with rage; "where have you fought that you dare to murmur at the *guardon* for your service? Are Rivoli, Arcole, the Pyramids Marengo, Austerlitz, Jena, written upon your brow, or do honours fall more thickly in the salon than on the battle-field? Take this (giving him a packet addressed to Marshal Soult), and see that your conduct in the field to-morrow merits the reward of which you seem to be so covetous; but beware! I will check that spirit of cavilling which seems to have taken possession of thee, or worse may come of it."

Le Beaujolais, not less thunderstruck by this unexpected scene, than we who had witnessed it, sneaked off, and soon the clattering hoofs of his retiring charger gave evidence that one part at least of the Emperor's mandate had been obeyed.

On the 8th, at break of day, the enemy began the attack by a brisk cannonade on the town and St. Hilaire's division. Napoleon, with Augereau's corps, advanced, and opened a battery of forty pieces. The enemy's troops, ranged in dense columns, received the whole of the discharge, together with that of some howitzers, and appeared determined to escape this murderous fire by an attempt to turn our left; but the tirailleurs of Davoust's division came upon their rear, while Augereau's division debouched at the tame time in columns to engage the centre. Thus hindered from attacking Davoust, he hesitated, and St. Hilaire's division appearing on the right, a series of manœuvres were executed for the purpose of uniting these two latter divisions with the former. Hardly had these commenced, when a thick snow came on, covering both armies and concealing them from each other.

This obscurity, which lasted for half an hour, caused Marshal

Augereau to lose his point of direction, and he moved too much to the left; but at the moment the air became clear, Napoleon happily perceived the mistake, and ordered Murat and Bessières to turn St. Hilaire's division, and fell upon the Russians—a bold manœuvre, rendered necessary by the position of our columns. The enemy's cavalry which opposed this movement were annihilated, after having rallied again and again; while two lines of Russian infantry shared the same fate, and gave us the victory.

Nevertheless, although the disasters of the Russians had been great, our loss was considerable. Three hundred cannon had vomited destruction on our ranks for at least twelve hours, and the victory for a long time rendered uncertain by the mistake of Augereau, was only decided when Davoust debouched on the plain and fell upon the enemy. If Bernadotte had come up in time to have taken part in the action, the whole Russian army must have succumbed; as it was, many escaped; and we had to regret the loss of several brave officers and men, among whom was General Haultpoult, who fell while leading on his regiment of cuirassiers.

The enemy, completely hemmed in between Ney and Davoust, and fearing to have his rear guard cut off, resolved at eight o'clock in the evening on a night attack, to retake the village of Schanaditten, then occupied by one of our regiments. Several of his grenadier battalions which had not been engaged advanced to take the village, but being warmly received, were beaten off, and, thrown into disorder, quickly retired.

On the morrow we advanced to the Frickling, hanging on the enemy's rear, who was obliged to retire behind the Prégel. He left the field of battle, at Eylau, covered with dead, lost 12,000 prisoners, eighteen standards, more than fifty pieces of artillery, with equipages in proportion, and found himself, as the consequence of this bloody reverse, thrown back upwards of forty leagues from the Vistula. This event allowed our harassed troops some days of rest and repose.

On the 9th Napoleon personally inspected the position occupied by each corps on the preceding day; the country was entirely covered by a thick snow, through which peered the bodies of the slain, and the fragments of the battle field, every here and there a patch of blood, presenting an awful contrast with the whiteness of the earth elsewhere. The spots which had witnessed the charges of the cavalry were especially marked by the number of horses, dead, wounded, and abandoned, while detachments of our troops, and large bodies of the Russian prisoners were seen employed on every side, turning over the vast masses on this field of carnage, and carrying the wounded towards the ambulances or the town.

Long lines of Russian carcasses, wounded, mutilated, dead, and dying, arms and haversacks, marked the spots where each battalion had fallen; each squadron been mown down. The dead were heaped upon the dying, in the midst of caissons, burnt or broken, of guns dismounted or overthrown.

Napoleon stopped before each lot of the wounded and addressing them in their own language, promised them assistance, and offered them consolation. Many were dressed in his presence, and the Chasseurs of his guard transported them on their horses, while the officers of the household were desired to assist them. The Russians, in place of that death which they awaited with resignation, in accordance with the absurd prejudices which had been inculcated, found a generous conqueror, and in their astonishment prostrated themselves before him, raising their stiffened limbs towards him in token of their gratitude. The consolatory regard of that great man seemed to soften the horrors of death, and to diffuse around this horrible scene some scattered grains of comfort and hope.

After the battle, one of the general officers of the Emperor seeing him distressed at the loss of so many of his veteran troops—troops who had given him such constant proofs of their attachment and their bravery—observed to him that the loss had been exaggerated.

"A father who has just lost his children," said Napoleon, "does not appreciate the victory; when the heart speaks, even glory is robbed of its illusion." Nothing can be more correct or more touching than these words; and the Emperor, who felt them more forcibly than any other man, was always greatly distressed whenever in the battle he saw fall around him more of his veteran troops than he had feared before its commencement.

Our troops now made a retrogade movement, to wait for a season more congenial for military operations. As a thaw had rendered the roads impassable, it was impossible to advance, and ten days after the battle of Eylau the army retired into winter quarters.

Bernadotte occupied Braunsberg, Fraunsberg, Elbing, and Preusch Holland; Soult, Liestadt and Mohrungen; Ney concentrated his corps at Gutstadt and Heilsberg; Davoust was at Allenstein, Warterburg, Passenheim, and Ortelsburg; Lannes and Massena were stationed on the Omulew and the Naren, as far as Ostrolenka; while Augereau's troops were distributed among the different corps of the array; and Napoleon, with the guard, established his headquarters at Osterode.

In this order the Emperor disposed his army, and awaited the return of a more genial season; the disposition of the troops presenting a good line of operations, free from all danger of surprise, at the same time affording the necessary supplies.

CHAPTER 37

Osterode

Notwithstanding the in activity of the main body of the French army, daily skirmishes took place at the distant outposts, but the difficulties of the roads, the accumulation of frost and snow, together with the severity of the weather, prevented any great movement, and we fell into that inactivity at Osterode which, if not the parent of evil, proved the origin of as fatal consequences, for I have invariably found that during the listlessness entailed by garrison duty in winter quarters, attachments, or rather those *liasons* which are too often dignified by the name of attachments, spring up "thick as the leaves in Valambrosa."

Our occupations were confined to those watches and necessary parades which our presence in an enemy's country rendered indispensable, but the inclemency of the season prevented field-days and the mere routine of guard was easily dispensed with; added to which our quarters were not the most comfortable—though by those who had braved Nature in the region of eternal snows, during the passage of the St. Bernard, the comforts of a barrack were unheeded.

My brother, warned perhaps by my fate, mindful of my experience, or of a less inflammable temperament than myself, had never yielded himself a slave to the *beau sexe,* and consequently had not been the victim of those indiscretions into which young men on their first entering into life usually fall. It was my care sedulously to watch over him, and to inculcate those lessons and that information which subsequent events in the service had impressed upon me as so necessary to his advancement, and thus had many a weary hour been lightened of its dullness—many a lingering watch enlivened.

Thus time sped, and our sojourn at Osterode was rendered more pleasant by the good luck of getting into the house of a citizen who was what is called "well to do in the world"; and thus pleasantly matters might have gone on, but for an event which I am about to relate.

Attached to the Chasseurs of the Guard in the capacity of suttling woman was Christine Legrot, whose husband, Antoine Legrot, had fallen at Marengo, leaving her, with an only child, to the mercy of the wide world and the fortune of war. Little Annette was an universal favourite; and as she advanced to womanhood, not few and far between were the soft speeches poured into her ear by the gay youngsters of the different corps; and yet, though her manners were free—free as the license of a camp and her situation allowed, still no breath of reproach had sullied her fair fame—she had as yet passed through the fiery ordeal untainted.

In the Grenadiers of the Guard was Augustin Noel, a sub-officer, who was said to be the last representative of a family which had seen better days; if this were the fact, no one would have believed it on seeing him, for assuredly nature had not shown much regard for his external appearance, having bestowed upon him a coarse and forbidding exterior, and an absolutely ugly countenance. Dirty and untidy in his person, the disgrace and ridicule of his company, Augustin seemed to pursue the even tenor of his way, and had made the different campaigns without aspiring to a higher grade than that which he acquired at Marengo. I had known him for some time, having been on guard with him frequently. Forbidding as was the external man, his heart seemed as sensible to the softer emotions as that of the handsomest fellow in the army, and, strange to say, Annette became the object of his passion.

The noise of this attachment was bruited abroad, and the subject of it most unmercifully roasted by the youngsters; still he persevered, and surprising as it may appear, that a young woman, adorned with all the graces of youth and beauty, should marry a man who, in point of years, was much more suitable as a helpmate for her mother, it actually took place; and shortly before the battle of Jena they were united; but what means were used to induce two such incongruous beings to plight their faith to each other was a mystery, though rumour occasionally whispered that the mother had been detected by Noel in some peccadillo, from which nothing but the sacrifice of her daughter's hand could rescue her. Some such overwhelming influence must have operated on the mind of Annette to induce one so young, so gay and beautiful, to link her fate with that of a man so many years her senior—one who was ugly, ignorant, and morose.

Though a change had come over her manners, and the gay and lively girl had sobered into the sedateness of married life—though her face had lost its freshness, her cheeks the roses, her eye the brightness that charmed all who knew her, Annette never complained, but continued to serve the mess to which her mother was attached, if not with her former readiness and pleasure, at least with every appearance of content; and although many tales of her attachments were occasionally noised abroad, her conduct as a wife was irreproachable. At times, however, when her brute of a husband came home in a worse temper than usual, the big tear would silently steal down her cheek, and her manner become sad and *distrait,* yet word of complaint never passed her lips, and after a desperate effort at composure, her mind seemed to recover its wonted firmness.

She was a general favourite, and oftentimes after the fatigues and dangers of the day, the mess provided by Annette welcomed the survivors, and warmed their hearts towards the young being whose lot seemed cast so differently to what it should have been.

And thus the time passed away, Christine becoming more fat and immoveable, Augustin more morose and unkind, Annette more careless, till at last the flatteries of our sex, and her lonely condition, exerted their baneful influence upon her, and she became a wicked, wilful, malicious coquette, yet though nothing tangible had been proved against her, dark whispers of secret meetings, and stealthy assignations, began to dim her fair fame.

Jaques had long been one of the crowd of idlers who had basked in the sunshine of her smiles, and had for some time suspected the author of these rumours, who, himself a disappointed suitor for her favours, had threatened her with exposure unless she consented to give him a meeting, and this, from fear for the result, she was silly enough to do. Having overheard this appointment, my brother determined to be an unseen witness of it, and, concealing himself, was pretty soon convinced that however presumptuous the wishes of Dupont may have been, they bad no chance of being gratified. The brute tried force, and a scream soon bringing Jaques to her assistance, the ruffian fled; when thoroughly convinced of her innocence, he lectured her for her imprudence, and saw her home.

"Ah! lieutenant," she exclaimed, as together they threaded the dark and narrow street of Osterode, "you little know the persecution that I have endured from that man. Fool that I was to listen to his vows, brainless idiot to suppose that one like him could have any affection for me, I ought never to have given him the meeting; a meeting which but for your timely assistance would have rendered me the scorn of every café and cabaret to which the wretch can get admittance. How shall I ever repay your kindness in thus rescuing an innocent but imprudent girl from what would have been worse than death?"

"But Annette," said Jaques, "you ought to be aware that an act perfectly innocent in itself may wear the appearance of guilt, quite as plainly as if the crime had been committed; why then give him room to talk by affording him this interview?"

"Alas, you know not the influence be possesses over me. To fear, not love, was it accorded, but it shall be the last."

Poor Jaques, thus suddenly become the confidant of a young and lovely woman, was soon sensible of the peril of his position. I had marked his frequent visits to her home, and, exerting my influence, persuaded him to absent himself. For a few days they did not meet, till a casual rencontre in the street, in which she reproached him for his unkindness, again induced him to return, fancying that he might enjoy her society as formerly, without the danger of becoming attached to her. Again his visits were renewed; again he and Annette met even more often than before, and my absence for a short time having removed his monitor, he was seldom long from her presence, till like the insect fluttering round the flame, he approached too near, and he gave himself up to her entirely. Need I say he loved—ardently, devotedly, passionately—and yet so frequently had he watched her flirtations with others, that he thought he could bear them when addressed to himself, and when the unwelcome truth forced itself upon him, he was in despair.

No spark of jealousy had inflamed the mind of Augustin; possessed of her as his wife, he abandoned her to whatsoever society she thought fit, passing most of his time, when not on duty, in a cabaret hard by, caring little for her presence, or the comforts of her home, till at length the usual sequel to such attachments ensued, and Annette fell; and now rumour, with her hundred tongues, became more busy than before, but so well had they arranged their assignations, that no party was privy to them, and though Christine suspected her, Augustin still was silent, and if the breath of reproach did rest upon her, there, was many a fine fellow in the camp ready to wash out the blot in the blood of the utterer.

It was Jaques's first passion—intense, absorbing, consuming—the food on which he lived, the air he breathed; and when the spring approached, and returning vegetation gave us notice that we must soon be stirring, and that there was every probability that they must separate, Jaques urged her to abandon her husband, and fly with him. She had appeared devoted to him, and listened patiently at first, seeming to approve the proposal, but latterly it appeared more distasteful to her, added to which, a gay cornet of dragoons had seemed to find favour in her sight; and Jaques, whose attachment remained undiminished, was occasionally reminded that his presence was *de trop*. During the early period of their acquaintance, he had forced upon her a few trifling presents which she had accepted with reluctance; now, what ever was offered, was received with cordiality, nor did she scruple to wear in his presence the *cadeaux* of his rival. Still, at times, as if the feeling were only glossed over, not obliterated, a portion of her wonted warmth returned—she rallied Jaques on his jealousy, as if she, who had vowed to love but him, could ever forsake him for another; and he, poor fool, cajoled by her wiles, shut his eyes and ears to the evidence of his own senses. The truth was, that Annette was incapable of a firm and lasting attachment; but to a devoted mind nothing can give such pain and uneasiness as the belief that the being on whom its affections have been lavished is unworthy of them. Jacques had not yet learned the unwelcome truth, though it was gradually forcing itself upon him—yet was he unwilling to acknowledge it.

The dragoons were ordered to move, and, the morning they departed, Annette was absent from her home. In vain Jaques sought her in her accustomed haunts—the too damning fact at last became apparent—she was gone! and gone with the man whose attachment and attentions she had encouraged, while she professed to ridicule them. And this was woman's love! and thus was another chapter added to the dark history I had learnt.

Bright days beamed anew for us. Dantzic was invested, and opened its gates to General Lefebvre, affording us supplies in abundance. The Russians approached the Passage, a little river of which we occupied the right bank. Many skirmishes took place prior to the 5th of June, on which day we advanced in columns by different directions on Heilsberg, situate on the Allé, twelve, leagues south of Konigsberg, where the enemy's force was united in a camp, the position of which he had rendered impregnable by entrenchments and numerous batteries, to establish which had caused him four months uninterrupted labour.

On the evening of the 10th, we approached the Russian lines, and our light troops made a slight attack on the advanced works, but intimidated, no doubt, by the audacity of the French, and the preliminary movements of Napoleon, the enemy declined the battle.

On the 11th, the Emperor, in person, carefully examined the position of the Russian General, Beningsen, and decided on his movements and the order of battle.

CHAPTER 38

Friedland

General Beningsen having discovered that the various manœuvres of the French were made with a view to force him to an engagement, which he wished to avoid, or else to hem him in his formidable position, prudently retired in the night, and passed to the right bank of the Allé; yet, able as this movement was, it only retarded his defeat two days.

On the 12th of June, the Emperor having received reports, of the position of his force, fixed his head quarters at Eylau. The troops were ordered to march immediately; Murat, Soult, and Davoust being instructed to advance on Konigsberg to cut off the enemy's retreat, while, at the head of the corps of Ney, Lannes, Mortier, Victor, and the Guard, he himself moved on Friedland, a town situated about ten leagues to the south east of Konigsberg.

On the 14th, at three o'clock in the morning, the enemy debouched on the bridge of Friedland. A heavy cannonade commenced, when Napoleon exclaimed, "It is a day of good fortune,.. it is the anniversary of Marengo."

Lannes and Mortier were first engaged, and were supported by Grouchy's dragoons, and Nansouty's cuirassiers. Divers movements, and different changes were made, but the enemy was unable to carry the village of Posthenem. Believing that he was attacked by a division of the army too small to cause him serious inquietude, the Russian general continued his march, for the purpose of investing Konigsberg.

At five o'clock in the afternoon, the different corps of the army having moved into place—Ney on the right, Lannes in the centre, and Mortier on the left, the reserve consisting of the Guard and Victor's division; Grouchy's cavalry supported the left, Latour Maubourg's dragoons the right, those of Lahousaye and the Saxon cuirassiers drawn up behind the centre. This order of battle was magnificent though simple, and might serve as. an example at all times and in all places; it presented a centre, right and left wings, and a reserve, supported by divisions of cavalry. and numerous batteries, and thus displayed on a field of battle, whether it remain fixed or deploys, is extended or concentrated, an army is invincible.

The enemy developed all his force, extending his left Friedland, and his right to the extent of a league on the villages Mullin and Denn.

Napoleon soon reconnoitered his position, exposing himself the greatest dangers; he knew perfectly well that the general in chief ought rarely to run such risk, but such was the strength of his heroic valour, that he often advanced where men less timid dared not to go for fear of being accused of fool-hardiness. He resolved to carry the village of Friedland at once, by executing on the instant a change of front. The right moved up first, and the attack commenced by the flank of that wing, during which, the left formed the pivot for the execution of the movement, keeping the enemy in check, a manœuvre always imposing and advantageous, whether the columns arrest or pursue their march, because it is executed without confusion.

At half-past five, Ney, with his accustomed audacity, threw himself into the thick of the battle, a discharge of twenty pieces of cannon being the signal for his advance. At the same moment, Marchand's division took the direction of the village, and advanced with fixed baronets, while Buisson's division supported it on the left. When the enemy perceived that Ney had quitted the wood, where his right was at the commencement in position, he advanced a column of cavalry, and a multitude of Cossacks, but Latour Maubourg's dragoons were formed at a gallop on the right, and repulsed the charge.

Victor had orders to place, far in advance of his centre, a battery of thirty pieces, which opened a murderous fire on the advancing columns of the Russians, who made different demonstrations to create a diversion, but they were in vain. Ney marched at the head of his division, and was attacked on the right by sundry columns of the Russian infantry, but these were received on the point of the bayonet, and driven back on the Allé, where numbers of them met a watery grave. At the same time his left advanced to the ravine which surrounds Friedland, where the Russian imperial guard, cavalry as well as infantry, lay concealed, these, springing up, advanced with great gallantry, creating a momentary confusion on the left, but Dupont's division in reserve moved up, and meeting the advancing guard, gave them a considerable check.

In vain the enemy, by his reserve and centre, endeavoured to preserve Friedland; the town was carried at the point of the bayonet, the streets being literally choked by the slain.

At this moment the centre, under Lannes, was attacked. The effort which the enemy had made on our extreme right had been unsuccessful; he, therefore, tried a similar one on the centre, with the same result.

The charges of Russian infantry and cavalry failed to arrest the advance of our columns, which Napoleon accompanied, and encouraged; all the bravery—all the constancy of the Russians proved of no avail—they could not stop our career, and fell nobly before the advancing points of our bayonets. Marshal Mortier, who during the whole of the day had kept In check the enemy's right, now advanced, supported by the fusiliers of the guard under General Savary, and completed the discomfiture of the Russians, who in this affair lost 20,000 men killed, and a great number in our hands as prisoners; twenty generals, eighty pieces of cannon, a vast quantity of caissons, of standards, and baggage; the Russian cavalry especially lost an immense number of men and horses.

The retreat of the enemy on the Niemen resembled the most complete rout; at each step we received prisoners, caissons, arms, and baggage. On the 5th of June, the enemy, mistaking our inactivity, attacked us in our cantonments; by the 14th we had conquered at Gutstadt, Heilsberg, and Friedland. In a campaign of ten days we had taken one hundred and twenty pieces of cannon, seventeen standards, killed, wounded, or taken prisoners

60,000 Russians; stripped the army of the enemy of all its magazines, its hospitals, its ambulances; taken Konigsberg, with three hundred vessels found in the port, charged with every kind of munition of war, and 160,000 stand of arms, which had been sent by England to place in the hands of our enemies.

From the banks of the Vistula we had arrived with the rapidity of the eagle at those of the Niemen; and as at Austerlitz we had celebrated the anniversary of the coronation, so at Friedland we celebrated the anniversary of the battle of Marengo.

The battle of Friedland had indeed elevated the French army to the very pinnacle of glory; it had besides the happy effect of affording to an enemy, beaten, dispirited, and without hope, a sample of the conqueror's generosity. Overtures of peace were made and accepted. A raft established on the Niemen was the theatre of the first interview between Napoleon, Alexander, and Frederick William. The French army assembled on the banks of the river, piled its arms, and contemplated in silence the imposing spectacle of its general and emperor giving peace and repose to Europe.

On the 19th of June, Napoleon arrived at Tilsit; on the 7th of July peace was proclaimed, and the Emperor prepared to return to France. In the meanwhile, as the course of events has somewhat outstripped my narrative, I shall return to the morrow of the battle of Friedland, the 15th of June, 1807.

CHAPTER 39

The Hospital

One of the most distinguished of your poets has said:

The cold in clime are cold in blood,
Their love can scarce deserve the name;

but with Jaques, true child of the south, it was different. Since the discovery of Annette's intimacy with the dragoon, with whom she subsequently eloped, he had become an altered man. His love had been at times o'ermastered by a more intense feeling—jealousy—a feeling miserable enough when entertained without a cause, but ten times more miserable when cherished with some reason. Frequent altercations had taken place between the lowers—in vain Annette rallied him on his suspicions—she sometimes succeeded in lulling, though she never eradicated them; and then some secret whisper, some new familiarity, roused them up again, and they blazed as fiercely as ever. Naturally warmhearted, devoted to his first passion with an intensity which must be seen to be appreciated, Jaques had missed no opportunity of snowing her his fidelity; and when the blow came that convinced him of her worthlessness—when the blight fell upon his heart, its utter prostration was apparent.

There were times when, wandering forth alone, he felt oppressed by the sensation that he was entering into a new existence, an existence of penance for his faults, that he was endued with a capacity to suffer, but not one to enjoy; in fact, he began to doubt whether the transient state of this world could ever be one of happiness—or whether happiness were not an unsubstantial creation of the mind, ever apparently within reach but not to be attained—a baseless vision, beautiful to the mind's eye when clothed in the garments of anticipation, but vanishing on its approach like a sweet dream, from which it were misery to awaken. A change would then come over him, and, awaking as it were from the thrall that oppressed him, he seemed to overcome the repugnance to exertion which he felt stealing over him, benumbing his faculties, and devoting himself with more than common ardour to his duties, enjoyed at least for the moment a temporary relief.

On the morning after the battle of Friedland, I was ordered to command the fatigue party, whose duty it was to turn over the saps of mutilated bodies, and to rescue from impending death such of our wounded troops as lay upon the field. Jaques, (who since the departure of his beloved had fought more like a fiend than one of earth's denizens, and courted death in every charge, seeming to bear a charmed life which protected him from the shot of the Russians, no matter how murderous the fire,) formed one of the party, and amongst the earlier victims rescued from the embrace of the destroyer, was the husband of the very woman who had betrayed him—Augustin Noel. A ball had carried away his right leg, while his left arm hung powerless by his side, rendered so by the sabre of a Cossack, and in this state, insensible from loss of blood and the anguish of his wounds, we placed him on the ambulance and conveyed him to the hospital.

Notwithstanding his attachment, between him and Jaques there had always been a good understanding, the latter believing him blind to what was going on, a deception he favoured by not appearing to notice it. Although amputation was quickly performed, consciousness returned only to assure him that he was sinking rapidly, and when Jaques visited the hospital he declared his belief that a few hours only remained to him, and requested his attention to the following recital, which my brother repeated to me immediately on his return to our quarters.

"Lieutenant," said Augustin, speaking with great difficulty, for nature was fast giving way, and his articulation occasionally became low and indistinct, "I feel that my hours are numbered, and am anxious to employ the short space that may be allotted to me in endeavouring to obtain for my misguided wife a friend that may rescue her from her degraded state after I am no more. I know your love for her, passionate and devoted as it is, and though she has forfeited all claim to your affection, you will not refuse her your pity. Say, then, *mon officier*, will you befriend the unhappy girl should you ever have the opportunity?" Moved by his vehemence, Jaques gave the required promise and he resumed.

"No doubt you in common with the other idlers in the camp, have felt surprise that one so young and beautiful should have linked her fate with mine. No doubt conjectures have been rife and rumour busy to account for so strange a proceeding. Listen, and I will explain. Christine, her mother, and myself were children together, and our intimacy continued after she married; for though in circumstances we were upon a par, in birth I considered her my inferior, and when I declined her as a wife she refused to become my mistress. We did not quarrel, and the camp, which levels all distinctions of birth, soon made Antoine and I good friends, and when he was detained on guard I consoled the pretty Christine without once awakening the jealousy of her husband. He fell as a Frenchman should do, fell nobly on the field of battle, and the widow and her daughter were left without any protection save such as I felt disposed to afford them. I did not love the mother well enough now to tie myself to her, and yet in her distress I could not abandon her. Christine soon became careless of her good name, and was accused of robbing the mess by one who had long persecuted Annette with dishonourable proposals. Her daughter's honour was demanded as the price of his secrecy, and as the galleys would have been the alternative Christine entertained the proposal. Becoming: acquainted with the transaction, I determined to frustrate so infamous a scheme, for I loved Annette as my own child, and she entertained a filial affection for me; and knowing how she recoiled from the bargain, I offered to become her husband, assuring her at the same time that I would never claim a husband's privileges. Even death sooner than dishonour; and as she saw no other means of escape we were married. Thus armed, I challenged her persecutor, and he fell by my hand, and at this awful sacrifice was Christine's secret preserved. Heaven is my witness that through the whole affair I had but one motive, the preservation of her who was dear to me as my own child. I religiously adhered to the condition—was her husband in name only; and if after an evening spent in drinking I became sour and morose, it was with Christine, and not her daughter. True, that occasionally the silent tear rolled down her cheek, and looks of unspeakable anguish told of the conflict within; the babbling world ascribed them to my unkindness; she knew me better, and appreciated my forbearance. Knowing that in all probability her unoccupied heart would find some one of her own age with whom it might fall in love, I never felt annoyed at the admiration she excited, hoping that some worthy man would be her choice, and at my decease would make her happy. You know, lieutenant," said Augustin with a ghastly smile, "the lease of life for a grenadier of the guard is never a very long one; most of my companions have fallen around me, and I have long felt convinced my turn was not far distant. When I found that you were her choice, I shut my eyes to the probable consequences of your intimacy, rather rejoicing than otherwise that now she would have a protector, and I might depart in peace. I thought not of her fall, because I anticipated you would repair the fault, but fate decided otherwise; yet am I convinced that she loved you with a passion as intense as her nature was capable of entertaining. A longer experience in this world will convince you that most women are imbued with a spirit of coquetry, and will often flirt with one man, though their hearts be wholly devoted to another; and thus has many a constant heart been wounded—many a cherished affection been sacrificed, but why they should thus trifle with their own happiness I cannot discover. That Annette loved you I am convinced—that she cared little for Carlin, equally so—and yet she abandoned you, while he will use her as children do their toys, and when he is tired of her cast her forth upon the world. Let me then entreat you to seek the unhappy girl and rescue her from a fate worse than death. I do not ask you to do more for her than husband the little provision I have made which will keep her from want. I do not ask you to outrage your wounded feelings by having further intercourse with her, but endeavour through your brother to put her into some situation where she may be comfortable if not happy. Do this for the love you once bore her, and the blessings of a dying man shall ever rest upon you."

Though I have given this in a connected form, Augustin could only utter it in disjointed sentences, and towards the conclusion frequent applications to a goblet of wine became necessary, after which he rallied a little and resumed his narrative. Death, however, had marked him for his own, and the sands of life were few. After a few ineffectual attempts to address Jaques again, he turned in his narrow bed, his head dropped, fell back, and all was still—the husband of Annette had met the fate he coveted.

The task imposed on Jaques was anything but a pleasant one, for independent of the tie which formerly existed between them, and which Annette had so rudely and unceremoniously dissolved, he had a natural antipathy to an interference which he felt could be productive of no good, and might cause additional misery. However, the division of the army to which Carlin was attached was ordered to the south, while the guard prepared to accompany the Emperor to Paris, and thus any danger of a chance encounter was removed. Since the death of Augustin, Christine had followed her daughter, and I persuaded Jaques to let subsequent events take their chance, leaving all to time.

Napoleon now returned to France, and made his entry into Paris covered with a glory more brilliant than ever. He inspired all hearts with admiration, and his soul worthily appreciating the virtues of the French whom he cherished, responded to their love by an eulogy at once simple and true, "You are a great and good people."

Jaques and I took up our old quarters, and were soon immersed in the gaieties and dissipations of the capital. Though Annette's name was never mentioned, there were times when a dark shade passed across his forehead, marring the pleasure of the scenes in which he was engaged, and showing how intense the effort by which it was suppressed. I had gone through the ordeal and was free, but I could well feel for him over whom I had watched with a father's care.

CHAPTER 40

The Estaminet

Immediately after the conclusion of the campaign in Poland, Napoleon, with the hope of dazzling the world by a false light, and adding to the splendours of the throne he had mounted, as if the glory of the conqueror, or the love of a nation were not enough, created princes, dukes, counts, and barons, out of number, forgetting that the imperishable names of Hoche, Kleber, Dessaix, Massena, Jourdan, were of more value than all the titles in the world. It may be true that the dukes of Rivoli, Montebello, and Dantzic—the princes of Essling, Wagram, and Moscow, recalled the defeats of the Austrians, the Prussians, and the Russians, defeats which can never be effaced from the page of history.

Time's waves still rolled silently on eternity's vast shore, weeks and months elapsed, and still found us doing duty in the capital, gaudy satellites of that gilded sun, the court, reflecting back the borrowed lustre of its splendour. My commission gave me plenty of employment about the Tuileries, and this introduced me into the best society, to which my brother might also have had access, but that the recesses of his own chamber, and silent communings with his own heart seemed more to his taste.

Weeks and months sped on, bringing still the same unvarying round of duty, each day so like its predecessor, that they were only remembered in one conglomerate mass, or if by accident one gayer than another did occur, so trifling were the incidents they were soon blotted from the mind. Still onward moved the destroying scythe of time, slowly—silently, but surely—yet were his marks concealed by the brilliant display in Paris.

In October, 1808, Napoleon started for Spain, intending to join his brother Joseph, who had been elevated to the throne of that kingdom, at Madrid. Jaques and I, grievously to our disappointment, were left behind in attendance on the court, but our regiment having been employed in all the late campaigns, had suffered severely, and needed re-organization; this duty was entrusted to me with the grade of colonel. It was an arduous task, requiring me to be many hours daily in the saddle, but I was determined to render them second to none, and shall hereafter describe a scene which will prove my confidence was not unfounded.

On returning one evening from the palace to our quarters, Jaques and I feeling ourselves in need of some refreshment entered an Estaminet in the Rue St. Honoré not far from the Palais Royal. The room was crowded with people of both sexes, by far the greater portion of the men wearing the uniform of different regiments doing duty in Paris, all eager to hear the last news from Spain, the latest having led us to believe that Napoleon was upon the track of Sir John Moore, and that the English, under the latter, must either stand and fight, or make a precipitate retreat. Expectation was on tiptoe, and as we sipped our coffee, it was ludicrous to contemplate the various groups, who, with outstretched arms, and eyes intently fixed, were endeavouring to devour the words of the readers of the *Moniteur*, or the *Gazette*, as they fell from their lips, while ever and anon, muttered curses on *Les Anglais* were uttered, whenever there appeared anything which led them to anticipate that the much-hated foe would escape the fate to which they were one and all destined.

The evening glided away, and night approached, still we lingered, for the novelty of the scene diverted us, when we were disturbed by an altercation which proceeded from the farther end. of the room, and a momentary lull taking place in the babel of sounds by which our ears were assailed, Jaques became convinced that the accents were those of Annette. A sudden revulsion took possession of his whole frame, and approaching the spot, at the same time cautiously concealing himself in the crowd, he managed to get on the other side of the partition which separated the boxes unperceived, and became a hearer of the scene that followed.

He was not deceived. The inmates of the box were Annette, Carlin, and another woman, and the mutual flirtations of the two latter had roused the ire of their companion. High words ensued, till at last Annette burst out in a strain of loud invective, lamenting that she had ever quitted the side of one whose sabretache Carlin was unworthy to carry. "If, he were here," she added, "you would not dare to treat me thus, for fallen, worthless, degraded as I am, I should receive protection from him."

"Peace, minion," roared the half drunken dragoon, "would to Heaven your favourite were here! What was he but a raw beardless boy, unworthy the notice of a soldier of the Empire? I would serve him as I do you—thus," and the room re-echoed with the sound of a blow which the ruffian had inflicted on his victim.

To spring from his seat and draw his sword, ere I could restrain him, confronting Carlin almost at the moment that he uttered the words, was the ready action of my brother; and scarcely had the sound of the blow died away upon the ear, than in a voice hoarse with passion he exclaimed, "Behold I am here! Come forth, ruffian, or by the glory of him whom I serve I will stab yon where you sit."

Now, though half muddled in drink, Carlin was too perfect a master of his weapon to be encountered by a man in the mood Jaques then was; I therefore interfered, declaring I would cut down the first man who dared to advance a step. It was, however, of no avail, Jaques, more like a madman than anything else, threw himself upon his opponent, and a space being cleared at the end of the room, to it they went, Annette falling in a swoon on the seat. No heed, however, was taken of her; few knew the cause of quarrel, fewer still cared to enquire, all, with anxious looks, contemplating the scene, satisfied that amusement was in store for them, and regarding the event as unconcernedly as if it were a practice-bout in the *salle-d'armes*.

The first few passes convinced Jaques that he had an opponent of no common skill, and that if he had any hope of success, it was derived from the known confusion of vision which oppresses persons under the influence of wine. At each extraordinary lunge or parry, loud shouts would rend the air, till at length

Carlin, desirous of putting an end to the matter, made a feint, well known in the Italian schools, but imperfectly understood in the French. Here my careful attention to my brother stood him in good need; he had often practised and was thoroughly master of the manœuvre, which, being exercised with one who was believed to be a novice, was not over carefully done. In an instant Jaques saw his advantage, and availing himself of it, before Carlin could recover his position, his adversary's sword had entered his heart, the crimson tide of life fast flowing from the wound. He stood transfixed for a moment, and then fell weltering in his gore, while shrieks the most awful that ever saluted my ear made the room re-echo again. To hurry my brother into the street, and thence into the first *fiacre* I could meet (directing him to see the regimental surgeon and get his wound dressed, for Carlin's weapon had passed through the fleshy part of his arm) was but the work of a moment, and I returned to the wounded man, whose tide of life was fast ebbing away through a wound which had penetrated his chest, destroying one of the larger vessels. Though faint and sinking from the loss of blood, his countenance wore a demoniac scowl, and raising himself with difficulty on his elbow, he said, "Tell your brother my eternal curse shall rest upon him for this deed; bid him take the minion I have spurned, and would have abandoned ere the dawn of another day; may he be happy with her if he can." At every word he uttered with an effort, the crimson flood increased, and in a few minutes, still continuing to mutter the most dreadful imprecations, he fell back and expired.

Desiring his remains to be conveyed to his lodgings, I offered my services to his victim, then drowned in tears. Hers was not the grief of bereaved affection—not the anguish of having lost all it most prized in life—no, it was remorse that weighed upon her frame, crashing her energies to the dust. On our way to her lodgings she related the following particulars:

> What could have induced me to leave your brother for the brute who has just paid the merited penalty for his crimes I cannot imagine. Coquetry began what ended in my ruin; for, though I was satisfied with the devotion and

fidelity of Jaques, I was insane enough to feel pleasure in his jealousy, and, with the view of increasing this pleasure, gave liberties to Carlin which I loathed myself for bestowing. Still he haunted my footsteps, morning, noon and night was by my side, and as each succeeding visit seemed to add fresh fuel to the flame that burned in the breast of your brother, I often encouraged them, though they were in reality distasteful to me, while increasing coolness on my part served to widen the breach between us. Oh! what a fool is that woman who, satisfied with the devotion of a true heart, trifles with the happiness which she holds within her grasp, till at last it slips away, and she only becomes aware of the treasure she possessed when it is no longer her own. That I loved Jaques fondly, truly, with all a woman's idolatry, and all a woman's dependence, heaven is my witness, and often, when in the solitude of my own chamber I reflected upon the withering pain I was inflicting on one I loved so well—the uneasiness I was causing to a generous heart so thoroughly mine—I have resolved to do better for the future. The morrow came, and with it came my two lovers—the same scenes were re-enacted, until at last, stung by reproaches, which, though not merited, annoyed me, in a weak moment I yielded to Carlin's proposal and eloped. Four and twenty hours had not elapsed ere I repented—four and twenty days had not passed away before the brute's passion had begun to fade, and I found how wretched was the exchange. I reproached him, and he tauntingly bade me return; but as my mother had joined us, and still contrived to amass money, and his dissipated habits could not be supported by his own resources, he endured me for the sake of the gold she gave him, though his conduct was that of a monster. We went to the south, and early in the year my mother fell a victim to her love of gain, and died; while Carlin, having lost her assistance, had recourse to bad practices, and being detected in an attempt to cheat at play, was ordered to quit the army and return to Paris.

He would have abandoned me then, but that the order desired I should accompany him, and we had not arrived many days when it became evident that he could not support himself without my assistance. Spare me the recital of the scenes through which I have passed; ask me not to repeat the loathsome proposals I have been pestered with; to number up the blows I nave received because I have recoiled with horror and disgust. The tale would harrow up your soul. To-morrow, aye, to-morrow, if it come, I will resume this subject, but this night you must leave me to myself. Come again to-morrow, and till then farewell.

Poor Annette—for her the morrow never dawned, that night she died—died by her own hand.

Poor Annette, unable to bear the altered state of her fortunes after they had become known to those who used to be her friends, had put a period to her existence, but before we had become aware of the fact, Jaques had resolved on throwing up his commission, and returning, to spend his days in peace amid the scenes of his youth.

Under all the circumstances, this was perhaps the wisest course for him to pursue. Still a slave to the passion that had overmastered his reason, he could not banish her image from his heart, and it was better to avoid than come in contact with her. He started early in the morning, and years elapsed ere the news of the melancholy end of her he had held so dear was communicated to him, and even then so powerful was memory that he was affected to tears.

I lost no time in seeking the Minister of War, and explaining to him the full particulars, receiving in exchange permission for my brother to absent himself for a year. He never, however, returned to the service of France, but remained buried in obscurity on the paternal estate till the revolutionary troubles in Piedmont, in 1820, drew him forth. Joining the popular side, he was shot in the streets of Genoa, and thus perished as brave and fine a fellow as ever led a charge or mounted a breach; one who was a victim to that passion which has destroyed many a wiser and a better man.

Chapter 41

Eckmuhl

The year 1808 had passed away—an eventful year in the history of the world. To me it had produced little good commensurate to the loss I sustained, for it had robbed me of the society of a brother to whom I had been fondly attached. My regiment, however, had gone on famously; and when, on the return of Napoleon from Madrid, we were inspected on the *Champ de Mars*, we received from his own lips the most flattering commendations.

I confess I was proud of my fine fellows, and though, in losing my brother I had parted with one on whose zeal and attention to the service I could most implicitly rely, still, as I rode at the head of the regiment, with the crosses of the Legion and the iron crown of Italy hanging on my breast, I would not have exchanged situations with any monarch on earth. I knew my men were perfect; and as Napoleon, with a brilliant staff, slowly rode down our ranks, turning occasionally to make a passing remark to one of those whose daring acts had won a title, I felt that many there, like myself, had commenced as soldiers of fortune, and risen from the ranks to be the favourite generals of the first soldier in the world: high-vaulting ambition held out the same guerdon to me, and I resolved to obtain it or perish in the attempt.

The Austrian Emperor was making preparations for war, although his minister at the Court of the Tuileries continued to pour into the ear of the Emperor assurances of his master's friendship. He was not, however, deceived by his protestations, and remonstrated with the Court of Vienna, even offering to be guided by the mediation of the Emperor of Russia.

Futile proposal; it was declined. The Austrian had already made up his mind, and war became necessary.

Orders were now issued that such portion of the Guard as was serving in Spain, sundry regiments in Paris, and other troops then on the march to reinforce the army in the south, should turn their steps towards Germany, and at Ratisbon they were united to the division of the army of the Rhine that had remained behind, together with the troops of the Confederation. Napoleon himself went to Donawerth, which was the head quarters of the army, and on the 17th of April, the day of his arrival, addressed his first proclamation to the troops.

Napoleon conceived the happy project to act as it were in a manner directly the reverse of that of Prince Charles, and to concentrate his force as much as possible, at the same time isolating the corps of the enemy. He determined to advance rapidly on Vienna, to effect a junction with the armies of Italy and Dalmatia, and this determination inspired serious fears in the heart of the Archduke Ferdinand, who advanced into Poland against Generals Poniatowski and Dambrowski, then in position on the Vistula. The plan was admirable, and its execution promised the most brilliant success.

A commander who neglects to avail himself of any favourable incident when it does occur, rarely finds a second opportunity, besides which he cannot profit by the ardour of his troops, their good opinion, or the weakness of the enemy. It is well known that French troops will achieve wonders when they begin the action—the first advantage generally assures them of success for the rest of the campaign; and as Napoleon knew better than any one the dispositions of the men he had so often led to victory, he determined to make account of the inaction of Prince Charles, who, before the arrival of the Emperor, thought he should be able to prevent the union of the different divisions of our army, and beat them in detail. He appeared the more certain of success, because Berthier and Davoust, who had been in command during the absence of the Emperor, had made dispositions unworthy the reputation of good generals. This conduct had given a totally different appearance to the commencement of hostilities, and its influence on the progress of the campaign was incalculable.

The 19th of April was the first day we canoe to blows, at Psaffen-Hoffen and at Tann, where the Austrians met considerable loss; and immediately after these two affairs, measures were taken to attack and destroy the corps of the Archduke Louis and General Hiller, numbering together 60,000 men. The morrow we advanced to Abensberg, and Marshal Davoust received orders to hold in check Generals Hohenzollern, Rosenberg, and Lichtestein, while Napoleon, with the corps of Lannes, the Bavarians and Wirtembergers, attacked Prince Louis and Hiller, and cut off the enemy's communications by Massena, who was ordered to advance towards Freying, and from thence to the rear of the Austrians.

With his usual courage and sagacity, Napoleon determined on this occasion to lead the attack. Assured of the devotion of the French, he had his doubts about the Bavarians and Wirtembergers, and as he had a large number of them in the army, he began by flattering their military pride, and his presence in the midst of them inflamed their courage, rendering them only inferior to some of our veteran troops. In this he followed the example of that great master of the art of war, Hannibal, and with equal success. He assembled around him the officers of the allied troops, was prodigal of his commendations and praise, and directed them to execute such movements as he knew were suited to their particular character. Thus, these troops advanced on the enemy with great resolution, uttering loud cries of "*Vive l'Empereur Napoleon!*"

The assault was so like many others in which I had been engaged, that I will not stop to describe it, suffice it to say, that the result, in less than an hour, was, that the Austrians were repulsed, and lost eight standards, twelve pieces of cannon, and, besides a number of killed and wounded, 18,000 prisoners.

The result of this great success was, that the flanks and magazines of the enemy were exposed. At day-break Napoleon marched on Landshut, which Massena turned, and thus all obstacles were surmounted, the position, the bridge—although set on fire—and the town were carried. The enemy abandoned his magazines, his hospitals, thirty pieces of cannon, six hundred caissons filled with munitions of war, three thousand baggage wagons, three pontine bridges, and nine thousand prisoners.

Prince Charles, master of the Danube and of Ratisbon, had united Eckmuhl, a village situate between Landshut and Ratisbon, a force of a hundred and ten thousand men. On the 22nd at daybreak, Napoleon marched with the corps of Marshals Massena and Lannes, the division of Wirtembergers, and the cuirassiers of the Generals Nansouty and St. Sulpice; at two p.m. he arrived in front of the Austrians, and Lannes commenced the action by a movement on the left, while Lefebvre, Davoust, and Montbrun's light cavalry, who had held in check the corps of Rosenberg, Hohenzollern, and Lichtenstein, debouched.

The Archduke, attacked on all points at the same time, and his left extended in consequence of the rapid combinations of Napoleon, was obliged to retreat precipitately, leaving a large portion of his artillery, all his wounded, fifteen standards, and twenty thousand prisoners behind. My regiment had merely manoeuvred in the field, and the word was now passed, "Cuirassiers of the guard, move up, prepare to charge." It was our first appearance as it were on the field of battle, for though troops and detachments had partaken of a few skirmishes, the regiment as a whole had never been engaged. The eagle eye of Napoleon ran from rank to rank, as sitting immoveably on their horses, their features stern and rigid, each hand grasping a sabre, the men returned glance for glance, assuring him that they could be depended on. "Steady, men," said the Emperor, "remember you are not on the *Champ de Mars*, and let your first charge prove the soundness of my reliance on you."—"Colonel Gazzola," he continued, "you will charge the Austrian rear guard, and advancing to the walls of Ratisbon, support the division of Marshal Lannes. March! trot!" waving his hand, we were soon in motion, and coming up with a regiment of Austrian cavalry then covering the retreat, we bore down all opposition, capturing the regimental standard, together with several officers and men. The pursuit was continued till daybreak, even to the walls of the city, and in this pursuit our cavalry made many charges, all of which were eminently successful.

Marshal Lannes formed his troops in order of battle a short distance from the town, which was defended by six regiments, charged to maintain their ground till night, so as to protect the rear of the retreating army. Ratisbon was surrounded by a low wall, a ditch, and counterscarp, and presented little resistance. Immediately on their arrival, the French began the attack; the daring Lannes, instructed that a breach existed between the two gates, put himself at the head of his grenadiers, and descending into the fosse under a heavy fire of musketry from the Austrians, mounted the breach, penetrated into the town, and throwing open the Straubing gate, admitted a part of his corps. These soon gained the bridge, cutting off the retreat of the garrison, who, to the number of eight hundred men, laid down their arms.

In five days Napoleon, with that rapidity his extraordinary talents, and clear view, more bold and penetrating than that of an eagle, conduced to, destroyed every project of the enemy. In five days he beat the corps of Prince Louis and General Hiller, cut off at Landshut the Austrian centre of communication with their principal magazines and artillery, and defeated Prince Charles, at Eckmuhl, in a pitched battle.

On the 24th he thanked the army in one of his celebrated orders of the day.

Napoleon, who scores of times had been in danger of losing his life in battle, and who since he made war had never been wounded, was struck by a ball in the right foot before Ratisbon, during a conversation he held with Marshal Duroc. Any other prince than himself would have been vain of this wound, and Europe would have been filled with the noise of the event. To Napoleon it was a matter of small attention, he did not even afford time to his chief surgeon, Ivan, to dress it, but started off at a gallop, regardless of the observations made upon it, to discover what it was that impeded the advance of Lannes.

Displaying so perfect an abnegation of self, can you wonder at his being admired and cherished by his brave soldiers? Nevertheless they grumbled at his exposing himself so often. "What would you, my friends," was his reply, "is it not necessary that I should partake of your dangers and your fatigues?"

The different corps were in movement; Davoust pursued the Archduke Charles, who retired towards Bohemia, by Waldmunchen and Cham, his communications with the Inn and Vienna being cut off; Massena marched on Passau, by Straubing; Napoleon, with Lannes, advanced by Mulhdorf; the Bavarians advanced on Saltzbourg, while Bessieres pursued the troops of Hiller escaped from Landshut, in the direction of the Inn.

Massena passed the Inn at Schandnig, after having rendered himself master of Passau; Napoleon and the advanced guard entered Burckhausen; the bridge of Saltza was re-established., The corps of Oudinot occupied Ried; those of Lannes and Bessieres, Wells; while Lefebvre took Kufstein and Radstadt on the Ens, the routes which led to the north of Italy through the Tyrol.

Chapter 42

Essling

Matters now assumed a serious appearance, for the divisions of Lannes and Massena, uniting at Sieg-Harts-Kirchen, marched on the Austrian capital, where Napoleon himself arrived on the 10th of May. It was defended by the Archduke Maximilian and sixteen thousand troops of the line and landwehrs, and although the Faubourgs, which contained two-thirds of the population, were not fortified, and surrendered without assistance, the advanced guard, under Oudinot, having approached the esplanade that separates the Faubourgs from the city, were saluted with a heavy fire from the ramparts, which committed great havoc amongst them, and forced them to retire.

I was ordered to take a flag of truce, and to summon the town; but instead of obtaining that respect and attention which the nature of the duty I had undertaken ought to command, I was received with evident marks of distrust, and in a few minutes saluted with an attack.

Calling out to the Austrians by whom I was surrounded to respect the sacred office I was filling, the only reply was an attempt to hustle and throw me down. I therefore made the best of my way whence I came, and, returning to the Emperor, reported what had taken place.

"*Eh bien!*" was the short reply, "if they do not know the usages of civilised warfare, they must be taught; still we will not lose our tempers; let them violate the rights of war; I will not imitate so bad an example." So, summoning a staff officer, he directed his secretary to write to the Archduke, begging him to spare the miseries which must be necessarily entailed upon the city if he were forced to lay siege to it. To this the Archduke replied by a heavy fire from the batteries; and Napoleon, reduced to the dire necessity of bombarding Vienna, withdrew behind that arm of the Danube which separates the promenade called "the Prater" from the Faubourgs. A little edifice on the left bank was occupied by the Voltigeurs, for the purpose of protecting the troops employed in the erection of a bridge, which he determined to throw over the river at this point. The French army formed a circle around the ramparts, the left extending to the Danube as far as Dobling, the right at Simring, and the centre in the environs of Schoenbrunn, a country seat of the Emperor of Austria. For the erection of a battery of howitzers, the same spot was chosen as was occupied by the Turks in 1683.

The fire of this battery against Vienna commenced at nine o'clock in the evening. Eighteen hundred discharges took place in a very short time. Many hotels and large edifices in the interior of the city were soon enveloped in flames. Great was the consternation amongst the inhabitants, who found themselves crowded into a space much too small for their numbers. A flag of truce was despatched from them to say that the young Archduchess, Maria Louisa, she who afterwards became Empress of the French, was stricken with the small-pox, which had prevented her accompanying her father and family, and that her apartment in the palace was exposed to our fire; in consequence of which the Emperor, who declared that he warred not against women, ordered the direction of the fire to be changed.

Convinced of the futility of farther resistance, the Archduke evacuated the town with the troops of the line, and on the 12th, at day-break, General O'Reilly sent an officer to the advanced posts to demand a cessation of hostilities, and to state that a deputation of the principal inhabitants were about to pay their respects to the Emperor. A short time after this deputation arrived at Schoenbrunn, and were ushered into his presence, and informed that the same capitulation which he had afforded them in 1805 should be given on this occasion. The articles were signed that afternoon, and on the morrow Oudinot's corps entered the town, making the garrison prisoners of war.

In one month after the enemy had passed the Inn, on the same day at the same hour we had entered Vienna. The princes of Austria had abandoned the capital, not as men of honour who had been beaten by circumstances, but as fugitives who had met their reward. In flying from Vienna, their adieus to the inhabitants were fire and sword. *Like Medea, they had destroyed their own offspring with their own hands.*[1]

The corps of Marshals Massena, Lannes, and Bessieres were cantoned in the environs of Vienna, while the Imperial Guard occupied the palace of Schoenbrunn, where the Emperor fixed his head-quarters. Here he passed the troops in review, as soon as they arrived, distributing rewards to such as had distinguished themselves since the opening of the campaign, and ordering preparations to be made for the passage of the Danube.

Officers who had acquired an insight into military matters by the study of the operations of our best generals, and especially such as admired the tactics of Napoleon, no doubt remembered that this great master of the art of war, in place of pursuing in person the fugitive corps of the enemy after the battle of Echmulh, took another direction. Nevertheless, though some believed that he had committed a false step, others applauded it, for by so doing he rendered himself master of the enemy's line of operations. If Napoleon did commit a fault, which I am slow to admit, it was not appreciated by the Austrian generals; and who shall decide that he could have done better had he acted otherwise? He must have been his superior in genius, and where could he be found?

In following the. Archduke Charles into Bohemia with all his force, Napoleon would have afforded time and opportunity to the Austrian Emperor to have levied fresh troops, which, once organised, might have prevented our advance on Vienna; for our men, harassed with fatigue and badly supplied with provisions, which the Austrians took care to destroy in their retreat, would have been ill able to sustain an attack from fresh troops. In truth they had carried

---

1. Proclamation of Napoleon.

off their materiel, though they were obliged to destroy it, but had preserved their troops; and it is with troops rather than with guns and equipages that war is carried on and triumphs are achieved. Prince Charles, without doubt, thought that Napoleon would follow in his track, and that in this case the capital was safe; but he deceived himself. His adversary was too experienced to amuse himself with movements by which nothing could be gained, and when he became master of the Danube he could do as he liked with the capital, which soon became the centre of operations.

In charging Davoust with the pursuit of the enemy, and himself rapidly advancing on Vienna, Napoleon attained a desirable end, which rendered his junction with the army of Italy much easier, at the same time that it paralysed the efforts of his opponents. We cannot too much admire these well-planned movements, made day by day, according to circumstances; relieving Italy, opening to us, without defence, the barriers of the Inn, Saltza, and Traun, , with the whole of the enemy's magazines; Vienna surprised, the militia and the landwehr disorganized, terminating in the defeat of the corps of Louis and Hiller, and striking a fatal blow on the brilliant renown hitherto accorded to the Archduke Charles. It is well known that the greatest misfortune that can happen to an army is to lose the reputation of its general, a loss which infallibly destroys the confidence of the troops, which soon become demoralised, and are most easily conquered. It appears to me that the Archduke committed a great fault in abandoning the Danube; for had he fortified Ratisbon and Lintz, which were the keys, and concentrated his troops on that river, before the arrival of the Emperor, he might have avoided any serious engagement, covered Vienna, and so manœuvred as to prevent the union of the army of Italy with that of Napoleon.

On the 18th of May, we were in position as follows—The corps of Massena, Lannes, the Grenadier Guards of Oudinot, and the Imperial Guard, in Vienna; part of Davoust's corps was divided between that city and St. Polten; the Saxons and Wirtembergers, under Bernadotte, at Lintz, ready to advance on the capital the Bavarians, commanded by Lefebvre, at Saltzbourg and Innspruck.

Prince Charles, having made a long detour, arrived at the foot of Bisamberg, on the 16th of June, and having rallied his forces, and collected the scattered remains of Hiller's division, deployed in two lines on the plain of Marckfeld; his centre was placed behind Gerardsdorf, his right extended towards Stannersdorf, his left on Wagram, about three leagues distance from Vienna, while the. whole of his cavalry was in reserve behind his centre.

Napoleon, having visited the different points where it was proposed to establish bridges for the passage of the Danube, chose the island of Lobau, about a league and a half below Vienna, in front of the village of Debendorf. At this spot the river divides into three branches. The bridges finished, the Emperor passed over, and reconnoitered the position on the opposite bank, and being followed by the corps of Massena, Lannes, and Bessieres, formed them as they arrived. The left of the army was at Gross Aspern, the centre at Essling, and the right opposite Stannersdorf.

At four in the evening of the 2lst, the enemy attempted to drive our, advanced guard into the river, but were repulsed by Massena. In the. meanwhile, Lannes defended the village of Essling, and Marshal Bessieres with the light cavalry,.and Espagne's division of cuirassiers, covered the plain and protected Enzersdorf. The affair was warm, for the Archduke put in motion two hundred pieces of artillery, and deployed nearly a hundred thousand men.

Espagne's heavy cavalry behaved nobly, charging many squares, and carrying off forty guns, but their success was dearly bought, for General Espagne, an officer of great merit, was struck by a ball, and died nobly in the midst of his men.

During the night, Oudinot's corps, that of St. Hilaire, part of the guard, three brigades of cavalry, and a train of artillery, passed the Bridge and came up with the other troops, and at four in the morning of the 22nd, Massena put his men under, arms, and was soon engaged. The enemy made many desperate but ineffectual attempts to retake the village, but Massena, profiting, by a favourable movement, kept them in check.

As the flanks of Prince Charles were very far apart, Napoleon determined to endeavour to force his centre, and Lannes was quickly leading the attack, having Oudinot on his left, St.

Hilaire in the centre, and Boudet on the right. In one moment all was changed, Bessieres executing several beautiful charges, which were attended with the most brilliant success.

Matters were in this state when Napoleon received the news that a sudden rise of the Danube had put afloat a vast number of large trees and rafts, which had been cut and left on the banks of the river during the taking of Vienna, and that these had destroyed the bridge which connected the right bank with the Island of Lobau. All the parks of artillery in reserve, together with a large portion of the heavy cavalry, and Davoust's division, were thus cut off and left on the wrong side of the river, and this misfortune decided the Emperor to arrest the movement in advance. He ordered Lannes to guard the field which he had acquired, and to take position, the left being supported by a curtain which covered Massena, and the right at Essling. Perhaps it would have been better to have continued the battle, regardless of what was passing in the rear, and this temerity would no doubt have been crowned with success.

The enemy was in full retreat when he learnt the destruction of the bridge; the relaxation of our fire, and the movement to concentrate the army, confirmed the report of the terrible accident; in an instant he rallied, the regiments reformed, the whole of the artillery was quickly in line, and the most astonishing efforts were made, from nine o'clock in the morning till seven in the evening, to annihilate the French army. The intrepidity of our soldiers—the well-planned dispositions—the *sang-froid* of Napoleon—eight times snatched from the hands of the Austrian the triumph he thought to obtain, and at night he retired to the position from which he had advanced in the morning.

Their loss was great, for besides twelve thousand men killed and wounded, we took many prisoners, but if ours was less numerous, it was more cruel. France had to regret two of the bravest of her sons, Lannes was mortally wounded, as was St. Hilaire, and the loss of the illustrious marshal was equivalent to a defeat.

In this affair the Emperor preserved his presence of mind and rare courage, until assured of the safety and success of the brave troops who were placed between the enemy and the river;

but when he was informed of the accident to Lannes, his courage gave way, and his eyes became filled with tears. "It has happened," said he, when they carried near to him the body of the dying Marshal, "that on this day my heart has received a blow so severe, that I must abandon for other cares those of my army."

It was in the arms of Napoleon that Lannes recovered from his fainting fit, and casting his arms round his neck, he exclaimed—"In one hour you will have lost him who dies with the glory and the conviction of having been, and of being, your best friend." He was truly a noble soldier, and merited the glorious name of the "Bravest of the brave."

CHAPTER 43

The Passage of the Danube

On the 25th of June the army repassed into the island of Lobau and there took up a position which was fortified. We worked unceasingly at the re-establishment of the bridges. Bernadotte's corps arrived at Vienna, and the army of Italy, under the orders of Prince Eugene, having .been united to, and forming now the right wing of the grand army, was ordered to continue the pursuit of the Archduke John in Hungary. The army of Dalmatia, also under Massena, joined the, grand army, and formed its extreme right, under the orders of Eugene; and thus matters stood when we prepared for the passage of, the, Danube.

This river, perhaps one of the most rapid in the world, and nearly 400 *toises* wide, was crossed by a bridge of sixteen arches, erected in twenty days, under the, direction of General Bertrand. Over this three carriages might pass abreast. A second bridge of piles, eight feet wider, was established, for the passage of infantry only, and a third of boats, completed the means by which we could pass the river in many columns at once, and these were protected against injury from fire-vessels or other combustible machines by stockades of piles, constructed in different directions between the islands. These works were again defended by a *tête du pont* of sixteen hundred *toises*, formed by palisaded redoubts, strengthened and surrounded by moats, filled with water. The island of Lobau, thus rendered a stronghold, was a depôt for the magazines, and a hundred pieces of artillery of large calibre, and twenty howitzers, were placed in battery opposite Essling.

On the farther branch of the Danube was a bridge erected by Massena, and this bridge was covered by the works which had been erected for defending our first passage.

Napoleon having united the greater part of the divisions of the army, decided to carry them over the river, to debouch on the Austrian army, and give battle. The position of the French at Vienna was a very splendid one; they had in their grasp all the right bank of the Danube, Austria, a greater part of Hungary, and their supplies were abundant; but it would not do to remain quiet while the Austrians, separated by a canal of four hundred *toises*, were to be reached by means within our power. This would have been an assurance of the truth of the reports which the enemy industriously circulated in his own and the neighbouring countries, and have removed all doubts of the results of the battle of Essling—in fact, have given rise to a suspicion that existed of an equal force in two armies so differently constituted—the one stimulated, and in a measure rendered more powerful, by frequent successes, the other, on the contrary, depressed by great reverses.

All the reports which prevailed at our head-quarters relative to the Austrian army, agreed that it was very strong; that it had lately been augmented by the addition of considerable reserves; by recruits from Hungary and Moravia s by the whole of the landwehrs of' the provinces; that .forced requisitions had been everywhere made to remount the cavalry; in fact, that the strength of its artillery had been tripled by immense levies of carriages and horses.

To render all these chances more favourable, the Archduke Charles, who had extended his right to Gross Aspern, and his left to Enzersdorf, had covered the little town of Essling, Aspern, and the intervals which separated them, with redoubts, furnished with more than one hundred and fifty pieces of cannon, in position, drawn from the principal fortresses which yet remained in the hands of the Austrian government.

It appeared inconceivable that Napoleon, with his thorough knowledge of the art of war, should determine to attack works so strongly defended, supported as these were by an army of two hundred thousand troops of the line, militia and irregulars, and by an artillery of from eight to nine hundred pieces. It appeared more desirable to establish bridges some leagues lower down the river, and thus to prevent the advantages of a field of battle which the enemy had prepared with care, and knew perfectly. But on the other hand it was impossible to foresee all the means which it would be necessary to employ to obviate such accidents as had already failed to occasion the ruin of our army, and to prevent the destruction of the bridges recently constructed.

The situation of the French between these two difficulties had not escaped Prince Charles, who, besides, was aware that his Own army, too numerous and ill-disciplined for regular manœuvres, could not take the offensive without exposing itself to certain defeat, but he thought also that it would be very difficult, if not impossible, to drive him from his position. In maintaining it he covered Bohemia, Moravia, and a part of Hungary, but it could not protect Vienna, of which we were masters, although it preserved the left bank of the Danube, and impeded the arrival of the most necessary supplies for the subsistence of the capital. Such being the causes of hope and of fear which furnished matter for discussion and conjecture, both to the French and their opponents, Napoleon having declined to convey to any one the project he had conceived, the least indiscretion being sufficient to hinder execution.

At four in the morning of the 1st July, the Emperor returned to the island of Lobau, which had been named Isle Napoleon; a small island to which the name of Montebello had been given, over against Enzersdorf, had been armed with ten mortars, and twenty eighteen pounders; another island, named Espagne, had bit armed with six guns of twelve pounds, and four mortars, Between these two islands had been established a battery equal to that Montebello, and directed to the same point. These sixty pieces had the same direction, and in two hours could have razed the little town of Enzersdorf, driven out the enemy, and destroyed his works. On the right the island of Alexander, armed with four mortars, ten twelve pounders, and twelve six pounders, commanded the plain, and protected the bridges.

On the 2nd, Massena threw five hundred voltigeurs into the island of Moulin, the possession of which they retained, erecting works therein, and joining it to the main land by a little bridge, which reached the left bank. In advance was constructed a work called the little redoubt, and in the evening the enemy's redoubts at Essling, appearing jealous of it, not doubting that it was one of the first batteries that would be opened against them, commenced firing with great vigour. This was precisely the result which was sought by the occupation of the island, the attention of the Austrian being occupied, while the true intention of the operation was concealed.

On the 4th, at ten o'clock at night, fifteen hundred voltigeurs, of Oudinot's division, embarked in gun-boats, on the main branch of the Danube, passing thence below the island of Lobau. The enemy was quickly attacked, and driven from the wood to a village of Muhlleuten. At eleven, the batteries directed against Enzersdorf received orders to commence firing. The howitzers destroyed the little town, and in less than half-an-hour the enemy's batteries were silenced.

While the guns razed Enzersdorf, Massena crossed the little branch of the Danube, in boats, with two thousand men, landing them on the left bank below the town, at the same time the engineers threw a bridge, in one piece, of eighty *toises*, from one bank to the other. The infantry passed at quick march under a heavy fire from howitzers, bombs, and guns, both French and Austrian, which, discharged from either bank, flew over them.

Soon after, two other bridges were thrown over at a short distance from the first, and at three in the morning the army had four bridges by which it debouched; the left at fifteen hundred *toises* below Enzersdorf, protected by the batteries, and the right on Wittade; Massena's corps formed the left, that of Lannes, under Oudinot, the centre, Davoust's the right, Bernadotte's corps, those of Eugene, and Marmont, the Imperial Guard, and the heavy cavalry, composed the second line and the reserve. a profound obscurity, a violent storm, rain which fell in torrents, the thunder, the deafening roar of the artillery, the whistling of balls from howitzers, bombs, and muskets, rendered the night awful, but it was not the less favourable to our army.

With the earliest rays of the sun, on the morning of the 5th, every one discovered with admiration the project of Napoleon, who found himself and his army in battle array on the enemy's extreme left, turned his intrenched camps, rendered all his work and his toil useless, and obliged him to abandon his positions, and to fight on the ground which he chose. A great problem had been solved, and without passing the Danube elsewhere, without receiving any other protection than was afforded by the works erected, he had forced the enemy to a battle within three quarters of a league of his redoubts.

This prestige of success emboldened us, and we pictured to ourselves the greatest and happiest results.

At eight in the morning the batteries had produced such an effect that the enemy was obliged to abandon Enzersdorf, leaving four battalions .which surrendered to. Massena, while Oudinot, surrounded the *chateau of Sachsengang*, which the enemy had fortified, taking nine hundred-men who had defended it, and twelve pieces of cannon.

Napoleon now deployed his whole army on the plain of Enzersdorf, and the Austrians having recovered from their surprise, seized some advantages from this new field of battle. To effect this, Prince Charles detached several columns of infantry, a numerous train of artillery, and the whole of his cavalry, regular and irregular, to endeavour to turn the right of the French army. He soon occupied the village of Rutzendorf, which Napoleon ordered Oudinot to carry, to the right of which Davoust passed, to attack the head-quarters of Prince Charles, as he marched from the right to the left.

From noon till evening both armies manœuvred on this vast plain, taking all the villages, and hardly had we arrived at the entrenched camps of the enemy than they fell into our hands as if by enchantment, Massena occupied them without resistance, and thus we became masters of the works at Essling and Gross Aspern—works, the labour of forty days, which had proved of no use to the Austrians.

The enemy had his right from Standlau to Gerardsdorf, his centre from Gerardsdorf to Wagram; his left from the latter place to Neusiedel.. Our left was at Gross Aspern, the centre at Ruschdorf, our right at Glinzendorf. In this state of things the 5th was almost over, and it was necessary to prepare for the grand struggle on the morrow; nevertheless we attacked Wagram—our troops carried the village, but in the darkness a column of Saxons and another of French mistook each other for Austrians, rendering the operation incomplete—so we rested on our arms to await the break of day.

Chapter 44
Wagram

The battle of Wagram was inevitable, and we prepared for it. The dispositions of the two generals were diametrically opposite. Napoleon passed the night in concentrating his force on the centre, where it was hardly gun-shot distant from Wagram, Massena marched to the left of Aderklau, leaving a single division only at Aspern, and that was to retire on the Isle of Lobau if necessary. Davoust received orders to pass the village of Gross Hoffen, to approach the centre; while Prince Charles, on the contrary, enfeebled and weakened hit centre to augment his flanks, to which he gave a greater extension.

On the morning of the 6th, at break of day, Bernadotte, having Massena in second line, occupied the left, Eugene the centre, where Marmont, Oudinot, the guard, and the heavy cavalry division, formed many lines. Davoust marched from the right to arrive at the centre. The enemy put Bellegarde's corps in motion on Stadelau; Kallowrath's corps, and those of Lichtenstein, and Hiller, lay on the right of the position at Wagram, where was also Prince Hohenzollern; and on the extreme left, at Neusiedel, Rosenberg's corps debouched to intercept Davoust.

When the first rays of the sun broke forth, the order for battle was given. Napoleon was at the spot most menaced, and reinforced Davoust by a division of cuirassiers, taking Rosenberg's corps in flank, by a battery of twelve field pieces of Nansouty's division. In less than three-quarters of an hour, Davoust's corps had overthrown that of the enemy, who was driven back on Neusiedel, sustaining great loss.

During this time the cannonade extended along the whole line, and the dispositions of the Austrians became more developed every moment. The whole of their left was crowded with artillery, and it was said that Prince Charles did not so much combat for the victory as for the results that must spring from it, and this appeared so extraordinary that we feared some snare. For a long time Napoleon deferred making some manœuvres which he had determined to execute in opposition to those of his adversary, but this state of things could not last, and Massena was ordered to attack a village in the occupation of the enemy, which a little incommoded the extremity of the centre of the army, while Davoust was ordered to turn the position of Neusiedel, and fall on Wagram, for which purpose he formed in column Marmont and Macdonald's divisions, who carried the village just as Davoust debouched.

The enemy attacked the post which Massena had carried, with the greatest fury, throwing our left into some confusion, while a heavy cannonade extended as far as Gross Aspern, the interval between which and the village of Wagram appeared covered with an immense line of artillery.

Immediately orders were given to Macdonald's division to form in columns for the attack, and it was sustained by Nansouty's cavalry, the horse-guards, a battery of sixty pieces of the guard, and of forty others belonging to different corps. Three hundred guns started at a trot towards the enemy, advancing within half range, and then unlimbering, commenced a murderous fire which soon silenced the Austrians, sowing destruction in their ranks. Macdonald's division, supported by the fusiliers and tirailleurs of the guard advanced at quick time, the guard itself having changed front to render this attack certain.

In a second, as it were, the centre of the enemy lost its line of direction; the right, terrified by the danger of its situation, retreated in great haste, Massena threw himself on the leading columns during the confusion that ensued, while the enemy's left was briskly charged and repulsed by Davoust, who, after having carried Neusiedel, and attained the summit of the plateau, marched on Wagram. Oudinot had orders to advance on the village in support of Davoust, and this important position, which decided the fate of the battle, was carried.

By ten o'clock in the morning the enemy was in full retreat, at noon the affair was settled, and the Austrian army in disorder, and long before night Prince Charles, who was wounded, was out of sight. Our left now extended to Jetelsée, the centre was at Obersdorf, and our right at Shenhirchen.

At daybreak on the 7th, the army was in movement, and advanced on Korneuburg and Walkersdorf, with some troops at Nicolsburg. The enemy, cut off from Hungary and Moravia, found himself driven into Bohemia. He had lost on the evening before, and the day of, the battle, near sixty thousand men; our loss was infinitely less, although very considerable, and amongst the rest we had to deplore the death of General Lasalle, a brave and good officer, who was mortally wounded while cheering his men to the attack.

This battle, and never was one more memorable, took place under the eyes of a numerous portion of the population of Vienna, who, mounted upon the towers and the tops of the houses, were spectators of the defeat of their compatriots. The Emperor of Austria had quitted Walkersdorf on the 6th, at one o'clock in the morning, and was placed upon a terrace, from which he beheld the plain which enclosed fifteen hundred pieces of artillery, and four hundred thousand men, contending for victory under two of the most able generals of the age.

We continued to advance, and should, in a short time, not only have annihilated the remains of Prince Charles's army, but also the Austrian monarchy, if Napoleon had not generously granted an armistice to the Emperor Francis on the night of the 11th of July. The different corps of the army were ordered into position, Massena occupying the circle of Znaim; Davoust that of Brünn; Marmont, Korneuburg and its environs; Oudinot, Spitz; Eugene, Presbourg and Gratz. We of the Guard were established round the chateau of Schoenbrunn, which had been named as the head-quarters.

The fine dispositions of Napoleon at Obersberg, Landshut, and Eckmuhl; his march on Vienna instead of following the Archduke into the mountain fastnesses of Bohemia; the works on the Danube and at the Island of Lobau, which were planned by his genius and executed under his eye; the passage of that river; the manœuvre which placed our army on the extreme left of the enemy, rendering of no avail his strong entrenchments; the attack in force on one point only, and the occupation of Wagram, which taking place simultaneously decided the fortune of the day, form altogether a great and magnificent picture, which the generals of many an age to come will do well to study.

But if Napoleon acquired immortal glory in this campaign, Prince Charles was not for imitating him. What great fault did he not commit in withdrawing from bis line of operations on the Danube? He was very advantageously situated, having Ratisbon and Straubing on his right, Passau in the centre, Lintz and Ens on his left, and these might have been rendered formidable if the Prince had advanced on the Rhine before the arrival of Napoleon in Germany. In retiring, too, into Bohemia and Moravia, Prince Charles well knew he perilled the existence of the Austrian monarchy. Had be rallied the troops of his brother and General Hiller after the battle of Eckmuhl, and manœuvred on the van of his line of operations, he might have avoided the battle of Wagram; the country was difficult, his position with regard to Vienna respectable, and the day of Essling having been against him, he ought to have shunned this later engagement, especially with an army consisting mainly of recruits, and ill-drilled, who were more than intimidated behind their intrenchments, which many of them regarded as a position that was impregnable.

The armistice was prolonged, and on the 14th of October a treaty of peace was signed at Vienna. Thus terminated the campaign of Austria, and scarcely had we returned into France than measures were entered into for the dissolution of the bonds which united the Emperor to Josephine, and their re-construction with a daughter of the house of Austria, the princess, in fact, who, being ill of the smallpox, was left behind when her family evacuated the capital, and in whose favour Napoleon turned the direction of the artillery which was then firing on the palace. These affairs are too much matters of history to form part of my subject; I shall therefore content myself with saying that I returned to my old quarters in Paris, and resumed the usual duties of the guard at the chateau of the Tuileries.

CHAPTER 45

Russia—the Advance

There were gay doings in Paris on the arrival of the Arch-Duchess Maria Louisa, and I partook of them; still I could not but feel—and feel deeply—for the unfortunate Josephine, at whose hands I had received many acts of kindness, and who, as I heard from her attendants, was rendered miserable by her repudiation. She was one of those "children of the sun," who loved passionately, and the giddy height to which she had risen, and from which she was thus unceremoniously precipitated, had failed to obliterate either the feelings of the woman or the affection of the wife. Of the policy of the step, I am not competent to give an opinion; for, educated in a camp, questions of national policy were out of my way; but though the glittering pageant in which I bore a part, served occasionally to drive from my mind the injustice which was committed, it ever and anon revived, making me regret the cause that gave origin to the show.

I had passed so many years in the bustle of a campaign, that when on duty in the capital I often sighed to be with the gay and gallant hearts that were winning laurels in the field, and like the war-horse, champing his bit ere the encounter begins, I bore with little equanimity the duty that prevented me sharing their successes. But the end came at last; and when, in 1812, the Emperor Alexander, forgetting his defeats at Austerlitz, at Eylau, and at Friedland, determined on making preparations for war, and Napoleon, on demanding the cause, was assured that he remained faithful to the alliance he had formed, it required the re-union of eighty thousand men on the frontiers of Poland, to convince the

Emperor that his brother of Russia was no longer to be trusted. There can be no doubt that Alexander was jealous of the reputation Napoleon had acquired, that he was envious of his intrepidity, his genius, and his power, his great and brilliant glory, and that with a view of curbing the ambition of one who strove to rule the world, he sacrificed his honor, and risked his kingdom.

At peace with the princes of Germany, Napoleon accepted the defiance of his rival, and in so doing sought to effect three desirable ends—He was willing to free Poland from the yoke of the Czar; to destroy the commerce of England, which Alexander encouraged contrary to the faith of his treaties, during which he had prohibited that of France, and so to cripple the power of the Russian, by a quick and decisive campaign, as to induce him to withdraw from the English alliance, if he did not succeed in affording to Europe the peace it so much desired. He made levies of men, remounted his cavalry, provisioned his magazines and arsenals, demanded of the Emperor of Austria and the Confederation of the Rhine the contingents agreed upon in the treaties concluded between them, and succeeded in deciding the King of Prussia to arm in his favour.

Nevertheless, desirous of preventing the effusion of blood, he sent an ambassador to St. Petersburgh to demand the maintenance of the conventions, the continuance of peace and goodwill, which he affected to believe sincere, and on the left bank of the Niemen waited for an answer, while he organized and completed his army.

These pacific propositions were not acceded to, for his envoy was refused an interview, and then, justly incensed at so extraordinary a proceeding, he addressed his army—who attended with impatience the order to advance—in a proclamation, which recounted his wrongs and threatened redress.

The army was divided into ten corps, each having several brigades of cavalry, and well supplied with artillery, and these were entrusted to the command of Davoust, Oudinot, Ney, Eugene, Poniatowski, Saint Cyr, Regnier, Jerome, Victor, and Macdonald. The cavalry, independent of the brigades attached to each division, formed four corps under the orders of Nansouty, Montbrun,

Grouchy, and Latour Maubourg, who were subordinate to Murat. The Imperial Guard, both horse and foot, were commanded by Marshals Lefebvre, Mortier, and Bessières; while the Austrians formed a separate corps under Prince Schwartzenberg.

The Russian army was composed of six great corps, commanded by Generals Wittgenstein, Bagawout, Schmoaloff, Tulschkoff, Bragation, and Doctorow, all under the orders of Barclay de Tolly, who was himself commanded by the Emperor Alexander.

In order to reconnoitre the enemy, Napoleon ascended the heights which overlooked Kowno, a small town situated on the confluence of the Niemen and the Wilna, and having ascertained his position, our troops were soon in motion, passing the Niemen at various points, carrying Wilna, to which movement Barclay de Tolly offered no resistance; on the contrary, he retired in haste, having failed in an endeavour to destroy his magazines.

This bold manœuvre took the enemy's corps by surprise, threw them into difficulty and doubt, and the disorder prevented Bragation, who commanded the left wing and several other corps, from acting in concert with Barclay. The consequence was, these two generals were unable to unite their forces before they arrived at Smolensko, a distance of eighty leagues from Wilna, while we were left masters of the two fine provinces of Lithuania and Samogitia.

While the French army effected the passage of the Niemen, and advanced, its centre on Wilna, the left on Wilkomirz, and the right on Ossmiana, the Emperor Alexander abandoned himself to pleasure at the Chateau of General Beningsen, about half a league from Wilna, from which he was awakened by the thunder of our artillery. He then solicited an armistice, and begged Napoleon to repass the river; but as his design was only to gain time, so as to act with greater security, it was easily seen through, and Napoleon refused the armistice, but offered to negotiate a treaty of peace on the spot where the two armies were placed. Alexander, deceived in his hope, recalled his plenipotentiary.

On the 28th of June Napoleon entered Wilna, where he was met by a deputation from the confederation of Poland, who demanded the independence of their country. He received them with great honour, and answered in a remarkably moderate manner, declining to accede to their request so long as all the Poles were not united to preserve the liberties which they were desirous of recovering. He accepted a guard of honour, composed of young Lithuanians, under the command of Prince Ogienski, and some regiments of infantry were levied spontaneously. This guard afterwards became the second regiment of Polish light horse, commanded by General Konopka.

On the 30th, the whole of the army had crossed the river, and taken position, the guard remaining at Wilna.

Before he had crossed the Niemen, Napoleon had without doubt calculated (at least his ulterior operations indicated as much) that he should establish his head quarters at Wilna, Witepsk, Smolensko, and Moscow, by making march on many lines all the corps of the army, the movements of which would nave these four towns as the centre of operations. The execution of this plan, more or less understood by his lieutenants, proves how grand yet just were his calculations, and how superior he was in intelligence to his enemy. Thus was Alexander cruelly deceived, when the French army, which he thought was directed on St. Petersburg, by Courland and Livonia, advanced straight on Moscow, having passed the Niemen, and become master of both banks of the Wilna, separating the different corps of the Russian army, and having destroyed their line of operations from the Niemen to the Nieper.

From Wilna the Emperor advanced to Witepsk, with the whole of his forces, and on the 26th July arrived at Kukowiaizy, a village separated from the town by the wood of Ostrowno. During his march, the right ought to have entirely destroyed Bragations's corps, much weaker than itself, in a defile between Rieswig and Glusck, if Jerome Buonaparte and Davoust had acted in concert.

On the 27th, we discovered the Russian army in position on an immense plateau which commanded the place. The cavalry was partly drawn out in order of battle on the plain, backed by the Lutehse, a deep and rapid river. Napoleon approached within range to examine them, and an encounter took place between two hundred of our voltigeurs and the whole Russian cavalry.

During the examination, Murat pushed forward against the Russian cavalry a regiment of *chasseurs à cheval*, who being met would have been inevitably cut to pieces but that they were timely supported. The enemy on retiring fell in with 200 of our voltigeurs, and surrounding them prepared to put them to the sword. This was more easily said than done; they formed in square, and boldly resisted a mass of cavalry amounting to at least ten thousand men, bringing down upwards of three hundred with their first volley. This happened in the presence of both armies, who, placed on two small hills, which formed a sort of amphitheatre, could witness every movement. Napoleon dispatched an aide-de-camp to know to what corps these men belonged, and it being reported to him that they were of the 9th regiment of infantry, "Go to them immediately," said the Emperor, "say that they are brave men, and have well deserved to bear the cross of the legion."

On the morrow this mark of honour and of bravery was bestowed on every one of them.

Chapter 46
Smolensk

Barclay de Tolly being afraid to be forced from his position, although in command of eighty thousand men, withdrew his cavalry, and in the night effected his retreat on Smolensko, where he was joined by Bagration, but we were made acquainted with the movement by the ravages and fires which illuminated the whole country. In fact, whenever the opportunity offered, the Russians destroyed and ravaged the country, all the way from Wilna to Moscow, thus cutting off our supplies, and rendering the task of provisioning a large force one of great difficulty and danger.

In every case, whether the war be just or unjust, the generals forecasting or thoughtless, it is necessary that the troops should live and be clothed; and if the magazines of the army are insufficient for this, the country through which it marches must make up the deficiency. The conduct of the Russian General, therefore, exposed us to great privations, which were supported with resignation. We had never been plunderers; and even now, when want stared us in the face, Napoleon reminded his companions in arms that pillage dishonoured the brave, and ruined the people; that he had rather his army were resigned to the pains and privations they must necessarily undergo than, losing their respect for the orders of their officers, become the scorn of the world, and thus our brave fellows, jealous of their good names, proved by their discipline, that they could merit the good opinion of their Emperor by enduring, without murmuring, famine and fatigue, afterwards increased by the rigours of a season which cut them off by thousands. On the 4th of August, the head-quarters were at Witepsk, the right from Orsa to Mohilow; the left on the bank of the Dwina, extending to Wely; the centre in advance of Witepsk, and lying with its two wings and the cavalry at Rudine, the advanced guard at Inkowo.

Such was the disposition of the army, such the genius that had superintended the placing of each individual corps, so as eventually to protect and support each other, that Napoleon could at any one moment seize a large extent of country.

There were no suppositions engendered—no difficulties unforeseen—no accidents unprovided for when he felt disposed to move these masses; all was foreseen, everything ordered, and the execution could only be prevented by the ignorance or timidity of his officers, who were in general as brave as they were well informed.

These great corps were a load too heavy for any other hand, in which they would have been found without union, without accord, but with him every thing went smoothly, every movement was executed in the finest order, and always apropos. If anything went wrong his eye discovered the mistake, his genius rectified it, for his principal talent was to profit by the mistakes of others, and to turn them to his own account, instead of leaving them to be profited by his opponent. Did any one flag, Napoleon reanimated him, was his courage depressed, his example re-assured him; and, while the most implicit obedience was paid to his commands, his presence raised the spirits of all those who served under him, electrified all their souls—our troops could neither exist nor conquer without him—he was the idol of their hearts his smiles rendered them happy, his frowns miserable, with him there were no obstacles—no enemies invincible—privations, dangers, exertions—nothing diminished their confidence nor their affection.

Our men had need of rest, and that our illustrious chief well knew, but he also knew that it would not do to afford the enemy time to recover from his losses and surprise.

The army advanced rapidly and in good order on Smolensko, a large town, although thinly peopled. Our advanced guard fell in with the division of General Rewrerowski, in the defile of Krasnöe, and there attacked him with spirit. Notwithstanding a brave resistance, he was repulsed, losing many men and several guns. If our artillery had been brought up in time, the destruction of the division would have been complete.

At the news of this check, the Russians retired from Smolensko, but quickly returned. Barclay de Tolly had nearly one hundred and twenty thousand men, besides the division of the Prince Bagration, who was detached to cover his retreat on Dorogobuze, on the road between Smolensko and Viazma, thinking that Napoleon manœuvered towards this point. Barclay had lost his confidence when opposed to Napoleon, but having received orders from his sovereign to hold out Smolensko, even at the risk of a battle, he could not but obey. Alexander had prudently quitted the army and returned to his capital, where he passed his time issuing bulletins, setting forth the victories of an army, which at the moment was threatened on all sides with inevitable destruction.

Smolensko was surrounded by a wall, a league and a half in circumference, ten feet thick, and twenty-five high, flanked at short distances by enormous towers and bastions, mounted with heavy guns, and crenelled for musketry. Barclay had thrown 30,000 men within the walls, and drew up the remainder of his force on the banks of the Nieper, communicating with the town by bridges, which he had erected prior to the affair at Krasnöe.

Napoleon reconnoitred the enemy, whose principal forces on the right were near to Smolensko, and his left on the bank of the river, and then prepared for the encounter. Ney commanded the left, and advanced on the river; Davoust directed the centre, and attacked with great force the *faubourgs*, while Poniatowski, at the head of the right, was ready to advance to the river by changing front, as soon as the state of the battle admitted of the movement. The guard supported the centre, Eugene the left wing, the brigade of cavalry the right; the eighth corps of the army was on the extreme right, but Junot made a false movement, which prevented their taking any part in the affray.

Such were the dispositions of the two armies; but the same hopes did not animate the two commanders. Napoleon was certain of success; defeat never entered into his calculation; to fight and to conquer were things inseparable with him; but Barclay, on the contrary, was doubtful of the result, and half beaten before the battle commenced.

On the 17th of August, at noon, Napoleon, placed between the guard and Davoust's division, gave the signal. The *faubourgs*, entrenched and defended by heavy artillery, were carried at the point of the bayonet , amid loud cries of "*Vive! l'Empereur !*" Batteries were established, which thundered away at the ramparts, and those who defended them; while the enemy's masses formed on the banks of the river. We prepared for the assault, while Barclay reinforced the garrison by a brigade of the Russian Guard, and two divisions of the line, with the hope of affording Bagration time to come up to his support. But these reinforcements and new dispositions were of no avail, and only delayed the surrender of the town a few hours. Napoleon, after having directed a heavy brigade of cavalry to attack that of the enemy, which was posted on a plateau that extended to a bridge down the river, where was also a battery of sixty pieces of artillery, thundering away at the right bank, ordered Ney to carry the position, and to pursue the enemy to the glacis. Friand, Morland, and Gudin, were each ordered to turn a breaching battery of twelve pieces against the walls, to render the covered ways untenable by the garrison, and to enfilade the streets. These orders executed, the ramparts and covered ways were swept by our guns; and the Russians, finding the place too hot to hold them, set fire to it at various points, and fled, crossing the river, and, breaking down the bridges, continued their retreat by Prouditchi and Loubino, traversing several defiles and marshes.

On the 18th we entered the town, where we found two hundred pieces of cannon, five thousand killed, and seven thousand wounded, as well in the town as the environs. Our loss was proportionably severe, for we had three thousand five hundred men killed or rendered *hors de combat,* notwithstanding the ability displayed in the attack, and the vigour with which it was prosecuted.

At the close of this victory, Napoleon, according to his system of never letting his enemy breathe, a system which he often explained to his officers by the words, "Nothing is done while aught remains to do," hotly pursued the Russians. We came up with their rear guard on the plain of Valontina, called the "holy field," which, tradition said, was a happiness to the people. But it proved anything but that, for again were they attacked, and again defeated, although reinforced by a division under General Karpow, and supported by Barclay himself, who advanced each division as it arrived by *echelon*.

On the 19th, Ney and Murat attacked this position, carrying it, and covering the field of battle with the dead and the dying. The Russians lost a great part of the baggage which they had saved from Smolensko, and again would our success have been complete, had Junot seconded Ney by debouching on Koniecsewo, and cut off their retreat. Our loss was again severe, and amongst the brave men who fell to rise no more was General Gudin, an officer of great merit, of rare judgement, and cool intrepidity.

Napoleon passed in review the regiments which had been engaged at Valontina, and himself distributed the rewards. By well-merited eulogiums he inflamed the troops with the noblest enthusiasm, and was thanked by loud cries of "*Vive! l'Empereur*," without doubt making the day to him, as well as to them, the most pleasureable of the campaign. It was in truth an interesting spectacle to behold these brave soldiers surrounding their Sovereign, laying at his feet their best energies, for, although the field of battle covered with the dead and dying, proves beyond anything else that the French know how to appreciate and cherish the military talents of their chiefs, it is when the strife has ended that they show themselves aware of their virtues and their gratitude.

The victories of Witepsk, Smolensko, and Valontina, were not the only ones achieved by the grand army. The second, sixth, and tenth corps directed on the left, and the seventh, with the Austrians, on the right, gained some advantages, but the sixth, commanded by St. Cyr, was that which acted with the most vigour and determination. It obtained a marked success over Wittgenstein, at Polotsk, killing two thousand of his men, and wounding four thousand, besides taking many prisoners (amongst them were three generals,) and twenty pieces of cannon. For this brilliant exploit St. Cyr received the baton of marshal.

Before commencing his march on Moscow, Napoleon was desirous of being better supported by the reserve, and the corps which lay on either side the great road in the rear. Victor was ordered to advance rapidly, and establish his head-quarters at Smolensko, his right at Mohnow, his centre at Orsa, and his left at Witepsk. This reserve, destined to protect the march of Napoleon on arriving at the places fixed by him, had on the left the corps of Oudinot and St. Cyr at Polotsk and Swalnad; and of Macdonald at Dunabourg and Riga. In the rear of the centre were the corps of Regnier and Schwartzenberg, which Loison and Durutte's divisions from Konigsberg replaced on the Bug. On the right, at Bobruisk, was a part of the fifth corps commanded by General Dambrowski. The whole of these troops together composed a mass of one hundred and sixty thousand, which could easily be put in motion, besides which the Polish levies, and the reinforcements from France and Prussia, were on the march and had entered Russia.

Such were the dispositions on which Napoleon relied to support the army in its advance on Moscow, or if necessary protect its retreat on Smolensko. The most precise orders were given to fortify the towns and entrenchments—to form magazines and hospitals; in fact everything that genius could suggest or devotion achieve to second the projects of the Emperor was done.

Chapter 47
Borodino

After the action of Valontina, the French army continued in pursuit of the enemy, and arrived at Ghjat on the 1st of September. Here Napoleon concentrated his forces, and remained some days to allow the troops to recover from the fatigues they had undergone, and the stragglers to come up, as well as to prepare for the great battle which he foresaw must inevitably take place. He prepared to attack Kutusow, who had succeeded Barclay de Tolly as commander-in-chief, before certain reinforcements, which he expected from Moldavia, should come in.

The Russians were in position at Borodino, a village situate at the confluence of a small river with the Kalogha, on the route to, and within Borne twenty-five leagues of, Moscow. The place had been fortified. Murat established himself on the main road in the neighbourhood of Gridnewa, Poniatowski towards Budoiewo, Eugene on the left near Pawlowo, Davoust, Ney, and the guard around the Emperor.

Napoleon examined this position with great attention; not a movement of Kutusow escaped him, and prepared for the attack. Alexina and the surrounding woods, those of Elnia and the batteries constructed in the redoubt of Schwardino, a village opposite to Kalogha, between Borodino and the wood were carried, alter an obstinate resistance, but night coming on, the two armies remained under arms on the spot which they occupied; Poniatowski below Elnia; Ney at Schwardino, having Junot in reserve; Davoust in the centre, sustained by the horse and foot guards, Nansouty's, Montbrun's, and Latour Manbourg's corps of cavalry; Eugene on the road to Moscow, having as a reserve the Italian Guard and Grouchy's cavalry. Napoleon, with his staff, remained in the centre of the lines.

The enemy had only employed the troops which covered Elnia and Schwardino, and occupied as before the heights from Utitsa to Maslowa, that is to say, the whole space which exists between the old road from Moscow to Smolensko, and thence to the Moskwa. His centre extended from Gorka to Semenowska, advancing towards Borodino and the wood of Utitsa. The position was well chosen, being defended by the Kalogha and supported on the right by the Moskwa; the left by thick woods, with such necessary debouches as would enable him to effect his retreat, should he be desirous of evading an engagement. The dispositions of Kutusow were those of an able commander, based on the principles indicated by the best tacticians, nevertheless all these advantages vanished before the genius and valour of Napoleon.

Very contrary feelings prevailed in the opposing forces; the French were sustained by their confidence in the experience and courage of their leader, while the Russians were animated by an ungovernable fanaticism; thus the battle was sure to be terrible and bloody, for the two armies numbered from two hundred to two hundred and fifty thousand men in their ranks.

Napoleon never ceased, during the night, studying the plans of the ground occupied by the different corps of the army, which he had received from the commanders. He made some changes in the disposition of the cavalry, and ordered such parks of artillery as had not yet joined the army to move up more quickly, determined, if possible, that they should cover and support each movement. He then addressed a short but energetic proclamation to the troops, in which he reminded them of Austerlitz and Friedland, pointing out the glory that success would add to their names. Nevertheless, whatever might be his confidence in the courage and devotion of the men, to make assurance doubly sure, he again studied and calculated the position of the two armies, and on the 7th of September, all being arranged, we prepared for the attack.

The evening before, and during the night, the rain had descended in torrents; about five in the morning it cleared up, and the sun burst forth in splendour. "Soldiers, it is the sun of Austerlitz!" broke from the lips of the Emperor, who never appeared to more advantage than on this day, which was to decide the fate of his army. This exclamation flew from rank to rank, animating the hearts of the soldiery with the same ardour as inflamed their leader; regiment after regiment moved up at a quick pace, our artillery fired the signal, and the battle of Borodino began.

The divisions of Compans and Gerard soon carried two redoubts at the point of the bayonet, in vain the Russians strove to retake them, again and again they returned to the attack; the slaughter was terrific, the moats being choked by the dead and the wounded. Our cavalry drove their artillery and infantry back on Semenowska, General Friand carrying the redoubt in advance of this village by assault, Ney having been previously prevented doing so by a battery of seventy pieces which crowned the heights of Schwardino. This beautiful and daring manœuvre was supported on the right of the marshal by the corps of Davoust and of Poniatowski, and by a park of artillery, while Eugene advanced on the left. General Planzonne carried the village of Borodino, and fell at the moment of success. The intrepid Morand passed the Kalogha, and marched on the great redoubt established to the right of Borodino; the enemy in force, being in advance of Gorka, perceived the movement, and endeavoured to prevent it, but Morand halted a sufficient time for one of his regiments to turn the redoubt and carry it by assault, but so overwhelming was the force by which they were opposed, that after a short and obstinate resistance they were obliged to abandon their conquest.

The action had now become general, two hundred pieces of cannon pouring destruction on the two armies. Soon the Russians began to find out they could neither advance nor retreat, and there they stood under one of the most devastating fires the French artillery ever maintained. In an instant Napoleon, who was in the centre of his army, perceived the situation of the Russians; the batteries of the reserve were ordered to move up; a hundred pieces of cannon opened on the great redoubt and the enemy's centre at the same time, while our gallant leader supported the courage of his men, and incited them to more desperate efforts by addressing to each regiment as it passed, some short sentence, recalling to their minds the battles in which they had displayed the greatest energy and reaped the greatest glory. Thus animated by the voice and the example of their brave Emperor, the men surpassed themselves, and performed prodigies.

After having destroyed the greater part of the masses which were opposed to the centre, Napoleon manœvred the eighth corps, that of Ney and all the right, to turn the last position of the Russians. He ordered the guard, with all the corps of cavalry, to support this great movement; Eugene was directed to advance on the Kalogha, and the victory was decided—the day became our own; the Russians retiring towards Mojaisk, leaving on the field of battle seventy pieces of artillery, and fifty-five thousand men *hors de combat,* while amongst the latter were fifty general officers.

This affair, in which the soldiers of both armies behaved admirably, and even the losing party covered themselves with laurels, was certainly one of the most brilliant of Napoleon's achievements; never before had he directed so large a force with such consummate ability, and certainly his plans had never been more admirably carried into operation. The movements, the marches, the manœvres even, and the order of battle of the two armies—the one to defend its positions which were believed to be impregnable—the other to attack them because they fancied they could be carried—were all of the most perfect kind, and the result was only obtained by the most implicit obedience to the orders of our chief. Kutusow had doubtless forgotten the severe lesson he received at Austerlitz, or, perhaps, dazzled by ambition, he flattered himself that he was equal to Napoleon; in either case he found himself miserably deceived.

Napoleon remained master of the field of battle, and according to his noble and generous custom, no sooner was the affray ended than his attention was turned to those who needed his care. Orders were given for the accommodation of the wounded, both French and Russians, in the hospitals and magazines established in great numbers on the line of march, while those who had survived this memorable day were reminded that the city of Moscow was still in the bands of the enemy, and that its conquest was necessary to complete his plan of the campaign.

Towards this city Kutusow continued his retreat, and our expedition could not be considered over until we had paralysed his efforts by becoming masters of it. Then we might rest from our labours, and be reinforced by a portion of the troops left in reserve on the Dwina and the Nieper, which Augereau would replace with the eleventh corps of the army. Napoleon, therefore, pursued the Russians with the whole of his cavalry, supported by many divisions of infantry.

The enemy came to a stand again at Mojaisk, a town situated twenty-six leagues east of Moscow, and here he endeavoured in some manner to repair his awful disaster; but he had only time to set fire to the four corners of the town, having neither respect for the poor inhabitants of the place, nor humanity for the wounded, who were crowded into the churches, the hospitals, and even the private houses. He again retired in great haste, harassed by the French cavalry, which gave him no rest till he got beneath the walls of Moscow.

Napoleon moved his head-quarters to Mojaisk, and disposed of his forces as follows—The fifth corps to the right of the town; the fourth on the left, extending to Ruza, its advanced guard at Swenigorod; the third at Kubinskoe, on the grand route to Moscow; the first and the young guard between the third and the old guard, placed before Mojaisk; the eighth in reserve between Borodino and the Imperial head-quarters.

Napoleon has been blamed for remaining forty-eight hours at Mojaisk, but it is impossible to conduct a large army provided with considerable materiel, and an immense number of equipages, without halting occasionally to re-unite such parts of it as become dissevered either by a battle or the ardour of pursuit. It is necessary, though the enemy may be beaten and dispersed, that every movement should be covered, every advance supported. If we had immediately advanced on Moscow, the result would have been the pillage of that city, and the utter demoralization of our army, nor could we have avoided abandoning it, as we were afterwards compelled to do.

After our short sojourn at Mojaisk, the troops were again in motion, taking the same order as they had observed before the halt, each corps advancing directly on Moscow. Arrived there, we thought our toils at an end, and looked forward to comfortable quarters for the winter. As regiment after regiment came up, they were quartered round the city on the roads to Kolomna, Wladimir, Jaroslow, Twer, Woloklansk, &c, and the Emperor, with a portion of the guard, and the first corps, entered the city on the 14th of September. On the morrow morning, he fixed his residence in the Kremlin an ancient palace of the Czars, strongly fortified and situated in the centre of the city. Marshal Mortier was named governor of Moscow, and strict orders were given that we should treat the inhabitants with kindness and respect, the Marshal being specially commanded to prevent any act of plunder.

Here were we then, as in former campaigns, occupying the capital of our enemy's kingdom, dictating laws from his palace, regulating the government of his people. None knew better than Napoleon the value of time, none knew how to employ it better; and in thus concentrating his troops in the capital of Russia, he gave them an opportunity to collect the necessary supplies of which they stood in need, and to snatch a few moments of rest, of which they were in want; in the meanwhile a hot pursuit of the enemy was kept up by the cavalry.

Scarcely had he been well settled in the palace, than Napoleon sent for me. He was pacing the room, dictating to an aide-de-camp writing at the table, when I entered, and seeming much engaged, I did not immediately accost him. Years had elapsed since I first saw him in the Square at Mantua; nor had they passed lightly over his head, for the marks of time were evident. Though his figure had become fatter and broader, there was the usual restlessness of his manner considerably increased, and he took immense quantities of snuff, which he ever and anon drew from the pocket of his waistcoat. I could not help recalling to myself the many campaigns I had served under him, the numerous times I had followed him to victory; and if a doubt of our situation ever came across my mind, it was quickly re-assured. He was undoubtedly, the favoured child of fortune—would she desert him now?

"Gazzola," said he, stopping short in his walk, and rousing me from the reverie into which I had fallen, "I like not these Russians; let a strict watch be kept; and above all, let the men refrain from pillage. I feel I owe much to one who has served me so long and well as you have done. I will name you as one of my general officers, and on our return to France, should we be permitted to arrive there, will make you a Baron of the Empire. But remember the life of a soldier in an enemy's country must not be that of repose. Be watchful; and when we meet again you shall have no cause for regret." He held out his hand, which I respectfully pressed to my lips; and though years of captivity and misfortune have passed since then, I shall never forget that moment: it was the last interview I ever had with Napoleon.

Chapter 48

Moscow

I little thought how soon the Emperor's caution to be watchful would be proved to be necessary. I was returning to my quarters one night, after having gone the rounds, when suddenly my ear was saluted by the sound of an alarm bell, and this was quickly answered by several others. Every quarter of the city seemed in motion, while large sheets of flame burst forth in various places, throwing a lurid glare on the surrounding buildings, and illuminating every part of the city. It was evidently on fire on all sides, and as the alarm bells rung and drums were quickly put in requisition, it was not long before every one was astir creating a noise and confusion inconceivable.

The incendiaries, assisted by the convicts and other malefactors, who had been let loose on purpose, had fired the city on all sides, and being mostly built of wood, and a strong wind blowing at the time, the flames fled from house to house with frightful rapidity. All that men could effect to extinguish the flames was done, but although in some quarters their efforts were partially successful, the fire broke out anew in others, rendering the city a scene of tumult and confusion. The Russians, many of whom, rather than follow the army in its retreat, had hidden themselves in the cellars and other secret places in their houses, were now driven forth, and obliged to cast themselves on the mercy of the conquerors. Napoleon, always indefatigable when engaged in succouring the distressed, devoted himself to the relief of the wounded Russians, who filled the hospitals, already abandoned by those to whom the care belonged, and to such of the inhabitants as he found in the streets, deprived of asylum or shelter. He decreed the appointment of syndics, whose duty it was to search out all the miserable creatures who were without habitations or the means of subsistence. He opened houses of refuge to receive those who bad been burnt out, and promised them rations. He went to the Foundling Hospital, which had escaped the flames, and, summoning the director, General Toutolskin, engaged him to make a report to the Empress Mother, and to forward it by an *estafette*; but this was never replied to.

Most of the hospitals had been saved from the flames, and to these our especial care was devoted; but what was our astonishment to find that few of them were provided with the necessary succours, without medicines, firing, or attendants. We found an immense quantity of dead and wounded, for of the twenty thousand wounded Russians, more than one half had perished for want of proper attendance, and the remainder bid fair to follow them. Orders were dispatched to the different corps of the army—the surgeons came pouring into the city—an administration was quickly formed—the sick and wounded confided to their care were removed to convenient places, while reports of their state were drawn up and submitted to the Emperor. Food, furniture, money in large sums were distributed with no niggard spirit, and the wounded Russians blessed the hands that were thus stretched out to save them from perishing when their own countrymen had abandoned them to their fate.

Marshal Mortier, the governor, and General Milhaut, the commandant, were charged with the organisation of a municipality and an administration of police, to restore order in the town and provide the necessary supplies, while the Emperor placed fifty thousand roubles in the hands of the syndics for the immediate relief of the wants of the necessitous.

Many of the incendiaries had been caught, torch in hand, who were taken before courts formed by the officers of the army, and on being interrogated, one and all declared that they acted under the orders of Rostopchlin, the Russian governor of Moscow. Never was cruelty pushed to a greater extent; a paternal government would hardly devastate its own plains, burn its own cities, reduce to despair millions of its unoffending subjects; such conduct would be inexcusable on the part of an enemy, and should never be had recourse to by civilized nations. Its effects has been to make the name of the ferocious tyrant who gave the order more execrable than that of him who fired the temple of Diana of Ephesus.

What end was obtained by the pusillanimous cruelty of the Emperor Alexander in destroying Moscow and the other towns? He rendered them untenable by the French, it is true, but he could not cut off our retreat; that was provided for ere we advanced, and the benefit bore no proportion to the incalculable misery inflicted on his own people. He could not foresee the early setting in of the frost, and but for that the disasters which fell upon us had not occurred.

On the 18th of October the army resumed its march towards Kalogha, a town 38 leagues to the south-east of Moscow, and on the morrow Napoleon himself quitted the city with the Imperial Guard, ordering Mortier to abandon the Kremlin on the 23rd; after having destroyed its fortifications, and to take especial care that neither sick nor wounded were left behind, they were to be carried in the wagons of the Young Guard, and, if necessary, the cavalry was to be dismounted and marched on foot, to afford the means of transport to their disabled comrades.

Here then may be said to have commenced our retreat, a retreat memorable in the annals of the world for the immense destruction of human life—the wholesale abandonment of troops, material, and munitions of war. Never, in the history of warfare, was anything equal to it. May posterity never gaze upon its like.

The army made two marches on the flanks, and each division, as it arrived, took up its quarters at Borowsk. In the meanwhile the enemy effected a grand movement, for the purpose of concentrating his force on the heights, which commanded the the little town of Maloiarostawetz, situated on the Louja. Napoleon manœvred some corps for the purpose of forcing the Russians either to give battle, or to retire precipitately. Eugene had the principal direction of the attack, and received orders so to tune his movement as to allow Davoust to come up and take Kutusow in the rear.

On the night of the 23rd Kutusow established himself on the heights. On the morrow a brisk cannonade opened, and the action began. The town and the heights were taken and retaken several times, till Napoleon, having put himself at the head of Compans and Gerard's divisions, Davoust debouched, and Eugene, profiting by these circumstances, again drove the enemy from the heights and the town, possession of which he succeeded in maintaining. Napoleon expressed in lively terms his satisfaction at witnessing the determined bravery of the Prince, and the 4th division of the army under his command; and in the evening, having reconnoitred the position of the enemy, gave orders that the attack should be renewed on the morrow. But Kutusow retired, having lost ten thousand men, killed, wounded, or taken prisoners, and marched on Jonczarowo, which he hastily fortified, thinking Napoleon would pursue him. But however the latter might for one moment have contemplated such a thing, he quickly abandoned his intention. The hope of conquest had failed, and his whole energies were now directed to the preservation of his men. He changed the direction of his march, and returned to the great road towards Wiasma, for the purpose of covering Mortier, and the convoys of wounded, sick, artillery, munitions, and camp followers, which had been left exposed to the enemy, when he marched on Kalogha. This movement was followed and checked by the Russians commanded by General Miloradowitch, an officer more vain than able; but notwithstanding, on the 1st of November we entered Wiasma, after having repulsed the enemy near Utitsa, and continued our march to Smolensko, the rear guard constantly on the alert to resist the attacks of the Cossacks, immense numbers of whom hung upon our retreat, cutting off the stragglers.

On the 7th of November the frost set in with such intensity that the Russians themselves seemed unable to bear up against it. The population of these immense provinces, entirety destitute, reduced to hide themselves in the mountains, the deserts, and the woods, without habitations, clothing, or food, abandoned themselves to their fate, many lying down and being frozen to death. The Russian army fared no better than our own; but their losses even, then bore no proportion to their cruelties.

An armistice had been accorded, and Napoleon proposed peace; but this was not desired by Alexander, who, breaking his word, carried his duplicity so far as to attack our advanced guard, then established on the Nara. There he was beaten back, and forced to repass the river in disorder; but notwithstanding this success, we were obliged to continue our retreat.

Chapter 49

The Retreat

Thick and fast came the misfortunes of our retreating army, for although when the enemy really showed a front and awaited our attack we came off victorious, still the elements thinned our ranks with greater rapidity than did the weapons of the Russians. For some days the thermometer had stood from sixteen to eighteen degrees below the freezing point; the roads were like a sheet of glass; cavalry and artillery horses, as well as those of the baggage wagons and other equipages, died by hundreds in a night, obliging us to abandon the guns and other carriages to which they were attached. Heaps of carcasses strewed the way; men strayed from the ranks, and, quietly lying down by the way side, "slept the sleep that knows no waking." Harassed, dispirited, half-fed, and less than half clothed, our men gave way to despair. Whole regiments became totally disorganised, refusing to obey the orders of their officers, and only uniting for one common cause when the pursuing troops of the enemy became more daring, and charged up to the very points of our bayonets. Then a feeling of their former pride came across them, and the audacity of the Russians was punished; but, the excitement of the attack once passed away, they relapsed into their former state. In vain their officers endeavoured to re-animate their drooping courage—in vain appeals were made to their patriotism—in vain they were reminded of their former successes, and conjured to struggle on; even the master mind of Napoleon had lost its effect; and when on the 9th of November we entered the town of Smolensko, our numbers had diminished one half. The guard, however, preserved its well-merited character, and mustered strongly, taking up their quarters in the town and the faubourgs; the cavalry were quartered in the villages between the road to Krasnoi and the Nieper; the eighth corps on the road to Elnia; the fifth on that of Mstislaw; the first at Stughinwo; the fourth traversed the Wop; while the third was charged to defend the passage of the Nieper at Slapnerva. I have said the different corps took up their positions, I should have said the skeletons of the different corps, for to that they were nearly reduced, and even these had hardly arrived ere they were obliged to send to Smolensko for the means of subsistence. Here we remained only a few days, and advanced on the road to Minsk, but our difficulties were enhanced by the treason of Prince Schwartzenberg, who commanded the Austrians, and failed to oppose the Russian army, under Tchitchagow, which marched on Minsk, to cut off our retreat and to destroy the magazines that had been prepared for us. This he effected, and thus were our miseries augmented. In addition to this, York and Massenbach, both generals in the service of Prussia, abandoned us and passed over to the enemy, glorying in the greatest act of baseness a soldier can commit. Everything, in short, seemed to combine against us. The orders given by the Emperor to free the army from the convoys of the sick and wounded which impeded its advance as we arrived at Smolensko and Wilna, and to carry them to Konigsberg, Dantzic, and Warsaw, were not obeyed. The hospitals, the treasure, and the magazines were rendered unserviceable by the want of the necessary means of transport; and, unwilling to abandon them, yet unable to carry them with us, our embarrassment was increased, while the still excessive severity of the weather augmented the work of destruction.

    On the 14th we advanced, as yet ignorant of the fault of Schwartzenberg, who had retired on Warsaw, while the Russian general, having destroyed our magazines, had been reinforced by the army of Moravia, and had taken up a position on the Beresina. They awaited us in a ravine at Merlino, a village situated on the great road, intending to cut off our retreat on Krasnoi; but their project being discovered, matters were so well ordered that we opened a passage, and came off conquerors in the different skirmishes that took place, marching on Lyadi and Orsa, where we arrived on the 19th. Unfortunately the rear-guard, under the command of Ney, could neither force a passage nor turn the Russians, who, three or four times more numerous than his own force, threatened the French with annihilation.

We gave them up for lost; but the intrepid Marshal; with well-placed reliance on the valour of his troops, after having made two or three ineffectual efforts to force a passage, turned on the right towards the Neiper, and crossing that river on the ice at the height of Gusinoe, joined the main body of the army at the very moment when we had given them over. Napoleon, on bearing this happy news, seized the officer whom Ney had sent to communicate it by the two arms, and said to him, with the most lively emotion—"Is this true? are you quite sure?" The officer assuring him of the truth of the news, the Emperor added—"I have two hundred millions of francs in my palace of the Tuileries, and every one would I have sacrificed to save Marshal Ney."

But, brave as were our chiefs, devoted as were some of the troops, what could withstand the fury of the elements? From Smolensko to Orsa the cold destroyed men and horses by thousands; yet, spite of our loss, we had occasional brushes with the enemy, and generally came off victorious. On the 17th, the weather became a little warmer, and if it had not, not a man could have lived to tell the tale; but the relief was of little avail, for again the rigour of the season returned, and the same scenes occurred again and again.

No sooner had he arrived at Orsa, than the Emperor, without taking a moment's repose, busied himself in an endeavour to restore that order which the different engagements and the inclemency of the season had naturally deranged. He distributed an extra quantity of rations, of arms and munitions of war, and addressed us in one of his stirring orders of the day, reminding the men that in leaving their regiments they sacrificed their honour and the safety of the army. The desires of the Emperor were in some measure accomplished, and many of those who had quitted the ranks returned to their duty. Order and discipline were in some measure restored; we again showed a good front, and advanced by forced marches towards the Beresina, where we arrived on the 25th.

During the march from Moscow to this river, the different corps of the army, though supporting each other, had acted independently; now, however, the second corps joined that portion of the main body which was under the command of Napoleon himself, and with which he prepared to force the passage of the river.

The various other corps had separated as they retreated, each of them having suffered more or less severely by the harassing pursuit of the Russians: with them, however, after leaving Smolensko, we had nothing to do—each now more resembling an independent army than different corps of the same force.

CHAPTER 50

The Passage of the Beresina

The grand army arrived on the height of Borisow, a small town on the Beresina, on the road from Orsa to Minsk. Napoleon determined to force a passage of the river, with the hope of preventing the junction of Platow and Wittgenstein with Tchitchagow. In consequence, bridges were established at different points, and Napoleon manœvred all his corps to deceive the enemy, and conceal his true intentions. He raised sham batteries opposite those of the Russians, and with great ostentation drew together such materials as were necessary for the construction of a bridge; but while he made these preparations at Weslowo, and his artillery traversed the causeways raised in the marshes, which the thaw had rendered practicable, he himself superintended the erection of the bridges he meant to use. When those on the right were completed, Napoleon passed under his own eye the second corps and the guard, and when the other bridges were finished be crossed to the opposite side, and placed himself on the heights at two hundred paces from the right bank, with the guard, to protect the passage of the remainder of the troops, while the second corps kept in check the troops of Admiral Tchitchagow.

The third and fifth divisions passed at once, and were ordered to support the second. On the 26th and 27th the other corps, with the camp followers and the women were left to cross, while Marshal Victor, who had the command of the left of the army, took position below Weslowo, where General Partouneaux ought to have remained to support him till the night drew on. He marched too soon, and falling between the corps of Platow and Wittgenstein, was taken prisoner, with the greater part of his division.

In the night of the 28th Victor crossed the river, and there only remained the carriages, baggage wagons, camp followers, infants and old men and women in the plain of Weslowo; or rather such of them as had failed to cross the Beresina on the previous days. At the approach of the Russians, these unhappy loiterers suddenly threw themselves on the bridge of Studzianka, which gave way. Who can describe the awful situation of those unfortunates that were thus placed between the fire of the Russians and the river? Swollen beyond its usual size by the snow, the few who dared the flood rather then remain, were rapidly swept away from before the eyes of their countrymen, who left nothing undone to save them; but, alas! our efforts were unavailing, and the number rescued from a watery grave was trifling in comparison with those that were lost.

At the same time that the enemy advanced on Victor on the left bank, Tchitchagow having united different corps, briskly attacked the second corps on the right bank, but they were supported by the third and fifth, who in turn were supported by the guard, led by Napoleon in person.

In the charge of the guard, just before the army had achieved the passage, I was struck with a musket ball in the leg, which, passing through the fleshy part, killed the horse under me. Stunned by the fall, and hampered by the carcase of the dead animal, I know not how long I may have lain, when the sound of voices roused me from my stupor, and a party of our men relieved me from my situation, and carried me to a tent which had been used as a temporary hospital. As the shades of evening approached, I found that our troops, hard pressed by the Russians, had retired, leaving 95 poor miserable objects to the mercy of our enemies, or to that which proved as little merciful, the sharp biting frost of a November night.

I could never rightly describe the horrors of that scene. Men in every stage of life, from the trifling flesh wound to that mortal one which left the vital fluid fast hurrying from the body, broken limbs, broken heads, every description of wound that the casualties of battle render common to army surgeons, was to be found here, with not one of that meritorious body to rescue from the fangs of death those whom the iron hand of war had partially spared. Without fire, or food, or clothing, thrown side by side, or upon each other, as chance dictated, lay a number of miserable wretches, who had once formed part of the *élite* of a victorious army, while prayers, execrations, curses, loud cries for water, filled the air. As night advanced the cold became more intense, and the voices were gradually hushed. The pain from my wound was so severe that I could not sleep, but, as good fortune would have it, the party who had carried me in had thrown my cloak over me. Wrapping this around me as well as I was able, I awaited the dawn of day with feelings of more intense anxiety then I ever before remember, for sleep was banished from my eyes, and the frost had made an attack upon my foot.

At length day came, and with it came the Russians. Of the ninety-five men who were alive the night before but six survived, and one of them died ere he could be removed.

I was now a prisoner, and notwithstanding my wound, was soon made to feel that my lot was anything but a happy one. Kind, pitying woman, however, proved my guardian angel; the wife of one of the Russian soldiers payed me great attention, and to her succour and humanity I owe the preservation of my life, though even that could not preserve my toe.

When I was sufficiently recovered I was marched off with a number of other prisoners into the interior, and there led a life of suffering and hardship till Napoleon's abdication in 1814 allowed me to return to France.

ALSO FROM LEONAUR
AVAILABLE IN SOFTCOVER OR HARDCOVER WITH DUST JACKET

CAPTAIN OF THE 95th (Rifles) by *Jonathan Leach*—An officer of Wellington's Sharpshooters during the Peninsular, South of France and Waterloo Campaigns of the Napoleonic Wars.

BUGLER AND OFFICER OF THE RIFLES by *William Green & Harry Smith* With the 95th (Rifles) during the Peninsular & Waterloo Campaigns of the Napoleonic Wars

BAYONETS, BUGLES AND BONNETS by *James 'Thomas' Todd*—Experiences of hard soldiering with the 71st Foot - the Highland Light Infantry - through many battles of the Napoleonic wars including the Peninsular & Waterloo Campaigns

THE ADVENTURES OF A LIGHT DRAGOON by *George Farmer & G.R. Gleig*—A cavalryman during the Peninsular & Waterloo Campaigns, in captivity & at the siege of Bhurtpore, India

THE COMPLEAT RIFLEMAN HARRIS by *Benjamin Harris as told to & transcribed by Captain Henry Curling*—The adventures of a soldier of the 95th (Rifles) during the Peninsular Campaign of the Napoleonic Wars

WITH WELLINGTON'S LIGHT CAVALRY by *William Tomkinson*—The Experiences of an officer of the 16th Light Dragoons in the Peninsular and Waterloo campaigns of the Napoleonic Wars.

SURTEES OF THE RIFLES by *William Surtees*—A Soldier of the 95th (Rifles) in the Peninsular campaign of the Napoleonic Wars.

ENSIGN BELL IN THE PENINSULAR WAR by *George Bell*—The Experiences of a young British Soldier of the 34th Regiment 'The Cumberland Gentlemen' in the Napoleonic wars.

WITH THE LIGHT DIVISION by *John H. Cooke*—The Experiences of an Officer of the 43rd Light Infantry in the Peninsula and South of France During the Napoleonic Wars

NAPOLEON'S IMPERIAL GUARD: FROM MARENGO TO WATERLOO by *J. T. Headley*—This is the story of Napoleon's Imperial Guard from the bearskin caps of the grenadiers to the flamboyance of their mounted chasseurs, their principal characters and the men who commanded them.

BATTLES & SIEGES OF THE PENINSULAR WAR by *W. H. Fitchett*—Corunna, Busaco, Albuera, Ciudad Rodrigo, Badajos, Salamanca, San Sebastian & Others

AVAILABLE ONLINE AT
www.leonaur.com
AND OTHER GOOD BOOK STORES

www.ingramcontent.com/pod-product-compliance
Lightning Source LLC
Chambersburg PA
CBHW031620160426
43196CB00006B/209